# LETTERS OF
# MAX BEERBOHM
## 1892–1956

# LETTERS OF
# MAX BEERBOHM
## 1892–1956

EDITED BY
RUPERT HART-DAVIS

JOHN MURRAY

Beerbohm letters and drawings © Eva Reichmann 1988
Editorial matter © Rupert Hart-Davis 1988

First published in 1988
by John Murray (Publishers) Ltd
50 Albemarle Street, London WIX 4BD

Printed and bound in Great Britain by
Butler & Tanner Ltd, Frome and London

*British Library Cataloguing and Publication Data*

Beerbohm, Max, *1872–1956*
   Letters of Max Beerbohm, 1892–1956.
   1. English literature. Beerbohm, Max,
   1872–1956. Correspondence, diaries, etc.
   I. Title     II. Hart-Davis, Rupert, *1907–*
   828'.91209

ISBN 0-7195-4537-4

*This book is dedicated*
*by its editor*
*with love and gratitude*
*to Eva Reichmann*
*and to the dear memory*
*of her beloved husband*
*Hans*

# CONTENTS

———

# ILLUSTRATIONS
## (all but seven drawn by Max)

# INTRODUCTION

Max Beerbohm, like Charles Dickens, became famous in his twenties, and many people kept his letters. They are now scattered over the world, and there must be hundreds, if not thousands, that I have failed to trace. Of the hundreds I have collected many are what Henry James called "the mere twaddle of graciousness" – simple acceptances or refusals of invitations, bread-and-butter letters of gratitude, business arrangements, and so on. I have included here only letters that I found interesting, revealing or amusing. No doubt many more such will come to light.

Some letters here have been printed before in various forgotten books, some quoted, in whole or in part, by David Cecil in his biography of Max. I have reprinted them because they clearly deserve to be collected together.

Except for the first letter in this book, which has not been published before, I have included none of Max's letters to Reggie Turner, Will Rothenstein, or Siegfried Sassoon, since they have already been published.[1]

Max always loved drawing, which was as easy to him as breathing. Writing was for ever a labour towards perfection – often a labour of love, but during his twelve years as a dramatic critic a weekly chore. He always disliked writing letters, and in June 1945 he wrote to Violet Schiff:

> Lovely to hear from you again – and it would be so even if you weren't the born letter-writer that you are! You write just exactly as you talk; and that, of course, is the secret of good letter-writing. But I never have been able to master that secret, and almost always dread writing a letter, knowing it will be an entirely unvocal pen-and-inkish affair and as flat as the paper it is written on.

Readers of this book are unlikely to agree.

---

[1] *Letters to Reggie Turner* (1964), *Max and Will* (1975), and *Siegfried Sassoon's Letters to Max Beerbohm, with a few answers* (1986).

I have not included otherwise uninteresting letters which contain such snapshots of other writers as these:

*To Hugh Walpole, August 1927:*
Please give my best messages to "Elizabeth" [of the German Garden] when you write to her. I was reading *Love* in the Tauchnitz edition just before we came here. She writes as a lark sings, doesn't she? – or rather as a lark *would* sing if it had a powerful little brain in addition to its other advantages.

*To Jim Rose, October 1951:*
I wish I were not a heretic in the matter of C.P. Snow. Nowhere in his laborious account of that squalid little group of earnest drunkards[1] do I find one spark of evidence that he has even a rudimentary gift for the art of fiction. Let us hope that this failure to find is entirely my own fault, not his.

*To Sam Behrman, February 1956:*
The thought of him [William Morris] has always slightly irritated me. Of course he was a wonderful all-round man, but the act of walking round him has always tired me.

The letters to Florence Kahn, Max's future wife, present a special difficulty. They met in June 1904, and from then until their wedding in May 1910 Max wrote to her several times a week. More than a thousand of his letters have survived, and they can be divided into two very different groups. The first lasted from the beginning until November 1908. Except for the first few they all begin "Very dear little friend" and end simply "Max". As readers will see from my selection of the most interesting of these letters, they are full of tender brotherly affection and concern for her health, commiseration for all the important acting parts she failed to get, and details of his own character and of his doings. There are few jokes in them, for Florence had little humour and never enjoyed Max's jokes, which she often failed to understand. Nor is there in all these outpourings of four-and-a-half years a single suggestion of physical love or desire.

The last letter in this group (see p. 62) seems to me a key document in Max's life. I interpret it as meaning that if they were to become man and wife their marriage would never be consummated. Max was a natural celibate and I doubt whether he ever had a sexual experience of any kind. His brother Herbert once described him as "more brain than heart, and an entire absence of passion". In his youth his family worried

---

[1] *Strangers and Brothers* (1940), which Rose had sent him. Max's first comment read "Strangers to whom? Brothers to none".

because so many of his friends were homosexual – Oscar Wilde, Alfred Douglas, Reggie Turner, Robbie Ross – but, although Max greatly enjoyed their company, there is no scrap of evidence that he ever shared their sexual propensities.

He had already been engaged to two other actresses – Grace (Kilseen) Conover, whom he kept hanging about for six years before they agreed to break it off, and Constance Collier, who soon found a more satisfactory lover. All Max needed was a devoted and companionable woman to look after him, and this part was perfectly played, first by his mother and sisters, then by Florence, and lastly by Elisabeth Jungmann.

My further conjecture is that Florence was as undersexed as Max and accepted his confession with relief. Once that difficulty was out of the way Max felt able to give voice to his affection (Herbert was wrong about his heart), for in the next surviving letter (p. 62) "Very dear little friend" has changed to "*Darling* love", and the simple "Max" at the end has become "Your own loving Max. Kisses." All his later letters to Florence are in the same demonstrative vein. Another fifteen months were to elapse before their wedding, but now at last Max was engaged to the lady he was certainly going to marry.

He would greatly disapprove of this prying into his private life, but I feel it is necessary if one is to understand him fully. My theory may be quite wrong, but it does at least provide an explanation for the abrupt change in his letters to Florence.

I have printed only one letter to Elisabeth Jungmann, since from the time when she first arrived to look after Max they were seldom separated, and Max's written words to her consisted of tiny pencil notes of love and gratitude. Nobody, I believe, had ever loved Max so deeply, and looked after him with such tender efficiency, as Elisabeth did, and he loved her as perhaps he had never loved any other woman.

I have included twelve letters and two postcards *to* Max, for which I acknowledge with gratitude the generous permission of Messrs A.P. Watt Ltd on behalf of the Maurice Baring Will Trust; King's College, Cambridge, for E.M. Forster; Jennifer Gosse for Edmund Gosse; the Society of Authors on behalf of the Bernard Shaw estate; the Strachey Trust for Lytton Strachey; Auberon Waugh for Evelyn Waugh; and Professor Quentin Bell for Virginia Woolf.

All letters are printed in their entirety, and wherever three dots occur they are Max's. His very few slips of the pen I have silently corrected. The texts of all letters to the press are taken from the relevant newspapers.

All letters marked MS. have been taken from the originals or photo-copies. Those marked TS. Merton are typed transcripts made for David Cecil, with no note of the ownership of the originals. The few originals which have turned up show that the typing was accurate. In his last years Max drafted by hand letters which Elisabeth Jungmann then typed. Hence MS. Draft and TS. Draft.

Although these letters range from the skittish Oxford undergraduate to the venerated sage of Rapallo, they cannot be taken as anything more than an outline of Max's life, since there are lengthy periods from which no interesting letters have come to light. The Biographical Table on pp. xvi–xviii should fill some of these gaps.

For footnote-information I am greatly indebted to many old friends. Paul Chipchase has excelled himself in quickly ferreting out answers to my incessant and sometimes almost insoluble queries. Ernest and Joyce Mehew have, as usual, provided much valuable information. Dan H. Laurence from Texas, Owen Dudley Edwards from Edinburgh, and the late Oliver Stonor from Devon have contributed their expert knowledge. Douglas Cleverdon entrusted his precious originals to the post and also helped me to annotate them, but he did not, alas, live to see them in print. To the other private owners of letters I am equally grateful.

From librarians and others I have received ungrudging assistance. In particular I must thank Dr Roger Highfield and John Burgass of the Merton College Library, who from their huge Beerbohm collection have cheerfully sent me photo-copies of everything I asked for. My debt and my gratitude to them are immense.

I have also been greatly helped by the following: Sir Harold Acton; Peter Aldersley of the Savile Club; Barney Blackley of the Bodley Head; Carol Reid Briggs of the William Andrews Clark Library in Los Angeles; Mrs P.J. Burrough of the Somerset County Library at Street; Professor T.V. Buttrey; Herbert Cahoon of the Pierpont Morgan Library in New York; John Charlton of Chatto & Windus; Edward Craig; Professor Lawrence Danson of Princeton University; Rodney Dennis of the Houghton Library at Harvard; Ian Fletcher; Stanley Gillam; Miss C.M. Hall of the British Library; Professor N. John Hall of the City University of New York; Michael Hall; Dr Michael Halls of King's College, Cambridge; James Hart of the Bancroft Library at Berkeley; Cathy Henderson of the Humanities Research Center at Austin, Texas; Frances Hickson of the Society of Authors; Norman Higham of Bristol University Library; Dr Timothy Hobbs and David McKitterick of Trinity College, Cambridge; Michael Holroyd; Julian Jeffs, Q.C.; Lord Kennet;

Colonel Andrew Man; the late Professor Bruce R. McElderry Jr; Professor Ellis M. Pryce-Jones of the University of Nevada at Las Vegas; Dr J.G. Riewald; Mrs Tatyana Schmoller; Christopher Sheppard of the Brotherton Library in the University of Leeds; Faye Simkin of the Berg Collection in the New York Public Library; H.W. Smee of Brock's Fireworks Ltd; Dr David C. Sutton of the University of Reading; Richard Usborne; Alexander D. Wainwright of Princeton Library; Frank Walker of the Fales Library in New York University; Peter Walne, the Hertfordshire County Archivist; Gillian Walsh of the Athenaeum library; Isolde Wigram; Marjorie Wynne of Yale University Library; and Melanie Yolles of the New York Public Library.

If I have forgetfully omitted the names of other helpers, I can only beg their forgiveness and thank them *in absentia*.

RUPERT HART-DAVIS

Marske-in-Swaledale
April 1988

# MANUSCRIPT LOCATIONS: INSTITUTIONS

Bancroft         Bancroft Library, University of California at Berkeley
Berg             Berg Collection, New York Public Library
B.L.             British Library
Bodley           Bodleian Library, Oxford
Brotherton       Brotherton Collection, University of Leeds
Cambridge        Cambridge University Library
Clark            William Andrews Clark Memorial Library, University
                 of California, Los Angeles
Edinburgh        National Library of Scotland, Edinburgh
Fales            Haliburton Fales Collection, New York University
Georgetown       Georgetown University Library, D.C.
Glasgow          Glasgow University Library
Hertford         Hertfordshire County Record Office
King's           King's College, Cambridge
Lilly            Lilly Library, University of Indiana
London           University College, London
Merton           The Max Room, Merton College, Oxford
Morgan           Pierpont Morgan Library, New York
N.P.G.           National Portrait Gallery
Princeton        Princeton University Library
Sterling         Sterling Library in the University of London
Street           Somerset County Library at Street
Texas            Humanities Research Center, Austin, Texas
Toronto          University of Toronto Library
Trinity          Trinity College, Cambridge
Virginia         University of Virginia Library
Yale             Yale University Library

# MANUSCRIPT LOCATIONS: PRIVATE OWNERS

Brudenell | Edmund Brudenell
Cleverdon | Mrs Douglas Cleverdon
Hart-Davis | Rupert Hart-Davis
Hodson | Haro Hodson
Holland | Merlin Holland
Hyde | Mary Hyde (Viscountess Eccles)
Irving | Laurence Irving
Jebb | Louis Jebb
Lasner | Mark Samuels Lasner
Mix | Mrs Katherine Lyon Mix
Reichmann | Mrs Eva Reichmann
Rose (J) | Jim Rose
Rose (K) | Kenneth Rose
Sebag-Montefiore | Mrs Ruth Sebag-Montefiore
Waugh | Auberon Waugh

# BIOGRAPHICAL TABLE

| | | |
|---|---|---|
| 1872 | August 24 | Henry Maximilian Beerbohm born at 57 Palace Gardens Terrace, Kensington |
| 1881–5 | | Attended Mr Wilkinson's day school in Orme Square, Bayswater |
| 1885–90 | | At Charterhouse |
| 1890–4 | | At Merton College, Oxford |
| 1892 | August 30 | Death of his father |
| 1895 | Jan-April | Toured in America with the theatrical company of his half-brother Herbert Beerbohm Tree |
| 1896 | June 10 | *The Works of Max Beerbohm* published |
| | December | *Caricatures of Twenty-Five Gentlemen* published |
| 1897 | April 14 | *The Happy Hypocrite* published |
| | | Family moved from 19 Hyde Park Place to 48 Upper Berkeley Street |
| 1898 | May 28 | Succeeded Bernard Shaw as dramatic critic of the *Saturday Review* |
| 1899 | April 20 | *More* published |
| 1901 | November | First exhibition of caricatures at the Carfax Gallery in Ryder Street, St James's |
| 1904 | May | Second Carfax exhibition |
| | | *The Poets' Corner* published |
| | June | Met Florence Kahn |
| 1907 | April | Third Carfax exhibition |
| | November | *A Book of Caricatures* published |
| 1908 | April & May | Fourth Carfax exhibition |
| 1909 | October 12 | *Yet Again* published |
| 1910 | March 26 | Retired from *Saturday Review* |
| | May 4 | Married Florence Kahn |
| | | Settled at Rapallo |
| 1911 | April & May | First Leicester Galleries exhibition of caricatures |

| | | |
|---|---|---|
| 1911 | October 26 | *Zuleika Dobson* published |
| | December | *The Second Childhood of John Bull* published |
| 1912 | October 12 | *A Christmas Garland* published |
| 1913 | April & May | Leicester Galleries exhibition |
| | October 9 | *Fifty Caricatures* published |
| 1915 | | Stayed with the Rothensteins at Far Oakridge in Gloucestershire till 1917, with various *pieds-à-terre* in London. First at 26 Oxford Terrace W. |
| 1916 | February | Left Oxford Terrace |
| | April–June | At Bognor |
| | | Then rooms at 21 Southwick Street W.2. |
| 1917 | July 2 | Death of Herbert Beerbohm Tree |
| | | Rooms at 12 Well Walk, Hampstead, till 1919 |
| 1918 | March 13 | Death of his mother |
| 1919 | Oct–Dec | Flat in Grove Place, Hampstead |
| | October 30 | *Seven Men* published |
| | December | Returned to Rapallo |
| 1920 | December 7 | *And Even Now* published |
| 1921 | May–June | Leicester Galleries exhibition |
| | December 1 | *A Survey* published |
| 1922–8 | | Collected Works published in ten volumes |
| 1922 | September 28 | *Rossetti and his Circle* published |
| 1923 | June | Leicester Galleries exhibition |
| | October 25 | *Things New and Old* published |
| 1924 | November 6 | *Around Theatres* published as two volumes in Collected Works |
| 1925 | April–May | Leicester Galleries exhibition |
| | October 22 | *Observations* published |
| 1927 | | Met Elisabeth Jungmann |
| 1928 | June 28 | *A Variety of Things* published in Collected Works |
| 1930 | July 2 | Hon LL.D. at University of Edinburgh |
| 1935 | | Returned to England |
| | December 29 | First broadcast, 'London Revisited' |
| 1936–8 | | Back at Rapallo |
| 1938 | | At 62 Inverness Terrace, Bayswater |
| 1939 | February | At Abinger Manor Cottage, lent by Sydney and Violet Schiff |
| | June | His knighthood announced |
| | July 14 | Received accolade at Buckingham Palace |
| 1942 | | The Maximilian Society formed for his 70th birthday |

| | | |
|---|---|---|
| 1943 | May 20 | Delivered the Rede Lecture on Lytton Strachey in the Senate House, Cambridge |
| | June 25 | *Lytton Strachey* published |
| 1944 | August | Bombed out of Abinger cottage |
| | | Stayed with various friends |
| 1946 | August | Moved to Highcroft, The Edge, near Stroud in Gloucestershire, lent by Ellis Roberts and his wife |
| | September 2 | *Mainly on the Air* published |
| 1947 | September | Returned to Rapallo |
| 1951 | January 13 | Death of Florence Beerbohm |
| | | Thereafter Elisabeth Jungmann looked after Max |
| 1952 | June | S.N. Behrman's first visit |
| 1956 | March | Start of fatal illness |
| | April 20 | Married Elisabeth Jungmann |
| | May 20 | Died in Rapallo nursing home |
| | June 29 | His ashes buried in St Paul's Cathedral |

Max Beerbohm.
by Himself. 1892.

xxi

## To Reggie Turner[1]
MS. Toronto

[c. 17 January 1892]                                    *Merton College, Oxford*

My dear Turner, So glad you like the Lord Arthur Savile[2] and have got seats for the first night.[3] The bosom friend of whom you speak is who? If you do have the book bound do not forget to have those two pages interleaved. I would suggest pale sea-green rough leather with an oval-shaped label (on the back) of white calf with tiny black letters for the title. I hope the late Duke won't be buried on Thursday and the performance be postponed.[4] Your requests are endless but I send you a picture of myself.          Yours   MAXWELL BEERBOHM[5]

P.S. Perhaps our seats will be together – only my eldest sister and I are going to the first night. Don't I write just like Blanche Amory?[6] I think I am rather like her in all respects. Do you like this sort of handwriting? I see you have copied my margins but then margins are such very easy things to copy. To create a blank shews no vitality at all. It is as easy as not painting a picture. Have I been just a little too hard upon you? – Perhaps. Have I made clear my meaning? – Possibly.

[1] Novelist, journalist and wit (?1869–1938). He was now in his final year at Merton. Max's earliest, dearest and lifelong friend. See *Letters to Reggie Turner* (1964).

[2] Oscar Wilde's *Lord Arthur Savile's Crime and Other Stories*, published in 1891. Max had sent a copy to Reggie.

[3] Of Beerbohm Tree's production of *Hamlet* which opened at the Haymarket Theatre on Thursday, 21 January 1892.

[4] Prince Albert Victor (Eddy), Duke of Clarence, the elder son of the future King Edward VII, died at Sandringham, aged 28, on 14 January 1892. The military funeral at Windsor was on 20 January.

[5] Max's first caricatures to be published in a national periodical, "Club Types" in the *Strand Magazine* of September 1892, were signed H.M. Beerbohm, but the second and third instalments in the same paper of November and December 1892 were signed H. Maxwell Beerbohm. For his explanation see p. 138.

[6] The lovely scheming Sylphide whom Thackeray's Pendennis so nearly married.

# To the Editor of The Yellow Book[1]

Dear Sir, When *The Yellow Book* appeared I was in Oxford. So literary a little town is Oxford that its undergraduates see a newspaper nearly as seldom as the Venetians see a horse, and until yesterday, when coming to London, I found in the album of a friend certain newspaper cuttings, I had not known how great was the wrath of the pressmen.

What in the whole volume seems to have provoked the most ungovernable fury is, I am sorry to say, an essay about Cosmetics that I myself wrote. Of this it was impossible for any one to speak calmly. The mob lost its head, and, so far as any one in literature can be lynched, I was. In speaking of me, one paper dropped the usual prefix of "Mr" as though I were a well-known criminal, and referred to me shortly as "Beerbohm;" a second allowed me the "Mr" but urged that "a short Act of Parliament should be passed to make this kind of thing illegal;"[2] a third suggested, rather tamely, that I should read one of Mr William Watson's[3] sonnets.

More than one comic paper had a very serious poem about me, and a known adherent to the humour which, forest-like, is called new,[4] declared my essay to be "the rankest and most nauseous thing in all literature".[5] It was a bomb thrown by a cowardly decadent, another outrage by one of that desperate and dangerous band of madmen who must be mercilessly stamped out by a comity of editors. May I, Sir, in justice to myself and to you, who were gravely censured for harbouring me, step forward, and assure the affrighted mob that it is the victim of a hoax? May I also assure it that I had no notion that it would be taken in? Indeed, it seems incredible to me that any one on the face of the earth could fail to see that my essay, so grotesque in subject, in opinion so flippant, in style so wildly affected, was meant for a burlesque upon the "precious" school of writers. If I had only signed myself D. Cadent or Parrar Docks, or appended a note to say that the manuscript had been picked up not a hundred miles from Tite Street,[6] all the pressmen

---

[1] Max's satirical essay "A Defence of Cosmetics" appeared in the first volume of *The Yellow Book* in April 1894. This letter was published in the second volume (July 1894), from which the text is taken.

[2] In the *Westminster Gazette* of 18 April 1894.      [3] Poet (1858–1935). Knighted 1917.

[4] i.e. the New Forest in Hampshire, planted in 1079 and still called New.

[5] Barry Pain (humorist 1867–1928), in *Black and White* of 28 April 1894.

[6] Where Oscar Wilde lived.

would have said that I had given them a very delicate bit of satire. But I did not. And *hinc*, as they themselves love to say, *illæ lacrimæ*.

After all, I think it is a sound rule that a writer should not kick his critics. I simply wish to make them a friendly philosophical suggestion. It seems to be thought that criticism holds in the artistic world much the same place as, in the moral world, is held by punishment – "the vengeance taken by the majority upon such as exceed the limits of conduct imposed by that majority". As in the case of punishment, then, we must consider the effect produced by criticism upon its object, how far is it reformatory? Personally I cannot conceive how any artist can be hurt by remarks dropped from a garret into a gutter. Yet it is incontestable that many an illustrious artist has so been hurt. And these very remarks, so far from making him change or temper his method, have rather made that method intenser, have driven him to retire further within his own soul, by shewing him how little he may hope for from the world but insult and ingratitude.

In fact, the police-constable mode of criticism is a failure. True that, here and there, much beautiful work of the kind has been done. In the old, old Quarterlies is many a slashing review, that, however absurd it be as criticism, we can hardly wish unwritten. In the *National Observer*,[1] before its reformation, were countless fine examples of the cavilling method. The paper was rowdy, venomous and insincere. There was libel in every line of it. It roared with the lambs and bleated with the lions. It was a disgrace to journalism and a glory to literature. I think of it often with tears and desiderium. But the men who wrote these things stand upon a very different plane to the men employed as critics by the press of Great Britain. These must be judged, not by their workmanship, which is naught, but by the spirit that animates them and the consequence of their efforts. If only they could learn that it is for the critic to seek after beauty and to try to interpret it to others, if only they would give over their eternal fault-finding and not presume to interfere with the artist at his work, then with an equally small amount of ability our pressmen might do nearly as much good as they have hitherto done harm.

Why should they regard writers with such enmity? The average pressman, reviewing a book of stories or of poems by an unknown writer, seems not to think "where are the beauties of this work that I may praise

---

[1] W.E. Henley, poet and journalist (1849–1903), edited the *Scots Observer* from 1889 until 1890, when it was renamed the *National Observer*. Henley remained editor until 1894, after which its "reformation" made it very dull.

them, and by my praise quicken the sense of beauty in others?" He steadily applies himself to the ignoble task of plucking out and gloating over its defects. It is a pity that critics should show so little sympathy with writers, and curious when we consider that most of them tried to be writers themselves, once. Every new school that has come into the world, every new writer who has brought with him a new mode, they have rudely persecuted. The dullness of Ibsen, the obscurity of Meredith, the horrors of Zola – all these are household words. It is not until the pack has yelled itself hoarse that the level voice of justice is heard in praise. To pretend that no generation is capable of gauging the greatness of its own artists is the merest bauble-tit. Were it not for the accursed abuse of their function by the great body of critics, no poet need "live uncrown'd, apart". Many and irreparable are the wrongs that our critics have done. At length let them repent with ashes upon their heads. Where they see not beauty, let them be silent, reverently feeling that it may yet be there, and train their dull senses in quest of it.

Now is a good time for such penance. There are signs that our English literature has reached that point, when, like the literatures of all the nations that have been, it must fall at length into the hands of the decadents. The qualities that I tried in my essay to travesty – paradox and marivaudage, lassitude, a love of horror and all unusual things, a love of argot and archaism and the mysteries of style – are not all these displayed, some by one, some by another of *les jeunes écrivains*? Who knows but that Artifice is in truth at our gates and that soon she may pass through our streets? Already the windows of Grub Street are crowded with watchful, evil faces. They are ready, the men of Grub Street, to pelt her, as they have pelted all that came before her. Let them come down while there is still time, and hang their houses with colours, and strew the road with flowers. Will they not, for once, do homage to a new queen? By the time this letter appears, it *may* be too late!

Meanwhile, Sir, I am your obedient servant   MAX BEERBOHM

## To Ada Leverson[1]
MS. Texas

[*Late September 1894*]                                      *19 Hyde Park Place, W.*

Dearest Mrs Leverson, I am not surprised that our Worthing friends[2] think anything so witty as *The Green Carnation*[3] must have been written by you. Probably too they are anxious to believe it comes from one of the rival sex. I hope you won't be able to make them believe you just yet. The whole thing is very piquant. Of course they are not offended.

It is sweet of you to ask me to come and see you tomorrow. If they have arrived I will bring you the proofs of my literary guilt which have strayed from the Bodley Head to Broadstairs and are I believe on their hither way. What agitated discussions Bosie[4] and Osie must have had over the authorship of that book. I wonder if they thought of Hichens at all?

Till tomorrow                         Yours ever   MAX BEERBOHM

I hope this will catch the post.

## To Ada Leverson
MS. Texas

[*October 1894*]                                      *19 Hyde Park Place, W.*

My dearest Mrs Leverson, I was so very glad to hear from you today – such a very nice letter – and I think your idea for a parody quite lovely and delightful.[5] I lunched today chez Harland.[6] Miss Robins[7] was there –

---

[1] Ada Esther Beddington (1862–1933) married Ernest Leverson, the son of a diamond merchant. She contributed witty pieces to *Punch* and other periodicals, and later published successful novels. She was a faithful friend of Oscar Wilde, who always called her The Sphinx.

[2] Oscar Wilde spent August and September 1894 at 5 Esplanade, Worthing, where he wrote the greater part of *The Importance of Being Earnest*.

[3] An amusing story based on the friendship of Oscar Wilde and Lord Alfred Douglas, by Robert Hichens, was published anonymously on 15 September 1894, but its author was soon identified. At the time of Wilde's prosecution in 1895 Hichens withdrew the book, and it was not published again until 1949. Hichens (1864–1950) became a prolific and successful novelist.          [4] Nickname of Lord Alfred Douglas.

[5] Mrs Leverson published several parodies of Max's essays in *Punch*. This one, I think, must refer to "A Phalse Note on George the Fourth" in *Punch* of 27 October 1894, after Max's "Note on George the Fourth" in the October issue of *The Yellow Book*.

[6] Henry Harland (1861–1905), American novelist and editor of *The Yellow Book*.

[7] Elizabeth Robins (1862–1952), American actress and writer. She played several of Ibsen's heroines on their first appearance in London.

5

also Aubrey.[1] We fed by the light of candles, with nice thick green curtains between us and the day. Altogether a rather pleasing meal – save for the Robins. Do you know her at all? Conceive! Straight, pencilled eyebrows, a mouth that has seen the stress of life, hands that etc, as The Chief would say.[2] She is fearfully Ibsenish and talks of souls that are involved in a nerve turmoil and are seeking a common platform. This is *literally* what she said. Her very words. I kept peeping under the table to see if she really wore a skirt. Also I had to go by promise to Bobbie Ross.[3] Do not, please, walk about near your house. The stabbing lady seems to be here there and everywhere. Mrs Harland will not cross from doorstep to cab alone, for fear of this so-called New Woman.[4]

May I, instead of tomorrow, come to you Sunday? Harland wants "1880"[5] by then and my time will be full. I am *so* sorry about your hateful head. Have you taken any remedies? How is the nurse? I hope you will both be soon better. Do let me know, by return of post if possible, is Mr Leverson going to the dinner?     Yours ever   MAX

## To Robert Ross
MS. Hyde

[*14 November 1894*][6]                         *19 Hyde Park Place*

Dearest Bobbie, So glad to hear from you. When are you coming back again? I have seen old Oscar several times lately here and there – wonderfully hale for his great age.

Mrs Leverson is delighted at your saying that she almost persuadeth you to be a "mulierast". I am dining with her and Monsieur to meet the Oscar aforesaid. Also Frank Harris,[7] who greatly admires me. Dear Bobbie, do come and see me as soon as you come back – you never do.

[1] Aubrey Beardsley (1872–98), artist, art-editor of *The Yellow Book*.

[2] Henry Irving was known in the theatre as The Chief.

[3] Robert Baldwin Ross (1869–1918). Literary journalist and art-critic. Faithful friend of Oscar Wilde.

[4] "The two stabbing cases in the Kensington district are creating some excitement, in consequence of the allegation that they were perpetrated by a woman. In both cases the victims declare that a well-dressed woman, wearing a black costume and a thick veil, asked them directions to streets in the neighbourhood, and dealt them blows ere they could reply. The police theory is that a female lunatic of homicidal tendencies is at large in the neighbourhood. Strong patrols have been arranged for the district, and hopes are entertained of an early arrest."     (*Pall Mall Gazette*, 4 December 1894)

[5] Max's essay, which appeared in the January 1895 issue of *The Yellow Book*.

[6] When Aubrey Beardsley went to Malvern.  [7] Author, editor, and adventurer (1856–1931).

I saw Lambart[1] looking very voguish at the New English Art Club. Sickert is painting me.[2] I have told you a lot of news.

Yours   MAX

Poor Aubrey is going to Malvern today – he is to reside at the Hydropathic place there – isn't it awful for him?

I hear that Bosie has started a single eyeglass – after reading the Parkinson case.[3]

## To Robert Ross
### MS. Hyde

*Sunday [27 January 1895]*     *Union Club, Fifth Avenue & 21st Street*
New York

My dear Bobbie, Many thanks for your nice telegram. This is one page to hope you are happy and well, and to *implore* you not to look after Reggie Turner while I am away. He is very weak and you, if I remember rightly, are very wicked. Also you are a delightful person to be with and just calculated to lead poor Reg astray without intention. Do not see too much of him. I wish he could get into a good ecclesiastical set and become good again, as I am sure he very soon would. Also keep Bosie away from him (give my love to Bosie). Bosie is more fatal to Reg than you – if anything.

All this is quite serious. I really think Reg is at rather a crucial point of his career – and should hate to see him fall an entire victim to the love that dares not tell its name. You are a person of far stronger character and it doesn't affect you in the way that it would affect him.

I am becoming enamoured of New York. At first I hated it – the dreadful passage, with the sea like a lake of glass and the vessel pitching like Hell and the disembarking at the hideous harbour with the statue of Vulgarity towering over us. It was awful. I told a reporter that I did not like the statue and said to him "It must come down".

I am trying to establish a monarchy here and rather scandalise these old-fashioned Republicans.

---

[1] Alfred Charlemagne Lambart (1861–1943), a kinsman of the Earl of Cavan, lived mostly abroad. He was twice married and was always very correctly dressed.

[2] Walter Richard Sickert, artist (1860–1942). He painted and drew a number of portraits and caricatures of Max.

[3] Major W.H. Parkinson was arrested in Southwark on "a shameful charge", and on 9 November 1894 he cut his own throat with a piece of broken glass in his cell at Holloway Prison.

We are at the Waldorf – a very Byzantine place, and altogether I am very fairly happy – but I don't like the custom they have of keeping the streets artificially cold.

And how is dear London? Do write to me a lot of news and *at once*, please. Does the scarlet carcase of G.S. Street still make the thoroughfares impassable?[1] Do write to me. We are here for the present. Herbert begins acting tomorrow.[2]                                              Yours ever   MAX


## To Ada Leverson
MS. Clark

*9 April 1895*                                                *The Waldorf, New York*

My dearest Mrs Leverson, *What* must you think of me for not having written all this long time? I missed two mails running and then I could not find a good excuse nor much news – and oh you know how one puts off writing, especially if one receives *very* charming, amusing letters which are difficult to answer at all worthily. You have told me so much that is cosy and funny about the people who amuse us – poor Frank Harris and Walter Sickert and so forth – and I can tell of no-one except Mrs de Rosen and Mrs Chatfield Taylor. Do the names suggest much to you? I have enjoyed myself very much but am longing to see you and talk with you as of old. Do you remember Broadstairs and our nice times there? What fun we had and how long ago it does seem! I feel so old. Even my writings in *The Yellow Book* are rather early '95. Younger men, new ideas have come into being since the days of Aubrey Beardsley. I don't profess to keep pace with them. I look around me and sigh when I see so many younger men with many months of activity before them. I don't think I shall do much more creative work in literature. Is your creative work, by the way, in *this Yellow Book*? I do hope it is. The thing was becoming rather dull.[3]

Poor Oscar! Why did he not go away while he could?[4] I suppose there

[1] George Slythe Street (1867–1936), journalist and author of *The Autobiography of a Boy* (1894) and other books. He had just overlapped with Max at Charterhouse, but they never met there. Rothenstein recounts how "they met one night at Solferino's. Street, like Max, was something of a dandy. Each aspired to be more coldly aloof than the other; but finally warmth crept into the party, and there and then a close friendship began." (*Men and Memories*, Vol. 1, p. 287.)

[2] Tree's American tour opened at Abbey's Theatre, New York, on 28 January 1895.

[3] Ada Leverson's short story "Suggestion" appeared in Vol. V of *The Yellow Book* (April 1895).                    [4] Oscar Wilde was arrested on 5 April 1895.

has *never* been so great a scandal and sensation! Over here the papers have been full of it. We are all so fearfully sorry about the whole thing. Poor Mrs Robinson too![1] John Lane, publisher,[2] was [*The rest of this letter is missing.*]

## To Leonard Smithers[3]
MS. Clark

[*Postmark 9 September 1895*]                    *19 Hyde Park Place*

My dear Smithers, Here is Roberts[4] – I think it is good. What about the rest? I had a letter from Raven-Hill[5] yesterday, asking me for some proofs. Do let me have them.

Could you also let me have £3 of which I am in violent need – it was what we arranged for last *Savoy*. If you would entrust it to the messenger – many thanks.                    Yours sincerely    MAX BEERBOHM

## To John Lane
MS. London

[*Early 1896*]                    *19 Hyde Park Place, W.*

My dear John Lane, Here are three *Unicorns*[6] – the fourth and last (October 2) I cannot find – but it contained nothing signed of mine. My two signed things are in numbers 2 and 3.[7] I have been laughing over the Bibliography – it is awfully good![8]

[1] Presumably the fashionable fortune-teller who had prophesied a brilliant life for Wilde.

[2] (1854–1925). In 1887 he founded the Bodley Head in conjunction with Elkin Mathews. He was to publish *The Works of Max Beerbohm* on 10 June 1896.

[3] Publisher of dubious reputation (1861–1907). But he did publish Oscar Wilde's last three books (*The Ballad of Reading Gaol*, *The Importance of Being Earnest* and *An Ideal Husband*), also Aubrey Beardsley's *A Book of Fifty Drawings* (1897) and *A Second Book of Fifty Drawings* (1899), and the monthly *Savoy* (January–December 1896).

[4] A caricature of the comedian Arthur Roberts (1852–1933), which appeared in the July 1896 issue of the *Savoy* and was reprinted in *Max's Nineties* (1958).

[5] Leonard Raven-Hill, *Punch* cartoonist (1867–1942). He wrote an introduction to Max's first book of drawings, *Caricatures of Twenty-Five Gentlemen*, which Smithers published in December 1896.

[6] The *Unicorn*, a monthly paper, lasted only from May to October 1895.

[7] "Notes in Foppery" (18 and 25 September 1895), which were amalgamated with "Dandies and Dandies" (*Vanity*, New York, 7, 14, 21 and 28 February 1895) to form "Dandies and Dandies" in *The Works*.

[8] At the end of the tiny quarto 160-page *Works* Lane added an accurate bibliography of Max's writings and drawings to date, with a gently amusing Preface, treating Max as a distinguished elder statesman of literature.

It has just struck me that when you speak of my "difficulty in hearing" as one of the few signs of my great age people will think I *am* actually deaf. Could you alter it to "the pathetic stoop and the low, melancholy voice of one who, though resigned, yet yearns for the happier past?"[1] – or something of the kind. What do you think?

I will come in and see you again on Tuesday.　　　Yours  MAX


## To John Lane
MS. London

[*c. April 1896*]　　　　　　　　　　　　　　*19 Hyde Park Place, W.*

My dear John Lane, I am sorry you haven't had the manuscript before. I have been in an agony of difficulties over the Dandies and trying to get one thing to fit into another in vain – at last I have done it, I think.

Also I send "Cosmetics" – which I have taken out of another old and very much torn copy we had.

Romeo Coates I will send by Tuesday – direct to you, so as to save time. I do not suppose Harland will mind.[2]　　　Yours  MAX


## To Edmund Gosse[3]
MS. B.L.

*Monday* [8] *June 1896*　　　　　　　　　*19 Hyde Park Place, W.*

Dear Mr Gosse, I send you a copy of my first book, and my excuse is that you, unconsciously, suggested the title of it. One afternoon of last summer, in the garden of a certain club, you were complaining of the folly of journalists, and you declared that, next time they asked you what works you had found most "helpful", you would say, "The Works of Max Beerbohm". So I send you the little monster that has been born of your *mot*, hoping you will be one of its keepers.

Yours very truly　 MAX BEERBOHM

---

[1] Lane duly inserted these words in place of his own.

[2] "Poor Romeo", the story of Romeo Coates, had appeared in the April 1896 volume of *The Yellow Book*.

[3] Poet, critic and autobiographer (1845–1928). Knighted 1925.

## To the Editor of the Daily Chronicle[1]

*28 July 1896*                                    *19 Hyde Park Place*

Sir, Are they really, as you suggest, going to raze the wall that hides Devonshire House from Piccadilly? I hope not. The unseen courtyards that still remain before a few of the greater residences in London – Devonshire, Lansdowne, Marlborough, and other houses – always strike me as peculiarly charming and impressive. I wonder that you, sir, who have so often and so well protested against the destruction of interesting pieces of architecture, should say no good word for these walls, also. Are they, like the toll-gates, an insult to democracy? To me it seems that they are only an odd relic of days when the people were so democratic that they actually broke ducal windows, of days when Disraeli could put into the mouth of an Eton boy that fine speech, "My father says that every nobleman's house should have a courtyard".[2] I have known many persons of taste, notably the late E.W. Godwin, distinguished among architects,[3] who held the arrogant mystery of these walls to be one of the most fascinating things in London, and I am told that Mr William Morris[4] (surely no champion of the *noblesse*) has often praised them. I hope they will stand. As for the "improvement" of Piccadilly, to that the razure of the Duke's wall could hardly contribute. Devonshire House itself is one of the ugliest sights in London.

Yours obediently   MAX BEERBOHM

## To John Lane
MS. London

*August 1896*                              *Berkeley Hotel, Bognor, Sussex*

My dear John Lane, I am glad you like the *H.H.*[5] and I expect you are right in thinking it too short for a book. With two other stories it would make a jolly book, though, and I like your idea about "wicked men". Also I should like the *H.H.* to go into the next *Yellow Book*[6] – *but* I

---

[1] Where it appeared on 29 July. Max enlarged it in "If I were Aedile" in *More*.

[2] *Coningsby*, Book I, Chapter viii.

[3] 1833–86. Lover of Ellen Terry. Father of Edy and Gordon Craig.

[4] Poet and craftsman (1834–96). Organiser of the Socialist League.

[5] *The Happy Hypocrite*, which Lane published in paper covers as No 1 of the Bodley Booklets in April 1897.       [6] It was first published there in the October 1896 volume.

really cannot let it go for less than £25. It is close on 15,000 words – three times the length of *George IV* – for which I got £10 – two years ago! Don't think me grasping. You see I am not and, if you don't think the story worth £25, I really can't part with it. I am staying here another week at any rate – so if you will write me a line – write to this address. Afterward I am going to France for a short time with one of my sisters. I suppose Owen Seaman[1] did the *National Observer*. Is he a very disappointed man? He is certainly smart. I am enjoying Bognor, though it is so small and so full that one can't get rooms for more than three days together, and I sleep already in my fourth bedroom!

Yours   MAX

## To Alfred Harmsworth[2]
MS. Merton

*30 November 1896*           *19 Hyde Park Place, W.*

Dear Mr Harmsworth, Since I saw you, I have had a bad chill and was unable till lately to write anything. Now I am sending you two instalments of my things – one about sign-boards, the other about the fire-brigade.[3] The second is the more sensational of the two – but you will know which of the two would be the best to lead off with. I hope you will like both. I think each cost me six guineas-worth of labour and time – so perhaps that sum might be fixed as my price. As you will see, I have given "A Commentary" as general title.

Yours very truly   MAX BEERBOHM

---

[1] 1861–1936. Editor of *Punch* 1906–32. Published much light verse.

[2] Later first and last Viscount Northcliffe (1856–1922). Journalist and newspaper proprietor. Founded the halfpenny *Daily Mail* in February 1896.

[3] "An Infamous Brigade", which appeared in the *Daily Mail* on 5 December 1896, was the first of a series of weekly pieces by Max which continued until 17 April 1897. "Sign-Boards" (12 December) was the second. Both were reprinted in *More*.

## To Bernard Shaw[1]
### MS. B.L.

[12] *April 1898*                               *48 Upper Berkeley Street, W.*[2]

My dear G.B.S., I was very much pleased, as you may imagine, to receive your letter and the great compliment it implied. But your decision to retire from dramatic criticism rather depresses me – and I hope that you will still reconsider it. You may be tired of the job, but "stale" you certainly are not – you are a weekly marvel of freshness and agility – and you certainly don't repeat yourself, though I am sure you would bear repetition.

Whether *I* could succeed you, I am by no means certain. There would be several difficulties. My mind is not very fertile, and any success I may have had is due to my own shrewdness in not doing much. I am afraid I might come an early and a nasty cropper off the hebdomadal tightrope. Also, I have no enthusiasm for the theatre – in fact I don't care a damn about the theatre. This would handicap me for decent criticism. Also, I have a big brother at Her Majesty's, and he would be rather compromised by my position, and I by his. Also I am an amiable person, and might be unable to speak ill of any bad actors, except those whom I have never met. And I have met so many, so many!

However, the position of dramatic critic to the *Saturday* is a dignified position – and regular emolument must be very nice. And I will wait and see what Frank Harris says – and whether you remain adamant.

The most obvious difficulty for me would be in following you. You have done so much in dramatic criticism, and I should be always tripping up in your large and deep footprints.

Meanwhile I am sincerely yours    MAX BEERBOHM

---

[1] Shaw (1856–1950) had been dramatic critic of the *Saturday Review* since 1895. He was now preparing to retire and in his final article on 21 May 1898 he wrote: "The younger generation is knocking at the door; and as I open it there steps spritely in the incomparable Max", whose first dramatic criticism appeared on 28 May 1898. Frank Harris had bought the paper in 1894, and had enlisted many leading writers as contributors.

[2] To which the Beerbohms had moved in 1897.

## To the Editor of the Pall Mall Gazette[1]

*5 May 1898*                                        *48 Upper Berkeley Street*

Shakespeare's Sonnets

Dear Sir, Your reviewer complains that in Mr George Wyndham's edition of the sonnets there is no note upon that much-debated line:

Time doth transfix the flourish set on youth.

Various editors have sought to elucidate this line in various ways, but, so far as I know, none has hit upon the following explanation, which seems to me to be the only one that is quite plausible. In all ancient books of heraldry one finds that the chief escutcheons bear on either side certain wing-like appendages, which are technically called "flourishes". Each of these appendages signified "a noble Place or Poste under the Crowne". The tenure of a Royal seal or charter, for example, or admission to the Privy Council, entitled a nobleman to add one of these flourishes to his arms. But if for any misdemeanour he forfeited his privilege the heralds caused a line to be drawn through his flourish, which was thenceforth described by them as a "flourish transfix". Thus in Hort's *Compleat Booke of Antient Heraldrie and the Devices*, published in 1653, one finds that the arms of the Earl of Forde had as many as nine flourishes, two of which were crossed – one "transfix in the yeare 1540 for Rebellion". All flourishes were abolished by Charles II, soon after the Restoration, when it was found that many noblemen had contrived to embellish their arms with flourishes to which they had no right.                     I am your obedient servant     MAX BEERBOHM


## To the Editor of the Pall Mall Gazette[2]

*25 May 1898*                                        *5 Thornhill Square, N*

Shakespeare's Sonnets

Sir, A letter signed "Max Beerbohm" in the *Pall Mall Gazette* for May 7 has come under my notice. The letter mentions a line in Shakespeare's sixtieth sonnet which certainly presents some difficulty:

Time doth transfix the flourish set on youth.

[1] Published there on 7 May 1898.

[2] Published there on 28 May 1898.

According to Mr Beerbohm the line contains a metaphor borrowed from heraldic usage. "Flourishes" were appendages to coats-of-arms indicating honours attained. Misconduct might be punished by a line "transfixing" the flourish. An alleged case in point is that of "the Earl of Forde", for information concerning which we are referred to "Hort's *Compleat Booke of Antient Heraldrie and the Devices*, published in 1653". Mr Beerbohm's suggestion would have been not without value if verification had been possible. Unfortunately this is not the case. No such work as that mentioned is to be found in the British Museum catalogue, or in that of the Bodleian or of the Huth Library, or in Moule's *Bibliotheca Heraldica*, or in other well-known lists. Dr Furnivall,[1] who has taken a good deal of trouble in the matter, wrote to a friend of his, a distinguished member of the Heralds' College; but this gentleman knew nothing of "the Earl of Forde", and did not believe in "transfixed flourishes". I do not like to come to the conclusion that Mr Beerbohm's letter was a practical joke; but if so, it can scarcely be regarded as other than very objectionable. Appearing in a journal so well known and so influential as the *Pall Mall Gazette*, it may, as Dr Furnivall points out, crop up again fifty years hence; and even now it may lead astray German or American students, who are unable to consult the great libraries of this country.     I am, Sir, your obedient servant   THOMAS TYLER[2]

## *To the Editor of the* Pall Mall Gazette[3]

*30 May 1898*                                      *48 Upper Berkeley Street*

### Shakespeare's Sonnets

Dear Sir, I am sorry that serious men have been taking me seriously as a commentator on Shakespeare, and I hasten to admit that my theory of the heraldic metaphor was but an essay in fantastic erudition, or, as Mr Tyler rather crudely conjectures, "a practical joke". To Dr Furnivall

---

[1] Frederick James Furnivall, eccentric and formidable philologist and editor (1825–1910).

[2] Shakespearean scholar (1826–1902), who produced the theory that the Dark Lady of the Sonnets was Mary Fitton. Shaw in the preface to his play *The Dark Lady of the Sonnets* described Tyler as "a gentleman of such astonishing and crushing ugliness that no one who had once seen him could ever thereafter forget him".

[3] Published there on 2 June 1898.

I have already confessed, receiving a genial absolution.[1] To the others I apologise also. But have I really wasted anyone's time? The true scholar loves research for its own sake. The exhilaration is in the chase itself, rather than in the "kill". That is a metaphor drawn from fox-hunting. It can be verified in the Badminton Library.

I am your obedient servant   MAX BEERBOHM


## To Edmund Gosse
MS. Berg

*20 November 1898*                                    *48 Upper Berkeley Street, W.*

My dear Mr Gosse, I am sorry to say that I could learn nothing very definite about the *Saturday's* future last night.[2] I kept trying to lead up to the subject – but at the beginning of dinner everyone was too discreet to commit himself – and at the end of dinner everyone was too sentimental. There were many speeches, made by Harris, Runciman[3] and others, with many references to "the ship", "the crew", "dropping the pilot", "stormy waters", "steering safe into harbour" and so forth. And at every nautical metaphor everyone shed a tear, and drank another liqueur, and drummed on the table with a fork. Later on, we adjourned to Southampton Street[4] and continued our emotions, and it was only when I walked some of the way home with Runciman that I was able to learn that Lord Hardwicke meant to instal a new *political* editor – (keeping Runciman, I think, as general editor) – but hoped that the rest of the staff would remain. Also, I understood that in future things would be conducted in a more business-like way. I am afraid there is no very important information in this letter. But it is the only information I could gather. And I send it to you for what it is worth.★

[1] On condition that Max should subscribe ten shillings to the Esperance Girls' Rowing Club at Hammersmith, in which Furnivall took "a very human interest" (*Men and Memories, Vol. I*, by William Rothenstein, 1931). There is a splendid photograph of Furnivall with a buxom eight in *Caught in the Web of Words* by K. M. Elisabeth Murray (1977).

[2] Frank Harris was now selling the *Saturday Review* to a South African syndicate backed by the sixth Earl of Hardwicke.

[3] John F. Runciman (1866–1916), outspoken music critic of the *Saturday Review* and Harris's understudy. He was then temporary editor.

[4] i.e. the offices of the *Saturday Review*.

With kindest regards to Mrs Gosse,

                    I am very sincerely yours    MAX BEERBOHM
★ This sounds rather Esterhazian![1]

## To R.B. Cunninghame Graham[2]
MS. Edinburgh

*8 February 1899*                    *48 Upper Berkeley Street, W.*

My dear Mr Cunninghame Graham, I am glad the caricature did not offend[3] – my caricatures generally do, I am sorry to say. *Contempsisti barbarorum gladios, non pertimesces meos,*[4] I suppose.

I have been revelling in *Mogreb-El-Acksa,*[5] certain passages of which I know by heart. It is refreshing and delightful to have such a book, and I firmly demand another.

                    Yours very truly    MAX BEERBOHM

## To Edmund Gosse
MS. Brotherton

*25 March 1899*                    *48 Upper Berkeley Street, W.*

My dear Mr Gosse, Many thanks for your letter. I need hardly say that I appreciate the kindly feeling which prompted you to write it, and that I value your good opinion far too highly not to take your bad opinion to heart.

[1] Commandant Marie-Charles Ferdinand Walsin-Esterhazy (1847–1923) had in September 1898 admitted that he had forged the *bordereau* which caused the innocent Dreyfus to languish on Devil's Island for five years. His hastily written book *Les Dessous de l'Affaire Dreyfus* had just been published, and on 19 November the *Pall Mall Gazette* published translated extracts. Hence Max's derision.

[2] The most picturesque Scot of his time, traveller, horseman, writer, and Socialist campaigner (1852–1936).

[3] Max's first caricature of Graham appeared in the *Academy* on 28 January 1899. It was reprinted in *Max's Nineties* (1958).

[4] "You despised the swords of the barbarians; you will not be terrified by mine" (adapted from Cicero's *Second Philippic*, ch. 118). Graham had been badly wounded and arrested in the Trafalgar Square affray on "Bloody Sunday", 13 November 1887. He was found guilty of riotous assembly and served four and a half weeks in the insanitary squalor of Pentonville Prison. "Sursum Corda", his account of his incarceration, was published in the *Saturday Review* on 19 June 1897 and reprinted in his book *Success* (1902).

[5] *Mogreb-El-Acksa: a Journey in Morocco* (1898). Shaw said that without it he couldn't have written *Captain Brassbound's Conversion*, and Conrad called it "the book of travel of the century".

17

I meant no "insolence" when I wrote the little note for this week's *Saturday*.[1] Still less have I the dreadful joy of being concerned in any "ignoble commercial intrigue" against Swinburne, or the Elizabethan Stage Society, or, indeed, anyone, or anything.[2] To "carelessness" I must, however, plead guilty. The Elizabethan Stage Society never sends a seat to the *Saturday*; but I had been particularly anxious to see *Locrine* and had intended to apply for a seat. On Saturday night I caught a chill, which developed into a kind of influenza, and so I did not, as I had intended, send a messenger to St George's Hall on Monday morning. In saying that I had "nothing to write about", I ought to have inserted that I had not seen *Locrine*. I forgot; and I am sorry.

In the more general part of your letter, you complain that every week I write "so badly" and "so insincerely". As I am never *conscious* of insincerity, I cannot admit the second half of the indictment. But the very fact that I am not conscious of writing badly does but make me the more uncomfortable about the first half. It makes me feel that such literary talent as I had must have been gradually debased and blunted by my indulgence in the hebdomadal habit.[3] This much I can say with perfect truth: I have acquired no journalistic *fluency* in writing – I still take as much trouble as I ever took. If I scamped my work, then your letter would be only a sharp prick to my conscience – I could "pull myself together", as you urge, and forthwith write something that would please you. As I do *not* scamp my work, your letter comes as a rather forcible suggestion that my talent has been diminishing, deteriorating, and that I am no longer capable of writing well. You hint that while I take less trouble with my writing I take more trouble with my humour. You say that I "force the giggle". Well, in point of fact, such jests as I make come as easily to me as they ever did. If, in print, they seem

---

"SILET, SAPIT"

[1] "This week I have nothing to write about. I am as the cuckoo in a clock that has not been wound up. Striking-time has come round, but the folding-doors fly not open, and I cannot hop forth to coo. Mr Hare has produced *Caste*, but that is not nearly enough to set the mechanism going. I have already explained, at great length, why Tom Robertson's plays are impossible in modern costume, and (except that *Caste* in such costume seemed to me even more drearily impossible than *School*, and that in the costume of its period it might have been even more amusing than *Ours*) I have nothing to say of the production. Having whispered thus through the crack of the folding-doors, cuckoo is silent." (*Saturday Review*, 25 March 1899).

[2] *Locrine*, Swinburne's tragedy in five acts, published in 1887, was presented by the Elizabethan Stage Society in St George's Hall on 20 March 1899.

[3] i.e. his weekly dramatic criticisms in the *Saturday Review*.

18

"forced", that simply shows that they are less good than they used to be, and that my sense of humour is on the wane. Altogether, I seem to be in a rather bad way. And since I cannot, on the one hand take less trouble with my jokes, nor, on the other hand, more with my actual writing, and since my bad opinions are the result of bad judgment, not of dishonesty, I cannot hold out much hope of my immediate improvement. Some day, perhaps, I shall be cured of the hebdomadal habit – the "gold-cure" is the only cure I know for it! – and then I may re-emerge as I was in the beginning – possibly as something even better. Meanwhile, it is some consolation to know that among the first to congratulate me on my redemption will be Edmund Gosse, to whom no young writer owes more gratitude than the young writer signing himself "MAX"

## Edmund Gosse to Max[1]

*29 April 1899*                                                   *29 Delamere Terrace*

My dear Max, You will, I hope, forgive my delay in thanking you for the kind thought you had in sending me your new volume of essays.[2] I wanted to read and re-read them before I wrote to you. Now, let me say to you how very highly I think of them. I weigh this little book against its predecessor, and I am astonished at the growth from the petulant, amusing, clever boy to the finished man. I do not think that there is an essayist living who is your equal now, *at your best*. But, bless me, how unequal you are! What rejoices me about the little book is that I find you throughout (or almost throughout) the rigid censor of your own things. You select for permanent form only your best, and I observe the revisions made since the first periodical appearance of the essays – always for the better.

Well, this really answers my anxiety and my indignation. The bad things don't matter, if you only reprint good ones. The newspaper is lost, the book remains. Our duty is towards our books. A little essay of yours is a sonnet, really; no one turns out the classic "*sonnet sans défaut*" every time. The fatuous essayist thinks they are all equally good, and his are all equally bad.

[1] Text from *The Life and Letters of Sir Edmund Gosse* by Evan Charteris (1931).

[2] *More*, published on 20 April 1899.

Now, about *More*. I should bore you if I told you all the reflections which have occurred to me in reading it. You are now a finished master in the form of your best groups of phrases. I am in despair: I have been trying to see where the magic of some of your sentences comes in, have even (for purely self-educational purposes) been trying to imitate some of them privately. Your constructions, at their best, have now become miraculously characteristic, in their solidity and lightness. You have an instrument quite your own, and you know how to use it. Beware – oh! good gracious, what is the good of being ware of anything, when one writes so well as you do?

Still, in pure priggishness, I will give you one or two warnings:

In these delicious little affairs of yours the balance is so exquisite that the least failure in tact vexes the reader. However, one or two little unfitting projections of yourself make me wince. You speak of yourself *humorously* with absolute success. But sometimes I am hurt when you speak of yourself *seriously*. You say your reviews of Ouida and again of Mrs Meynell caused in each case a revolution of taste.[1] This is not the voice of Max, but that of ——. Ah, how much more delicately Max could indicate what here has a touch of coarse vanity. Do think of this, and of the rare sensitiveness of the ear to the proper sounding of the ego.

Then, sometimes, you – whose whole function is to be on the side of the angels – fight abruptly with the fools. The essay in *More* which I like least is the Aedile one. I don't like you to be obvious. Now, there are a thousand journalists in London whose ignorance and whose insensibility to impressions render them entirely capable of approving or of signing your remarks on sculpture, which you will forgive me, my dear Max, if I tell you are quite unworthy of you. If you are insensible to form, sculpture may give you no pleasure, as music gives me none who am insensible to tune, but I have always refrained from saying that there is no difference between good and bad music, and that all music is insufferable. Don't let us insult the arts; it is such a stupid thing to do.

I could go on long talking about your delightful little book: but I must weary you.

Most truly yours    EDMUND GOSSE

---

[1] In his essay on the novelist Ouida (1839–1908) Max said that her work was as undervalued as that of the post Alice Meynell (1847–1922) was overpraised.

## To Edmund Gosse
MS. Brotherton

*30 April 1899*                                                    *Savile Club*

My dear Mr Gosse, Thank you for the very great pleasure your letter
has given me. I am delighted to think that my little book interested you,
and I have been reading over and over again the subtle and charming
things you say about it. I have never had, before your letter, any *technical*
criticism of my writing, and it is no exaggeration to say that your letter
gives me as much pride as Hall Caine[1] would derive from a "twenty-
fifth edition".

I see how right you are in your objection to the passages about myself
and my contribution to the Ouida and Meynell controversy. And if ever
I have a chance of re-revising *More* those passages will disappear or, at
least, be transformed. But as to *sculpture*, I think you have a little
misinterpreted my meaning. What I meant was that no *modern* statues
were valuable. I did not mean to decry the art of sculpture.

It was really most kind of you to write to me as you did, and – but I
need not labour the obvious point of gratitude. With kindest regards to
Mrs Gosse I am sincerely yours                    MAX BEERBOHM

P.S. It is appropriate that I am writing to you from this address, which
I owe mainly to you.[2]


## To William Archer[3]
MS. B.L.

*24 November 1899*                                    *48 Upper Berkeley Street*

My dear W.A., Thanks for your kind and charming letter. I readily
admit that you are not a poet, nor erratic; as to genius I am not so sure.
Perhaps you are not a genius in your sense of the word. But anyone who

---

[1] Prodigiously successful novelist (1853–1931). Knighted 1918.

[2] Gosse had recently proposed Max for the Savile Club, and he remained a member
until 1918.

[3] Scottish dramatic critic (1856–1924). Early friend, translator and champion of Ibsen.
On 18 November 1899 Max published in the *Saturday Review* an article entitled
"William Archer and A.B. Walkley", in which he compared the two critics and their
latest books. (It was reprinted in *Around Theatres*.) Archer had responded, and this is
Max's riposte. For his obituary tribute to Archer see *A Peep into the Past* (1972), p. 53.

is (in my opinion) an "ideally good critic" must have (in my sense of the word) genius for criticism. In case this sounds patronising and impertinent, I hasten to repeat that ideally good criticism does not much appeal to me. I "lugged in" Henley and George Moore as being men who have done a good deal of criticism in their time – the kind of criticism which I really enjoy: the stimulating prejudices (with rare flashes of inspired rightness) of men whose minds are involved in and limited by some kind of creative work. I think it rather disgraceful of me to prefer their criticism (if one can call it criticism) to yours; and I hope to outgrow the taste. However, that is my taste at present, and Henley and Moore were not really "irrelevant" to my article. By the way, when I spoke of Moore's criticism I meant his literary and dramatic criticism. In his criticism of painting he seems to me dreadfully sane; the cause of his sanity being that he can only paint like a schoolgirl: his love of the art is not absorbed by creative power into one strait channel. Whistler, of course, is the "art"-critic who gives me keenest delight.

As to Mrs Craigie,[1] I am sorry I implied that you wanted her to devote herself entirely to serious (or, as your typewriter calls it, *sarious*) work. But you did advise her to be serious occasionally. Man, you say, cannot live on trifle alone. Isn't that a false analogy? It would be sound enough if Mrs Craigie were the only living playwright. As she is not, and as there are few light comic dramatists, why urge the poor little lady to flounder? She is bound to flounder in serious work. Think of her last book, if you read it![2] Also, *A Repentance*[3] – but you had flown to America on the eve of that production – you whose advice, I am sure, was responsible for her shameful attempt. I think the least you could have done would have been to stay and see the unfortunate girl through her trouble.

Forgive this enormous rigmarole.            Yours very sincerely   MAX

---

[1] Pearl Mary Teresa Craigie (1867–1906). American novelist and dramatist as John Oliver Hobbes.

[2] *The School for Saints* (1897).

[3] A one-act play, first performed at Carisbrooke Castle 1899. It was described by the author as "a psychological diagram of the Carlist question".

## To Mortimer Menpes[1]
MS. Clark

*22 December 1899*                    *48 Upper Berkeley Street, W.*

My dear Menpes, I went to the Savile today, and found there your note, and the brilliant "Coquelin".[2] Very many thanks. Almost persuadest thou me to be a portrait-painter. I wish thou couldst enable me to be one. As it is, I can only gape and wonder how on earth you can distil a man's quintessence and at the same time not make a guy of him. It is absurd of you to compliment me on my decoctions, when you can do the trick so much better, without sacrificing the dignity and humanity of your subject – and of yourself.         Yours   MAX BEERBOHM

## To D.S. MacColl[3]
MS. Glasgow

*23 November 1900*                    *48 Upper Berkeley Street, W.*

My dear MacColl, Will Rothenstein[4] and Bobbie Ross have, at one time or another, flattered me by telling me that my caricatures amuse you. And so I am sending you the Xmas Number of the *World*, which contains a galaxy of my efforts. I should like you to see them, but please do not think that I am inflicting on you the necessity of sending me a letter of thanks. I am sure you loathe letter-writing as strongly as I do, and if I thought you would bother to reply I should forego the pleasure of sending you drawings.

I look forward to "D.S.M." week by week (always hoping, in a corner of my heart, that he will fall beneath his usual form and so allow me to read my own article with complacency. And always I am disappointed).
         Yours very sincerely   MAX BEERBOHM

P.S. I cannot remember your address at Hampton Court, so I send this note through the *Saturday*.

---

[1] Painter, etcher and author, disciple of Whistler (1859–1938).   [2] See footnote on p. 34.
[3] Dugald Sutherland MacColl, Scottish painter, author, art critic (1859–1948). Keeper of the Tate Gallery and the Wallace Collection. His art criticism, signed with his initials, appeared in the *Saturday Review* alongside Max's drama criticism. They remained friends for life.
[4] Artist (1872–1945). For his friendship with Max see *Max and Will*, edited by Mary M. Lago and Karl Beckson (1975). He married Alice Knewstub in 1899 and was knighted in 1931.

## To Ada Leverson
### MS. Texas

*5 June 1901*                              *48 Upper Berkeley Street, W.*

My dear Mrs Leverson, Yes, I shall be delighted to come and lunch with you next Sunday. Am so looking forward to seeing you.

I cannot remember Marjorie's[1] telephone number; nor yet the name of her landlord, under whose name you could find it in the book. But I will find out forthwith and let you know.                    Yours ever    MAX

*Scene*: Café Royal
*Time*: A few evenings ago. Enter Will Rothenstein, who espies at a distant table Frank Harris, whom he has not met for some years. He hurries, full of cordiality, to F.H., who stares at him with marked coldness and hostility.
*F.H.* "You've grown older ... *I* have grown younger."
*W.R.* "Oh well, my dear Frank, there was plenty of margin for that on either side!"

[Collapse of F.H.]


## To Robert Ross
### MS. Hyde

*Friday* [*November 1901*]                 *48 Upper Berkeley Street, W.*

My dear Bobbie, I will come on Monday to Carfax[2] and do all you ask. Monday at 12 shall we say?

The Henley idea appeals to me. But I think your suggestions are rather *too* bitter.[3]

How would it be to do Henley in tears, with the legend "And immediately the circulation of the *P.M.M.* growed. And Henley went out and wept bitterly"?

---

[1] Marjorie Battine, *née* Trevor (1883–1966). A beauty who was a friend of Max and other writers.

[2] The Carfax Gallery in Ryder Street, St James's, which Ross was running. Max's first exhibition of caricatures opened there in November 1901.

[3] In the December issue of the *Pall Mall Magazine* (which was available in November) W.E. Henley (1849–1903) published a savage essay on his old friend Robert Louis Stevenson, who had died in 1894.

Or Henley as Brutus, in the tent-scene of *Julius Caesar*, with R.L.S. as the ghost, and Whibley[1] as the sleeping Lucius?

Anyhow, I will do something.[2]                    Yours ever    MAX

## To the Editor of the Academy
MS. Texas

*[Postmark 2 December 1901]*

*The two new Books which have pleased
and interested me most in 1901 are:*

If in 1901 the firstlings of only two among my personal friends had been shown to the public, I should be yielding as gladly as anyone else to your annual temptation. But this has been a *Wunderjahr* for my personal friends, in that no fewer than six of them have "commenced author". The pleasure of awarding two wreaths is not so keen as the pain of inflicting four wounds. So you will excuse me.

MAX BEERBOHM

## To G.K. Chesterton[1]
TS. Merton

*4 May 1902*                                            *Savile Club*

Dear Mr Chesterton, I have seldom wished to meet anyone in particular: but you I should very much like to meet.

I need not explain who I am, for the name at the end of this note is one which you have more than once admitted, rather sternly, into your writings.

By way of personal and private introduction, I may say that my mother was a friend of your grandmother, Mrs Grosjean, and also of your mother.

As I have said, I should like to meet you. On the other hand, it is

[1] Charles Whibley, author and journalist (1859–1930), was Henley's henchman on the last two of the papers Henley edited.

[2] Max's caricature in the 1901 exhibition was headed "R.L.S. - W.E.H." "Out, out, brief candle" and showed a small Henley vainly attempting to extinguish the flame of a large candle bearing Stevenson's features.

[3] Poet, novelist, critic and essayist (1874–1936).

quite possible that *you* have no reciprocal anxiety to meet *me*. In this case, nothing could be easier than for you to say that you are very busy, or unwell, or going out of town, and so are not able – much as you would have liked – to lunch with me here either next Wednesday or next Saturday at 1.30.

I am, whether you come or not, yours admiringly    MAX BEERBOHM

P.S. I am quite different from my writings (and so, I daresay, are you from yours). So that we should not necessarily fail to hit it off.

I, in the flesh, am modest, full of common sense, very genial, and rather dull.

What you are remains to be seen – or not to be seen by me, according to your decision.

Any answer to this note had better be directed to
                48 Upper Berkeley Street, W.
for the porter of this club is very dilatory.


## To William Archer
MS. B.L.

*14 May 1902*                                    *48 Upper Berkeley Street*

My dear W.A., "The little feeble talents of the critics who still, from time to time, make Mr Pinero the butt of their lofty 'literary' scorn" ...

Now isn't this rather a deflexion from your usual and admirable *urbanity*, and as such isn't it to be deplored?

Of course, I shouldn't address to you this "humble remonstrance" if I supposed myself included in your attack. A man cannot bob up and say "I'm *not* feeble!" But, some time ago, when you wrote in a similar, though gentler, vein about "Anti-Pineroites", and I made some comments in the *Saturday*, you wrote to me, telling me to set my mind at rest, for that you had not been thinking of me at all, but of "George Moore, Shaw, and critics of that kidney, who" (I quote from memory) "never can mention Pinero's name without being unmannerly". So I conclude that it is on Shaw and Moore and those others that you are still harping. Wherefore I can in a quite detached way put it to you that, when you reach the point of calling people like Shaw and Moore feeble, you must have got somehow off the proper and safe track of controversy. Moore isn't, and Shaw mayn't be, a good dramatist. But of course you are not trotting out the silly little old fallacy that a man's criticism of an art is to be discounted by his failure to create well in it. What you do suggest, evidently, is that Moore and Shaw, as critics, are feeble creatures. And that is absurd, I think. I think that you, too, meant to oil with argument the stiff knees of those heathens. But to try to frighten them by substituting for argument a contempt which you do not feel – surely that is an ineffectual way out of your duty.

I am afraid this "humble remonstrance" may seem to you something very like an impertinence – in the common sense of the word. Indeed, as I read it over, it seems so to me.

My only excuse is that I have always admired you so much as a controversialist, and that if you throw away that *urbanity* which has always been one of your chief advantages over your opponents, then one of my little intellectual pleasures will be the necessity of sitting down to manufacture an answer.

If you do make any answer at all, let it be to the question whether you could, and would, lunch with me somewhere on Saturday week. If you say 'yes', then I will write to fix the place and the hour.

Yours very sincerely   MAX BEERBOHM

## *To the Editor of the* Daily Chronicle

*20 May 1902*[1]                                     *48 Upper Berkeley Street, W.*

### A POINT IN LITERARY ETHICS

Sir, Accept these premisses:
(a) When a man, writing for print, deletes a passage from his manuscript, his motive is a wish that this passage be not printed.
(b) Ruskin[2] was a careful artist in literature.
(c) Mr George Allen, Ruskin's publisher, is full of piety for Ruskin.
(d) So are Mr E.T. Cook and Mr Wedderburn, who superintend the new edition of Ruskin's works.

You will not wonder now at the wonder in which I have been reading what Mr George Allen has been saying to a representative of you. Mr Allen, I gather, is the pious possessor of Ruskin's manuscripts, which, I gather, teem with second thoughts. "For instance," says Mr Allen,

---

[1] On this day the *Daily Chronicle* published an interview with Ruskin's friend and publisher George Allen which suggested that all Ruskin's excisions from the manuscripts of his books were to be restored in the big Library Edition of Ruskin's works, edited by E.T. Cook and Alexander Wedderburn.

[2] John Ruskin. Prolific art critic and writer on social conditions (1819–1900).

"an examination of the manuscripts of *The Seven Lamps* shows that it contains about eight thousand words which Ruskin had deleted." "Well," chirps the interviewer, "what will now be done in such a case?" Surely a foolish question, to which there could be but one answer? Not at all. "It will lie with Mr E.T. Cook and Mr Wedderburn to decide what additions should be made to the text."

This amazing pronouncement is explicable only through one or the other of two hypotheses. Either Messrs Allen, Cook and Wedderburn are willing to win for their enterprise a fillip at the expense of their piety, or, despite their piety, they believe that they know better than Ruskin what Ruskin was about.

In either case, poor Ruskin!

It is bad enough that a dead man cannot be saved from those friends who, so frequently, nose out and retrieve for us this or that separate work which he himself had hidden as unworthy. It is much worse that he should be at the mercy of friends who will insert into his published works passages which he himself had deliberately expunged. No one with any sense for the art of writing will dissent from me when I say that to insert into a dead man's work what he had written and rejected is nearly as impious as to insert words written by yourself, or by Tom, or by Dick, or by Harry.

Let Messrs Allen, Cook and Wedderburn cooperate in making Ruskin "live" by any means but that of making him turn in his grave. I am yours obediently                                               MAX BEERBOHM[1]


## To the Editor of the Daily Chronicle[2]

*24 May 1902*                                          *48 Upper Berkeley Street, W.*

Sir, I am glad that the obvious inference from Mr George Allen's words, as given by his interviewer, was not the right inference. That the passages deleted by Ruskin should appear in footnotes is much better than that they should appear in the text. But I am unshaken in my opinion that they ought not to appear at all. It is amusing and instructive, no doubt, to trace the secret workings of the method of a literary artist, to investigate his means to his ends, as revealed by his rejections and

---

[1] Max's letter was published in the paper on 23 May, with a brief reply from George Allen saying that Ruskin's text would not be altered, but "hitherto unprinted matter" would be included either as footnotes or addenda.

[1] Published in the paper on 26 May 1902.

amendments. But I think that we owe it to him to deny ourselves this pleasure. He takes infinite pains that his work may be a smooth and flawless whole. He does not give it to us until he has carefully refined away everything that has seemed to him a blemish. He means us to receive of his best, and of that only. His pride therein would shrink from the proposal to make us privy to his second-best. And so I think that Ruskin's executors, in their piety, ought to give us Ruskin's work only in that first and final form in which he himself gave it to us. Perhaps this will seem to most people a rather pedantic view; but it is the view which I take; and it is, surely, the view taken by anyone else who has any true insight into the temperament of a literary artist, and any true sympathy with that rare thing. I am yours obediently

MAX BEERBOHM

## To Theodore Watts-Dunton[1]
MS. B.L.

[26 July 1902][2]                    48 Upper Berkeley Street, W.

My dear Mr Watts-Dunton, From day to day I have delayed writing to thank you for your delightful letter, because I have been hoping to be able to suggest to you a day on which I could avail myself of your very kind invitation to come and lunch with you.

And this suggestion I have again and again been prevented from by a terrible amount of work – (new work and arrears of old work) – that has held me mercilessly captive.

I wonder whether I might come down one day next week, now that the load is somewhat lifted. Monday, Tuesday, Wednesday, or Thursday would suit me equally well.

I cannot say how much pleased and honoured I was by your letter in which you agreed with me about the raking-up of Ruskin's rejected passages.

When I wrote to the *Chronicle* I felt that perhaps my letter expressed a somewhat "crankish" and over-fastidious sentiment – a sentiment, of course, none the less sincere for that. And when your letter came to me my self-respect was wholly restored. I saw that my view was the *right* view – not merely *my own*.

---

[1] Poet, novelist and critic (1832–1914). Guardian and protector of Swinburne for the last thirty years of the poet's life. For Max's visit to them, see "No 2 The Pines" in his *And Even Now*.

[2] So dated by recipient.

And so basely selfish is my nature that I was glad to find you saying in a letter to me what you might have said in print to "the giddy vulgar".

With kindest regards, I am very sincerely yours   MAX BEERBOHM


## To Bernard Shaw
MS. B.L.

*11 November 1902*                              *48 Upper Berkeley Street, W.*

My dear G.B.S., This is a begging letter, written by the President of the Playgoers' Club (myself!). Could you, would you, read or speak a lecture (of any length, and on any subject related to drama) to the Playgoers, in one of the first three months of 1903?

I don't approve of this kind of begging, in the ordinary way. But I don't mind begging a lecture of you, for I know that self-expression is a natural instinct in you, and that you have so much to express that your one serious difficulty is in finding a sufficient number of vantage-places.

And the Playgoers are at any rate as intelligent as most other audiences. So I hope you won't spurn them, and disappoint their wistful Committee and me.

Could you send me your reply before next Saturday?

I hope *Don Juan*[1] will soon heave in sight.

Please give my kindest regards to your wife.

Yours ever   MAX BEERBOHM


## Bernard Shaw to Max[2]

*12 November 1902*                              *Maybury Knoll, Woking*

Max Beerbohm, The bonds of friendship are now bursten. The cord is loosed, the bowl is broken, the grasshopper is become a burden. Damn the Playgoers! To the blackest pit with their lectures: they have too long profaned the Sabbath. Their laughter is as the crackling of thorns under a pot; and it generally comes in the wrong place. I have found some ray of grace in even the most degraded of other societies; but in this none –

---

[1] *Man and Superman*, which in his Epistle Dedicatory Shaw referred to as "a Don Juan Play". The dream-sequence *Don Juan in Hell* from Act III was first performed as a one-act play at the Court Theatre on 4 June 1907.

[2] Text from *Bernard Shaw: Collected Letters 1898–1910*, edited by Dan H. Laurence (1972).

absolutely none. The club is, and always has been, an eighth circle of hell, in which the male and female damned sit in rows and make one long for even devils from the higher seventh circle to bring into the stale atmosphere some breathable ether, were it only brimstone fumes. I have never been lured among them without longing to spring up and say "Do you know what is the matter with the theatre? YOU!" and stalk out. I do not believe that you are the President. I deny it, contradict it, repudiate it. The thing is eternally impossible. It may be that some fiend sits there in your semblance and invites me to lecture in your handwriting. But the lures of Satan are vain. *Vade retro.*[1]

You must come to lunch some day and be exorcised. I'll fix a date for the ceremony presently.

*Don Juan* is struggling through revision towards publication.

Yours ever    G. BERNARD SHAW

## To Bernard Shaw
MS. Morgan

*Sunday* [*16 November 1902*]                             *Savile Club*

My dear G.B.S., To have received and to possess your letter is better than to have secured your promise to lecture to the Playgoers. As a plain blunt Anglo-Dutch-German, I have interpreted that letter as a refusal to lecture. Am I wrong? Anyhow, I have told the committee that I have heard from you, and that though you were very much flattered by the invitation, and though nothing in the world would have given you so much pleasure as to come and lecture, extreme pressure of work, combined with modesty, forced you to refuse *for the present.*

Meanwhile, do please, when you are next in London, come and lunch with me, here or at the premises of the Playgoers, Clement's Inn, Strand, W.C., or elsewhere. I myself am a vegetarian in all but name, and the material side of the entertainment would be not at all disgusting to you. Will you let me know your movements, so that I could fix a date?

Yours ever    MAX

[1] Get thee behind me.

## To Olivia Truman[1]
MS. Merton

*7 April 1903*                                   *48 Upper Berkeley Street*

Dear Madam, I do not know where my brother is going to spend Easter; and really you must excuse me for not trying to discover the place and informing you of it.

You see, I have not the pleasure of knowing you (a pleasure to come, some day, I hope). Nor do you tell me what is your motive (or your anxiety). In this ill-regulated world one has to be careful; and for all I know, you may be an anarchist, eager to throw a bomb (skilfully disguised as an Easter egg) at my brother, as being a representative of "things as they are".

Probably you are not an anarchist at all. But you certainly are mysterious, and must, I repeat, excuse me. Faithfully yours   MAX BEERBOHM

P.S. You may, of course, rely absolutely on me not to show your letter to anyone.

## To Olivia Truman
MS. Merton

*Thursday* [*9 April 1903*]                      *48 Upper Berkeley Street*

Dear Miss Truman, Please don't speak of any "sacrifice of modesty". There is nothing for you to be ashamed of. Yours seems to me a very natural little case – a very usual little case. I myself, at your age, cherished a remote passion for an actress. And I remember that she too, in answer to one of my epistles, said that my insight into her character was "a great help" to her. All young gentlemen and most young ladies pass through this kind of phase, and the objects of their adoration always profess to be greatly helped by it.

"Profess" is not quite a just word, perhaps. They really are helped. It ministers to that particular kind of vanity which, whether they be men or women, the life of the stage fosters in them. I wish I were still young enough to help them thus. But my age is, alas! just about half-way between yours and my brother's. I can only contemplate these idylls from without. To be dragged into one of them as a go-between, I must

[1] A fervent fourteen-year-old admirer of Herbert Beerbohm Tree, who was trying to approach him through Max.

respectfully decline. I am very sorry indeed to refuse your request. But my sense of humour and honour and so forth prevents me. So here are the beautiful photograph and the beautiful letter and the sealed telegram which is, I am sure, as beautiful as they.

And I am, with many regrets,   MAX BEERBOHM

Olivia Truman

## To Olivia Truman
MS. Merton

*Savile Club*

Dear Miss Truman, Your last letter (which I should have answered days ago, only I have been away and had none of my letters forwarded to me) is (excuse that long parenthesis) full of fallacies.

1. I am not at all Scotch. That quality of caution which you contemn in me is due to an admixture of Dutch blood. (Beerboom is the original version of my name. Holland is a delightful little nation in its way, with a fine past; and I am sure you will be glad to know that my brother originates from it.)

2. I am always quite serious. Your notion of me as a compound of frivolity and caution is manifestly absurd.

3. I am not married.

Having ventured to correct these details about myself, let me now withdraw unreservedly my hint that yours was "a very usual little case". This I said merely to comfort you. I was conscious of having stumbled on a tremendous and soul-stirring tragedy. There never has been anything like it. I search the world's history in vain for any analogue to you or to my brother. I wish I were a poet and could hand you both down to posterity.

A mere prosaist, I find great pleasure in the prospect of meeting you both at tea. Please don't forget your promise to arrange that meeting, and believe me, Yours very truly   MAX BEERBOHM

## To Olivia Truman
MS. Merton

*21 April 1903* *48 Upper Berkeley Street*

Dear Miss Truman, I look forward to the postponed pleasure. But I am afraid the postponement may mean that the pleasure never will come off. "Going abroad" usually means staying in Paris on the way. I foresee you hopelessly in love with Coquelin *aîné*, and writing earnestly to Coquelin *cadet* to ascertain where his brother means to spend Whitsuntide, also to implore *cadet* to nip in the bud the dreadful stories circulated about *aîné's* private life.[1] I am very sorry that people are

[1] Benoît Constant Coquelin (1841–1909) and his brother Ernest Alexandre (1848–1909) were two of the leading French actors.

(apparently) talking scandal to you about my brother. But I don't think it really matters very much. Scandal always is talked about anyone worth talking about. If one happens to like the public person in question, one need only lay one's hand on one's heart and say that one's interlocutor is misinformed. This, at least, is what I always do. And in the case of my brother, I should be able to do it without violence to my conscience. Indeed, you are the nearest approach to anything scandalous known by me about him authentically. And this scandal consists merely in his having said that he finds your sympathy "a great help" to him – bless him!

I *don't* "hate" you, and you *are* "delightful". Excuse my negligence in not having till now paid you the compliments for which you had been so very patiently fishing. And believe me that the compliment is not the less sincere because you have (as who should say) used a landing-net.

To the possible pleasure of our meeting,

Yours very truly    MAX BEERBOHM

By "possible" I don't imply a doubt of the pleasure, on my side. Merely a doubt of the meeting itself. Coquelin is very overwhelming.

## *To E.F. Spence*[1]
MS. Yale

*31 May 1903*                                    *48 Upper Berkeley Street, W.*

My dear Spence, I was very much pleased and flattered by what you said in the *Sketch* about my caricatures. Thank you. But I don't agree with you that I get at the soul of a man without getting at his physical aspect. That would be an impossible feat, I think. When I draw a man, I am concerned simply and solely with the physical aspect of him. I don't bother for one moment about his soul. I just draw him as I see him. And (this is how I come to be a caricaturist) I see him in a peculiar way: I see all his salient points exaggerated (points of face, figure, port, gesture and vesture), and all his insignificant points proportionately diminished. *Insignificant*: literally, signifying nothing. The salient points do signify something. In the salient points a man's soul does reveal itself, more or less faintly. At any rate, if it does not always reveal itself

---

[1] Lawyer and writer (1860–1932). For many years dramatic critic of the *Westminster Gazette*, the *Scotsman*, and the *Sketch*.

through them, it is always latent in them. Thus if one underline these points, and let the others vanish, one is bound to lay bare the soul. But that is not sacrificing physical resemblance. It is simply an intensifying of physical resemblance. If, instead of intensifying it, one misses it, then one misses the soul also. It is because (and only because), or, let us rather say, when (and only when) my own caricatures hit exactly the exteriors of their subjects that they open the interiors too. Do I make myself plain? (I don't mean, do I caricature myself? I never do: I am much too sensitive: the bully is always a coward.) When one can *do* a thing, it is so difficult to explain, even to oneself, *how* one does it; and I suppose really one ought not to try; not for fear of being thought self-important, but because creative power does play the deuce with critical power and put its owner at a grave disadvantage in argument. But, in any case, you are on no account to trouble to answer this letter: it would not be posted except on that understanding. Let the matter rest till the first entr'acte of the next first night. Then you shall prove to me that I am wrong.                Yours very sincerely   MAX BEERBOHM


## To Olivia Truman
MS. Merton

*Sunday* [*? 7 June*] *1903*                *Hartley Grange, Winchfield, Hants*

Dear Miss Truman, No, indeed, I had not forgotten – but I had supposed you had by this time. Your fidelity to the ideal of my brother is very surprising and beautiful and touching. Alas, I shall not have even that modified meeting which you offer me for tomorrow night. I have promised to stay here for several days and cannot break my promise. I hope very much that the stars in their courses will bring us face to face before long, and that you will be duly dazzled by my reflected glory. You certainly have the power of exciting one's curiosity; you hint that you are "femine". Femineness must be a delightful quality – I shall not rest till I have beheld an example of it. Also, it seems, you are "unconspicous". That again is very rare. Finally you give me permission to call you a "prigg". What, oh what, is a prigg? It is quite awful to think that in stall sixteen of the upper circle will be sitting tomorrow night an unconspicous femine prigg and that I shall not be there to see. Beside me on this writing-table is a crystal – if only I were a clairvoyant!

I hope you will have a very nice evening. My brother has a very good part in the Kipling affair,[1] he dies on the stage and is covered with the Union Jack. Do not drown the stalls with your tears; buckets can be obtained from the attendants. I am, my dear Miss Truman,

Yours very truly    MAX BEERBOHM

I am flattered by your suggestion that I should write my memoirs, only my life has been so very uneventful; the nearest approach to luridness was that I almost met you, and it would hardly fill a volume to say "It was about this time that I almost met that remarkable woman Olivia Truman. Beautiful, in the strict sense of the word, she was not, but she had the remains of great prettiness, and was liable to become pretty at any moment. She had, moreover, her 'nice nights', one of which was the one on which I did not meet her. She is said to have been the one and only authentic prigg the world has ever known, and there is little doubt that she was conspicously femine. To have almost met her is to have lived not in vain."

### *To Bernard Shaw*[2]
MS. B.L.

*21 September 1903*          *48 Upper Berkeley Street, W.*

My dear G.B.S., Your "anticipation" of me is delightful, and is even now at the framer's. (I send you a picture which no framer would touch.)[3] And your letter, as soon as I have answered it, will be laid with lavender in that special drawer reserved for the engaging sophistries to which I am lucky enough to lash you every now and then.

Firstly (excuse my solid Dutch way of doing things), I am *not* a Jew. My name was originally Beer*boom*. The family can be traced back through the centuries in Holland. Nor is there, so far as one can tell, any Hebraïsm on the distaff-side. Do I *look* like a Jew? (The question is purely rhetorical.) Does my brother Herbert look like a Jew? (Still more rhetorical.) That my talent is rather like Jewish talent I admit

---

[1] Kinsey Peile's dramatisation of Kipling's story "The Man Who Was", which opened at His Majesty's Theatre on Monday, 8 June 1903.

[2] Shaw's play *Man and Superman* had been published in August, and Max had reviewed it at some length in the *Saturday Review* on September 12. Shaw fired back a long and lively broadside on September 15. (See his *Letters*, Vol. 2, p. 372.) Most of his remarks can be guessed from Max's refutations. The play was first produced at the Court Theatre on 23 May 1905, with Granville Barker and Lillah McCarthy in the leading roles.

[3] See page 39.

readily. And that is the sole reason for this pedantic denial and explanation. If I were a Jew, I should be rather a matter of course. But, being in fact a Gentile, I am, in a small way, rather remarkable, and wish to remain so. Suppose *you* were not an Irishman; and suppose someone, misled by your two chief characteristics – the love of dreaming dreams, and pugnacity – were to accuse you of being an Irishman: wouldn't you be annoyed, and eager to put him right? So forgive this momentary egoism. The rest of the letter shall be devoted to yourself.

Heaven forfend that I should try to convert you to Pater.[1] I hold no brief for that deceased. If you have seen the current *Saturday*, you have found me admitting that he was a poor creature enough, from the standpoint of wholesome humanity. Even had he been spared, he would never at Britain's need have dashed into the Volunteers, along with that prince of good fellows, Bill Archer.[2]

But, even if I idolised him, I shouldn't want *you* to see any good in him. If you could do that, you would be by so much the less your*self*. I delight in you as you *are*. Your limitations and wrong-headednesses are as dear to me as your powers and right-headednesses, of which they are the complement. But I, not being a man of genius, but a sound, eclectic, Batavian, critical person – an unprejudiced *taster* of things in life and literature – owe it to myself not to let go uncontradicted your notion that Pater's style was "a nerveless amateur affectation", and that he had "neither message nor vision". Personally, I think that the literary gift is a mere accident – is as often bestowed on idiots who have nothing to say worth hearing as it is denied to strenuous sages. You say that having "a vision and a message" makes a fine literary style. How about H.G. Wells, for example? *There*'s an evangelist and a seer, indisputably. But his writing!! Have you ever seen a cold rice-pudding spilt on the pavement of Gower Street? I never have. But it occurs to me as a perfect simile for Wells's writing.

But, granted for sake of argument your theory, your idealistic theory, that only the people who have something good to say know how to say it well, and that such people always are so blest, I maintain that Pater was master of a very exquisite prose. He *had* a message and a vision. He saw a great deal, and saw it very clearly, and ached to make other people

---

[1] Walter Pater, aesthete and stylist (1839–94), whose writings Shaw had demolished in his letter of 15 September.

[2] In 1899, at the beginning of the Boer War, William Archer's simple patriotism overcame his forty-five years of Liberal pacifism, and he volunteered for Home Defence with the Inns of Court Rifles, in which he served for the duration of the war.

Frontispiece for "Man & Superman"

anot

"Woman projecting herself dramatically by my hands"
(See Preface)

a man undramatically withdrawing himself

see likewise. To raw life and raw ethics he was quite blind. But when it came to art he was acutely sensitive, and was quickened to very genuine emotion. Heavens were opened to him, and Hells – not less real to him, in their way, than the Hells and Heavens which, in *their* way, gape to you and Bunyan and Martin Luther and Martin Tupper and H.G. Wells and W.T. Stead and ... but no: that's not fair: I won't take back the argument I granted as to literary ability. All I want to say is that your denial of Pater's beauty in prose is due to a misunderstanding of Pater's self. And even this I shouldn't say if I thought it would make the faintest impression on, and so mar my ideal of, you. *You*: that brings me back to my promise. I will divagate no more.

I admit that you score one true point against me. I ought, when I wrote about your play and said you have no real sense for human character, to have qualified and differentiated. I would have done so, but you know how hard it is, in writing a rough-and-ready article, to hedge without spoiling the effect. That is no real excuse, though. And I apologise. I should have been a fool indeed if I had not spotted how closely and finely observed are your American and the rest of your subordinate figures. Where it is a question of racial characteristics, class-characteristics, and so forth, you always do seem to me triumphant – "Hogarthian" quite. Where your vision seems to me blurred and false is in the deeper business of human character – character without the -istics.

You twit* me with wanting "the antique". I do want it, please. I admit the charm, or rather the interest, of your novelties. Only, as you yourself insist, mankind has not improved itself, nor how slightly soever altered itself even, since the dark ages: and therefore any departure from "the antique" in depicting mankind must be a departure, though it may be a fascinating and exciting departure, from the truth. Man doesn't strip to the Laocoön, nor woman to the Venus of Milo. Certainly not. But no more does man strip to wax, and woman to whalebone. Each strips to antique flesh and blood. Of course, I am talking at large. There *are* men and women like waxen John and whalebony Ann, possibly.[1] I object only to your pretension that they are the rule and not the rare, negligible exception.

* A word I have never seen outside the Parliamentary summaries in *The Times* – "The right honourable gentleman twitted members opposite with, etc". But I maintain that you have twitted me.  M.B.

[1] John Tanner and Ann Whitefield, the protagonists of *Man and Superman*.

And my objection goes deeper than you assume in your letter. I should not dream of denying the womanhood of a woman merely on the ground that she throws herself at the head of a man or at the heads of many men. Nor should I withhold the proud title of "brother" from a man merely because he isn't instantly responsive to the impact. True, I don't swallow your general theory that the sex-instinct proceeds more strongly from woman than from man: I believe the contrary. But that is beside the point. My specific objection to your John and Ann is that neither he in his passiveness nor she in her activity draws any ordinary human breath. Such life as they have comes by artificial respiration of your own wit and ratiocinativeness. Ann doesn't throw herself at John's head. You throw her. John gets slight concussion of the brain. If either had a heart, it would be a diseased one, and your rough violence would be dangerous. But there is no rudiment of a heart in either of them. In the average human being there is something more than a rudiment of heart. That is why Ann and John, as types, won't do.

They would not do any better in my eyes if I joined all the Borough Councils in England.[1] But I am not, despite you, going to offer myself for even one. Such limitations as I have I must guard jealously. On one condition I relent: will you offer yourself for matriculation at Balliol Coll., Oxon, next term?                    Yours ever   MAX

### To John Lane
MS. London

*15 April 1904*                           *48 Upper Berkeley Street, W.*

My dear John Lane, Here are sixty pages – type-written. Enough to show the *sort* of thing.[2] I began a "skeleton" of the rest; but found that, to give any right idea, this skeleton would have to be such a huge one – or rather a full-fleshed figure – that I had to abandon the attempt.

The dénouement is that the Duke and *all* the undergraduates, except Noaks, commit suicide for love of Zuleika; whereafter Zuleika, satisfied, but feeling at a loss in Oxford, goes on to Cambridge.

I can't describe the gradations to this without spoiling them: the whole thing depends so much on the *details* of treatment.

I hope you will like as much as there is here to read: of course it must

---

[1] Shaw had suggested that Max should stand for one.

[2] A progress report on *Zuleika Dobson*, which Max had begun in 1898 and was to finish in 1910. It was published by Heinemann in 1911.

be read from this standpoint: that it is not "a novel", but frankly the work of a leisurely essayist amusing himself with a narrative idea.

And now *bon voyage*, and many thanks for the very pleasant time I had with you this afternoon.          Yours ever    MAX

## To Florence Kahn[1]
MS. Reichmann

*5 July [1904]*                    *48 Upper Berkeley Street, W.*

Very dear little friend, It is too bad of you to *persist* in calling me "Mr Beerbohm", and you don't deserve that I should answer your letters when they begin in that way – that utterly ridiculous and unrecognisable way. "Mr Max" at any rate, *please*. At the same time *I* don't feel worthy to answer letters that are adorned with recondite Shakespeare quotations. "There is a soul of goodness in things evil" ... and ... "To be or not to be, that is ... " as far as I can go. What must you think of me, you dear little highly-educated, bronze-headed, April-mannered, un-earinged, telegram-to-bureau-showing, lilies-of-the-valley-to-my-mother-sending friend? I will restore the ear-ring to you tomorrow. I wish I could remember how its fellow was set. My mother was so delighted with the lovely flowers. I think it must be just a month today since first I met you. Such a happy little month for me.    MAX

## To Florence Kahn
MS. Reichmann

*27 July 1904*                    *Café des Tribunaux, Dieppe*

Very dear little friend, "Rain! So needed here", needed, at least, by everyone except me, who have to lie in bed till the time for second *déjeuner*, because of the torrents that splash continuously down on the cobble-stones beneath my window. In Dieppe everything depends on the weather: if rain, Hell; if sun, Heaven. If wind, then I cannot in this open café write to the dear little friend without the note-paper blowing away into the faces of the people at the next table. It is blowing *quite* a gale at this moment. However, I feel fairly happy today, yesterday having been a miserable day for me – a nightmare now past, and dear

[1] American actress, born 1876 in Memphis, Tennessee.

in the present. I wrote an article promised to the *Saturday Review. Such* an article: the sort of thing that might be written by a very small schoolboy as "English Composition", and written with the most awful efforts, at an awfully slow pace, with terrific agonies and shame. I never again must attempt to do anything when I am away from my home. I suppose this means that writing is not a natural function for me: just a talent which I have "faked up". You, if you had suddenly to act in Berlin, would be able to act as well as in America, I expect. "*Si liceat parvis componere magna*"[1] I *am* a very small writer though highly accomplished; where you, from all accounts, are a really great actress, with high accomplishment thrown in. How I wish I could see you act. But that could not give me nearly so much pleasure, dear, as seeing you yourself, with no footlights between us. You yourself with all your dear little graces and virtues, and moods of happiness and sadness, so utterly unlike all the other people I have known. Not necessarily finer, but more differently fine than they from the rest of humanity.

Goodnight dear   MAX

## *To Florence Kahn*
MS. Reichmann

*24 August 1904*
*St Bartholomew's Day*                               *Maison Lefèvre, Dieppe*

Very dear little friend, Today the Innocents were massacred, and I was born. It is the fifth birthday I have had in this dear little place, and as I am always, on the whole, happier here than I have been elsewhere, I reckon myself five years old. Thus extenuating and condoning all my failures and futilities, and seeing my grey hairs as hairs that will become duly brown, on a second crop, sooner or later. It is the first birthday I have had since I knew the dear little friend, and therefore a special birthday for me, and I wish her many happy returns of it, and of every day throughout all the year.                      MAX (*Aetat* 32)

---

[1] If one should compare great with small (Virgil, *Georgics*, IV, 176).

## To Frederick William Chapman[1]

MS. London

[1904–5]                                              48 Upper Berkeley Street, W.

Dear Mr Chapman, I am just back from the continent – hence the delay in my reply to your note about M. Boulestin[2] and *The Happy Hypocrite*.

I hope that in this instance Mr Lane will waive his claim (I am waiving mine) to any little fee that might accrue for rights of translation etc. The translation can hardly be regarded as a commercial undertaking: M. Boulestin and the *Mercure de France* expect to lose a little on the enterprise. They are doing the thing as a luxury for their artistic consciences – so far as I can gather. I know M. Boulestin quite well, and know him to be quite an honest person, who would not wish to deceive. Though commercially the undertaking is no good, it would be for Mr Lane and myself good in so far as it would be undoubtedly an advertisement for the book in England and America. There would be plenty of paragraphs in newspapers, I fancy.

Yours very sincerely   MAX BEERBOHM


## To Florence Kahn[3]

MS. Reichmann

*Tuesday* [*31 January 1905*]                          48 Upper Berkeley Street, W.

Very dear little friend, My letters to you always seem to me so very egoistic; and yet you say you don't know enough. Am I well? Am I happy? Quite well, thank you, dear. And nothing to complain of on the score of happiness. I don't think I ever am or shall be happy in the full sense, as some people are. As I think I told you, I can only stand life when it is made pleasant for me. Usually it *is* made pleasant for me. I have really been rather pampered than otherwise. So I have been all right, on the whole. But I do not like life when it does not offer me something nice every day. And if it ever offered me something *not* nice I should feel myself very much aggrieved. A *happy* person, it seems to

[1] 1863–1918. Manager of the Bodley Head.

[2] Xavier Marcel Boulestin (d. 1943) was music-critic, novelist, actor, caricaturist and designer before he found fame in England as cookery expert and restaurateur. *L'Hypocrite Sanctifié*, his translation of *The Happy Hypocrite*, was published by the Société du Mercure de France on 20 May 1905.

[3] Who had returned to America in November 1904.

44

me is the sort of person who requires no aids to happiness – who can grapple with life on any terms. And I never shall be that sort of person. That is all I have to complain of. And it is little enough in comparison with average grounds of complaint. So *there*, dear, I have told you as fully as I could – at tedious length, I am afraid. But you did ask me to tell you.

No more news as yet about the likelihood of your acting. I *am* so looking forward to hearing definitely. It must have been nice – it sounds very nice, as you describe it – to see Clara Morris[1] acting. Exactly ten years ago I was in New York. I suppose you were still in the South, at that time. But it seems odd that I should have been even on the same continent with you and yet not have known you.

Yesterday the Stage Society performed a comedy by George Street – a very good little comedy;[2] and I really should have enjoyed it if I hadn't got to write an article about it. Aylmer Maude has, I think, at last withdrawn from the scene. I was growing very tired of him.[3] Tonight I am dining with the Chestertons. Guess where. The Lyceum Club. That name pursues you even across the Atlantic.

Goodbye, dear, till Friday   MAX

## To Florence Kahn
MS. Reichmann

[*c. 20 February 1905*]                    *Savile Club, 107 Piccadilly, W.*

Very dear little friend, I was so very glad to have your nice letter, telling me that the rehearsals are going smoothly. I hope the headache under which you say you wrote the first part of the letter has quite gone away ... well, of course, it has quite gone away: I mean that I hope it won't

---

[1] American actress (1848–1925)

[2] *Great Friends* by G.S. Street, produced by the Stage Society at the Court Theatre on 30 January 1905. Max reviewed it favourably and at length in the *Saturday Review* of 4 February.

[3] Author and translator of Tolstoy (1858–1938). In the *Saturday Review* of 31 December 1904 Max praised the Stage Society's production of Tolstoy's *The Power of Darkness*, but lambasted the English translation by Maude and his wife Louise. In the issue of 7 January 1905 Maude replied, and Max contributed a brief reply, which ended: "To be a decent translator is certainly difficult. My point is that Mr Maude is not the man to cope with the difficulty." In the issue of 14 January Bernard Shaw urged Max to write "two columns, conveying a canon of translation for plays written in slang and dialect". Max obliged in the issue of 21 January. Both his articles reprinted in *Last Theatres* (1970).

return. Tonight I am dining with some people to meet Rodin,[1] the sculptor, who came over the other day to open the Whistler exhibition. It is rather touching: he has a hair-dresser twice a day to curl the grey lock on his forehead, so that he may do full justice to the fuss that is being made of him by the smart people. Thus do great artists end their days.

Dear, let me know when the out-of-town performances begin. I remember Abbey's Theatre (it was Abbey's then) very well indeed. My brother Tree had his performances there.

Goodbye, dear little friend   MAX

## To Florence Kahn
### MS. Merton

*Sunday [July 1905]*                                    *Café des Tribuneaux, Dieppe*

Very dear little friend, No – I never heard of horse-psychology. It sounds *very* German – and I suspect you of having invented it. In France animals are not supposed to have any souls: that is the one thing I don't like about the French people. Horses, dogs, cats, and the rest, are pariahs here except in so far as they can be made useful – a piteous, nervous, rib-showing race of creatures. The best horses here are the "little horses" which spin round at the Casino: they are kept brightly varnished – but only to make one lose one's francs in backing them. Not bad, too, are the horses in the merry-go-round at the Fair which is an annual institution here. Have you such things in America? I am very fond of them. I have had many nice rides this year – renewing my youth. It is quite sad how young I can feel, at a pinch. I, who might be the father of a large family, am always quite capable of behaving like a schoolboy, and only afterwards do I detect the impropriety. One midnight last week found me, in company with one or two men as old as myself, depositing an array of empty champagne bottles, noiselessly, in the bedroom of a chauffeur who lay sleeping innocently on his bed – also putting his watch back by two hours, and performing similar tricks which, lamentable as they seem in narration, thrilled me through and through with happiness at the moment of performance. Other practical jokes, too – writing letters in disguised handwriting with a view to ridiculous complications – what *would* you think of me – poor old me? You really ought to go to some Berlin library and read up Professor

---

[1] Auguste Rodin, French sculptor (1840–1917).

Pumpelsdröck or another on *"Praktikaljokimus"* and try to explain me to myself . . . What a lot of writing about myself! But it isn't egoism in the ordinary sense of the word. I am not thinking that "I am I" and must be interesting to everyone else. I am something more than I – a detached and puzzled spectator – detached, yet knowing more about myself than about any other subject, and offering myself humbly for the inspection of others. I think there is a difference between this and egoism. I don't know whether I have expressed it. But I think it is there. Poor little friend, I simply mustn't bore you any more. I talk of myself, but I think much more about you – and I do so very much look forward to the time when I shall see you again – whenever that may be. How about your going to Paris? You really and truly ought to. Duties are not the less duties for not being painful – are they, dear?     MAX

## To Florence Kahn
MS. Reichmann

*Friday [15 September 1905]*                    *48 Upper Berkeley Street, W.*

Very dear little friend, I saw *Billy's Little Love Affair,*[1] and remember it was *very* Esmondine; but I cannot remember which of Esmond's horrors it was. "Memory, first and greatest of the artists" has rejected it. I wonder if you did play Tess? I imagine you would make a splendid Tess. Why don't you wish to play Portia? I do hope you will have your way about *Herod.*[2] Mariamne ought to be a great chance for you, and you for Mariamne. I saw Gillette play on Wednesday night, and have written about him.[3] Have you seen or heard of Miss Marie Doro? She is his leading lady. I thought she acted very prettily and well. "Greenwich Park" sounds very European. And do you pronounce it Green-*w*ich, as you were going to, but didn't, at the ticket office when you were going to see the pictures? . . . No, that was Dul-*w*ich, of course. I have read a capital novel by W.B. Maxwell (a son of Miss Braddon) – *Vivien* – a blend of the old-fashioned romance and the modern realistic novel –

[1] A comedy in three acts by H.V. Esmond, produced at the Criterion Theatre on 2 September 1903.

[2] A three-act verse tragedy by Stephen Phillips, produced by Tree at Her Majesty's Theatre on 31 October 1900.

[3] William Gillette, American actor and playwright (1853–1937). His play *Clarice* was produced at the Duke of York's Theatre on 13 September 1905 and torn to pieces by Max in the *Saturday Review* on 23 September 1905.

really well-done.[1] Also *The Wrong Box* by Stevenson, which I had never read before. That is *too* exquisite. That that poor dear weak gentleman allowed himself to be diverted from his true function in writing by the elderly prigs who surrounded him, is a real tragedy. But perhaps one wouldn't revel so much in his fantasies if they were not so few. Write to me, please, dear, and don't tire yourself by too much rehearsing. You ought to eat a lot now that you are working so hard. I hope you do?

MAX

## To Florence Kahn
MS. Reichmann

*Friday* [*20 October 1905*]                                     *Savile Club*

Very dear little friend, How are you? I haven't heard from you since I wrote. Is Lady Macbeth stalking into the foreground of your thoughts? I have had a very theatrical morning – the most theatrical of my life: poor Irving's funeral in Westminster Abbey.[2] All the young and old actors and actresses there, and making such a show of suppressed emotion, with the sense that the whole Abbey's eyes were upon them, and comporting themselves with such terrific grace and seemliness. And outside the Abbey, hawkers innumerable selling penny-mementoes of "the late Irving" – driving their own humbler trade over the tomb. And, as I jumped into a hansom, "Don't forget the linkman today, sir. He's been *very* attentive." Funerals ought not to be held in so commercial a place as London; and "the histrionic temperament", moreover, mars them – what a blessing for you, dear, that you, with all your power for acting, haven't got what one calls "the histrionic temperament" in private life. Write to me, please                                     MAX

---

[1] Published 1905.

[2] Sir Henry Irving (born 1838) died on 13 October 1905, after a performance of Tennyson's *Becket* at the Theatre Royal, Bradford. His ashes were buried in Westminster Abbey on 20 October.

## To Florence Kahn
### MS. Reichmann

*Tuesday* [*20 March 1906*]                    *48 Upper Berkeley Street, W.*

Very dear little friend, I am going to see *Captain Brassbound's Conversion*[1] today – with Ellen Terry. I expect it will be rather appalling, as she is nowadays rather a clown than an actress. She can't learn two consecutive lines of a part, and has to rely entirely on her sense of fun and on the charm that is still hers. England is giving her a testimonial, shortly, to commemorate her fiftieth year on the stage, and a great deal of nonsense is being talked about her past triumphs. As a matter of fact, she never *was* an actress, in the strict sense of the word – only a delightful sort of a creature, symbolising (what one imagines to have been) Merrie England in the time of Elizabeth. I dine tonight with my old friend John Davidson,[2] who is spending some days in London. I never can read his writing – his violent buffeting of clouds may be very fine, but means nothing to me. But for himself I have a great affection. He is, in his way, authentically a man of genius; and has all the sweetness of his tribe. Dear, I hope I shall hear from you this week, and I hope you are very well and happy.                                                    MAX

## To Florence Kahn
### MS. Reichmann

*Friday* [*? March 1906*]                    *48 Upper Berkeley Street, W.*

Very dear little friend, No: I have never read *Corinne*.[3] I wonder if I ever *shall* have read something that you happen to be reading. Nothing, probably, that you are reading for the first time. Even with such things as Shakespeare, I shouldn't come out very well: I don't think I have ever read a single play of his straight through: I have always felt the need of plenteous skipping. And a good half of the plays I have never even dipped into. It is really rather odd that I am connected with literary matters at all, and I deem myself rather a fraud. The only writers who give me any pleasure are my contemporaries: I can't go with pleasure

---

[1] By Bernard Shaw. First publicly produced at the Court Theatre on 20 March 1906, with Ellen Terry in the leading part which Shaw had written for her. Max's review in the *Saturday Review* on 26 March was headed 'A Great Dear'.

[2] Scottish poet (1857–1909). Committed suicide.

[3] A long novel (1807) by Madame de Staël (1766–1817).

further back than Matthew Arnold: he (in small doses) pleases me and inspires me with a sort of affection. Had I never been at Oxford, I don't suppose even Arnold would waken anything in me. I do so greatly envy your power of projecting yourself into the mood for appreciating the best writers, no matter what their period or the direction of their genius. How are you, dear? I am very well. Tonight, as usual, I go to the Conders.[1] I long to hear about you and Europe.                    MAX

## To Florence Kahn
MS. Reichmann

*Friday 11 May 1906*                    *48 Upper Berkeley Street, W.*

Very dear little friend, I was delighted to have a letter from you yesterday, though you say nothing about Europe. I shall expect you till I *don't* see you! Bernard Shaw is back in London: I haven't seen him, but the newspapers are once more full of reports of speeches, interviews, etc.[2] It had been quite a welcome rest from him, during the past month or so: he has been in Paris – Rodin has been doing a bust of him, for Mrs Shaw and posterity. It is difficult to imagine that tremulous beard in marble – rigidly fluttering its way down the ages. I am going to call on the Conders this afternoon. Conder had an exhibition in Paris lately – not a success, I am sorry to say. But his wife has been ill, also, having fallen down in a sudden faint and cut her cheek seriously. I am glad you liked George Street's article.[3] I think it certainly is a good idea that I should write something about my contemporaries – but it could not be *published* before the twenty-first century.

Goodbye, dear, till Tuesday.                    MAX

---

[1] Charles Conder, artist (1868–1909), and his wife Stella Maris.

[2] Shaw returned to London on 9 May 1906.

[3] "Mr Max Beerbohm", a long and intelligent study of Max's books and caricatures in the *Tribune* of 17 April 1906. In it Street wrote: "I have never known an observer of character so swift, certain, and withal so subtle as Mr Beerbohm ... My hope is that he will write about character as well as draw it. He has the capacity and the opportunity to show his age something of the truth about its eminences".

## To Lady Desborough[1]
### MS. Hertford

*18 September 1906*                    *48 Upper Berkeley Street, W.*

Dear Lady Desborough, I am just out of my bedroom – a neat, slightly flushed convalescent, able to take nutrient – able to write to you in reply to that little note which I received from you when I was in the throes of the internal chill that laid me low. Feverish and much agonised though I was at the time, that note was such a pleasure to me; and I think my convalescence has been delayed by my troubled visions of how to reply worthily to it! What news could I invent for you? I who have no news at all, and am not in myself an exciting enough person to "carry" through the post without communicating some sort of exciting news... I fall back on inquiries – the refuge of the bad letter-writer – asking how you are, and stands Scotland where it stood – Scotland of which my only knowledge is two terrified visits to the Deeside, to stay with people who, because I wore trousers all the time and could not shoot or stalk or do anything out of doors, innocently expected me to be very amusing *indoors* – to improvise on the piano, recount the early struggles of Bernard Shaw, and generally make myself agreeable, and show off accomplishments that I haven't, alas, got – accomplishments without which I felt myself rather an impostor, and was glad when it was time to go to bed. But all this is autobiography, not news.

*News:* I am going to Italy a few days hence. I never have been there before. I should look very keenly forward to it. Only I am going there to *write* about it, and to write about it for the *Daily Mail*.[2] You scent sacrilege here; and so do I. But you probably don't scent so much *gloom* as I do. I remember you said last year of your coming visit to Venice "Is not that a blue window to look through?" I, too, am going to Venice – Venice first of all. But for me it is a black coal-hole to look down through. Because I have to go with a beastly professional eye for the beauties of it ... no, not the beauties of it, but just the *pegs* of it – the pegs on which to hang stupid little articles for the readers of the *Daily Mail* (of whom,

---

[1] Ethel (Ettie) Fane (1868–1952), granddaughter of the eleventh Earl of Westmorland, married (1887) William Henry Grenfell (1855–1945), all-round athlete and Liberal Member of Parliament. He was created Lord Desborough in 1905. Their home was at Taplow Court on the Thames near Maidenhead. Their eldest son was Julian Grenfell, the author of "Into Battle" and other poems. Max had visited Taplow in 1905 & 1906.

[2] "Max Beerbohm in Italy", a series of ten articles appeared in the *Daily Mail* from 8 November 1905 to 27 December 1906.

I hope, you are not one) to pull down into their eggs-and-bacon morning after morning. I am very querulous, you see – the privilege of the convalescent. I shall be quite the brutal, eupeptic, uncomplaining, rough-and-tumble globe-trotter next Sunday morning (the day when I hope to start) no doubt. And I shall be buoyed by the hope that you really will not forget or break your promise to send me some "Highland pages". Please do not forget or break. I am yours very sincerely

MAX BEERBOHM

## To Herbert P. Horne[1]
MS. Lasner

*October 1906*　　　　　　　　　　　　　　　　*Palazzo Bendini, Siena*

My dear Orné,[2] Just to say goodbye to you, and to Harris,[3] before I leave Italy. (I hope you will have remembered to say goodbye for me to your sister.) For the address that I have written above doesn't mean that I have bought the whole palace and am going to sit tight in it for ever. On the contrary, I find I can't blend Siena and solitude, by any means. The "portmanteau" positively insists on being driven to the station, and labelled, and hoisted into the van. Not such an easy matter, either, since I cannot understand even an English time-table, and not a soul in Siena speaks English. Perhaps they all *can*, but have the Pateresque prejudice against imperfection. However, I shall get off somehow, with the eyes of those damned Sienese-Chinese madonnas squinting me a farewell. Those madonnas are one reason for my departure. The *chief* reason is the aching void left in Siena by your and Harris's departure. The little restaurant seems dreadfully blank – all the more so because the waiter, at every meal, solemnly places before me the bottle of mineral water which you and Harris had not quite exhausted. And then there is the gulf that gapes between that waiter and me. I take a tumbler, and say "*piccolo*," and twirl my finger round and round

---

[1] Architect, writer and connoisseur (1864–1916). Edited a quarterly magazine *The Century Guild Hobby Horse* 1886–92. Thereafter he migrated to Florence, where he bought a palace, filled it with his pictures, drawings, furniture etc, and bequeathed it to the City of Florence, where it is known as the Musée Horne. He spent many years on his life of Botticelli (1908). Reggie Turner said "Dear Herbert Horne! poring over Botticelli's washing bills – and always a shirt missing!"

[2] The Italian pronunciation of Horne.

[3] Henry (Bogey) Harris (1871–1950), wealthy expert on Tuscan art. Great diner-out and party-giver in later life.

quickly in the tumbler's inside; but *cannot* make him understand that I want one of those sillabub things we used to have. Also, when I ask for the bill, I find myself asking for the night, and further confusing him. The climax of my disgust came tonight. I bought a copy of the *Vedetta Senese* as a charm against gloom. The leading article was entitled *Il Convitto[1] Tolomei*. I imagined that our friend with the poodle – the scion of the Ptolemies – had been arrested and summarily dealt with, on some dreadful charge. And, though I had to give up my attempt at understanding Italian journalism, my theory was borne out by the absence of the scion from his accustomed table. And now I have looked out *"convitto"* in my little dictionary. So there is an end of *that* excitement. And I am, I repeat, off. And good-bye, and very many thanks for all your great kindness.     Yours ever   MAX

Could you, within a week or so, be further so very kind as to send me a *line* to 48 Upper Berkeley Street, saying who sculpted the Hercules of the fountain in Florence, and who are the figures between his legs. Baedeker and Hare are silent.[2] Ashamed to bother you.[3]

## To Lady Desborough
MS. Hertford

*28 April 1907*                    *The Granville Hotel, Ramsgate*

My dear Lady Desborough, Abandon, I beg you, the idea of the luncheon-basket. Give Bury Street[4] a wide berth. Dismiss me from your thoughts. I do not say "lest a worse thing befall you", for I cannot imagine a worse thing befalling anyone than to see the streets peopled with my creations. It has never befallen *me*. Not that in drawing people I consciously exaggerate or distort them. I draw every man just exactly as I *remember* him. But when next I *see* him he looks something very different from my portrait, and quite his own bright self. He and all the other passers-by have for me quite a normal and unfrightening aspect.

[1] Not a convict, as Max clearly thought, but a meeting-place or college, in the Palazzo Tolomei in the middle of Siena.

[2] Karl Baedeker (1801–59) and Augustus Hare (1834–1903) both published popular guide-books to Italy.

[3] There is a statue of Hercules in Florence, but it is not on a fountain. Max was clearly thinking of the gigantic statue of Neptune by Bartolommeo Ammanati (1511–92), which is on a fountain. The figures below are Tritons, which form part of the stone block on which the huge figure stands.

[4] Where an exhibition of Max's caricatures had just opened at the Carfax Gallery.

More than once it has, indeed, occurred to me how awful it would be if my drawings *were* incarnated one fine morning – if the streets actually *were* peopled with carmine-faced gentlemen of balloon-like girth and legs only two inches long; ghostly and emaciated gentlemen towering high above the chimney-pots; gentlemen with globular heads and with all their other features pinched away into nothingness; and other gentlemen not less terrible. I have shuddered at this hypothesis, and rejoiced that it could not be realised. But for you, apparently, it *has* been realised. All around you you see my creatures alive and in three dimensions, when you take your walks abroad. Oh close your eyes. Exorcise me. Steep yourself in Fra Angelico. Else, inevitably, you will ride in a bath-chair along the esplanade of Ramsgate.

I came here last Friday in search of complete rest, which turns out to be a very fatiguing thing. Also, the place itself is depressing. I had imagined a scene of wholesome and refreshing vulgarity. But all the visitors who throng here are much too ill not to have every symptom of exquisite refinement. Among these "tottering and clay-faced marionettes" I have taken the greatest comfort and delight in your letter. What a charming letter! And such praise! I am more than pleased. I think you have picked out all the best for approbation, and of those picked out I think *I* like the Haldane best *as a caricature*, because it is so simple and definitive;[1] and the Alfred Rothschild *as an idea*.[2] The latter drawing gave me a lot of trouble. I had drawn A.R. looking from left to right, and MacColl from right to left, and had elaborately finished the drawing. But then I found a fatal flaw. It was absolutely essential that A.R., as not remembering Zion – at any rate not very vividly – should have his light-heartedness clinched by a flower in his coat. But flowers are worn on the *left* side of the coat. And therefore I had to do the whole drawing the other way round – tracing it laboriously through. If that isn't artistic conscience, what *is*?

Ever so many thanks again for your letter.

Yours very sincerely   MAX BEERBOHM

[1] Richard Burdon Haldane, Liberal politician, philosopher and lawyer (1856–1928). Secretary of State for War 1905–12. Max's 1907 caricature is entitled "8.30 p.m. Mr Haldane exercising a ministerial prerogative", and shows him in day clothes in the middle of a fashionable evening party.

[2] It is entitled "A Quiet Morning in the Tate Gallery", and captioned "The Curator [D.S. MacColl] trying to expound to one of the Trustees [Alfred Rothschild] the spiritual fineness of Mr William Rothenstein's 'Jews Mourning in a Synagogue.'"

# To Ronald Gray[1]

MS. Merton

*18 May 1907*                                      *48 Upper Berkeley Street*

My dear Ronald, Sunday week by all means: great fun. Caruso[2] behaved *fairly* well the other night. That is, he had tried to regularise his conduct so that he would not actually be liable to prosecution. To every lady in the room successively he put (in his quaint broken English) the old conundrum of Adam and Eve and Pinch-Me.[3]

Most of them replied cautiously "the third person on your list, Signor"; which seemed to annoy him horribly.

Yours ever    MAX BEERBOHM

---

[1] Painter (1868–1951).

[2] Enrico Caruso (1874–1921), one of the greatest operatic tenors of all time.

[3] The old riddle ran:
   Q. Adam and Eve and Pinch-Me went down to the river to bathe.
      Adam and Eve were drowned. Who do you think was saved?
   A. Pinch-Me [which was then taken as an invitation].

## *To Lydia Russell*[1]
MS. Princeton

*20 January 1907*                    *Taplow Court, Taplow, Bucks*

My dearest Lydia, I shall arrive at four tomorrow. Don't forget – please.

Rather an awful time here: my worst fears realised: all schoolboys – with a slight admixture of school-girls.[2] I rely on you to restore my sinking spirits.                                    Yours ever   MAX

This is how I feel!

---

[1] *Née* Burton. Married (1900) Walter Russell (1867–1949), artist, R.A. 1926. Knighted 1935. Lydia died 1944.

[2] This was the Cotillion Party of 18–21 January 1907. The schoolboys were Julian and Billy Grenfell and their friends Violet Asquith, Cynthia Charteris, Charles Lister and Venetia Stanley.

## *Fragment to Kathleen Bruce*[1]
### MS. Cambridge

[*1907*]

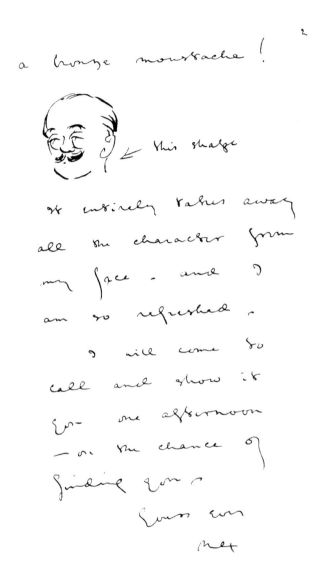

a bronze moustache!

← this shape

it entirely takes away
all the character from
my face — and I
am so refreshed —
    I will come to
call and show it
you — one afternoon
— on the chance of
finding you —
        yours ever
            Max

---

[1] Sculptor (1878–1947). She had executed a head of Max, which had been cast in bronze.

## To Kathleen Bruce
MS. Cambridge

*Monday [?23 June 1907]*                           *48 Upper Berkeley Street, W.*

Dear ~~Miss~~ Kathleen (I scratch out the middle word because, after all, it is about two years since I first met you). Also because you are lying down and can't spring up and say "Sir!" But *why* are you lying down? Do please be more explicit. What exactly has happened? Are you in pain? I am so sorry that *anything* should have happened to you of that kind – but, again, *what* kind? I suppose you, as a rationalistic open-air person, will think it very absurd of me; but *do* burn those peacock feathers. There are heaps of other kinds of feathers, just as pretty. Have some of them instead. I can't, of course, justify my distrust of peacock feathers. But, if it comes to that, what *can* one justify? There is no such thing as pure reason. At least we mortal creatures have never hit on it. We have to depend on superstitions, some of which *seem* reasonable, whilst others ... but here I am arguing about what can't be argued about, instead of merely begging you to destroy those beastly feathers. I shan't feel happy about you till you have done that. Really and truly. Do be afraid, *malgré vous*. Also, do please get well quickly, and tell me meanwhile what happened and how you are. And forgive me for bothering you.                                                      MAX

## To Kathleen Bruce
MS. Cambridge

*28 June 1907*                                      *48 Upper Berkeley Street, W.*

My dear Kathleen, A very delightful letter from you. But I do think you are as mad as a hatter, and stark staring mad, not to destroy the feathers once and for all. I am sure you won't get well, so long as you hang on to them, you foolish creature. Or at any rate, I am sure other unpleasant things will happen to you as soon as you do get well. Possibly shipwreck on your way to the Rocky Mountains. If you do get safely there, you won't catch any horses. Very likely they will catch *you*, and make an example of you. A furious breed. *I* know them. You wouldn't be ill now, but for the feathers. Your diagnosis about dancing and sculpting is all nonsense. But for the feathers, you might have danced all night and sculpted all day, you might have danced sculpting, and sculpted dancing, without being a penny the worse. All the fault of the feathers. Into the fire with them, this instant! Otherwise you are simply flying in the face of providence. This must be a very charming sensation for providence. But ... oh well, I suppose there is no use in adjuring you, so be a little sensible. How are you feeling? (Physically, I mean. Mentally I despair of you.) Much better, I hope? Nearly well? I do so look forward to the time when I shall have the privilege of seeing Miss K. Bruce again. Is there anything I can do for her, meanwhile? If so, let her "command" me. One thing I *can* do for her: the "patern" on her bedroom wall-paper is really spelt with two t's! Good night, and good morning, Kathleen.                                            MAX

## To Kathleen Bruce
MS. Cambridge

*8 July 1907*                                    *48 Upper Berkeley Street, W.*

My dear Kathleen, I was so *very* glad to see you; and I only wished you were as well as you looked. I did not stay long – tore myself away – partly because I supposed you ought to be "kept quiet"; and partly because I assumed that the American was in love with you; and partly because you may, for aught I know, be in love with *him*. The possible gooseberry, therefore, rolled down the stairs as it could, well-pleased, however, to be clasping to its rotund surface those feathers. As soon as I reached a place where the water flowed right up to the embankment, over went the feathers – gorgeously protruding from their envelope, and exciting utmost curiosity in the breast of a costermonger who was leaning over the parapet, and who, I do trust, didn't presently dive in to clutch them and present them to his donah.[1] *Such* a good day's work, I feel – taking those feathers away from you.

Lord Cromer had been for thirty years in Egypt; but who knows that his work will really benefit Egypt in the long run?[2] Whereas I know quite well that you are going to be completely well very soon, now that the feathers aren't there to bedevil you.

I suppose the American thought me *quite* mad; and perhaps Kathleen is rather of that opinion too.

Good night. Please let me know where it is you choose to go. Good-night again.                                            MAX

[1] Coster slang for sweetheart.

[2] Evelyn Baring (1841–1917), created Earl of Cromer 1901, was Agent and Consul-General in Egypt from 1883 to 1907.

## To Bernard Shaw
MS. Princeton

*11 February 1908*                    *48 Upper Berkeley Street, W.*

My dear G.B.S., Have you gone to see *Rosmersholm?*[1] If not, do go.
Two years or so ago, I wrote to Mrs Shaw, telling her about Miss
Florence Kahn, who was then in England, and who (I thought from
what Norman Hapgood[2] and other Americans had told me) would shine
in one of your plays. Now that I have seen Miss Kahn act, I think
Norman Hapgood and Co did not say half enough. A true tragedian,
with a quite extraordinary beauty of "style". Do go and see for yourself.

Yours ever    MAX BEERBOHM

A superfluous letter, this, I suppose; for you would be certain not to
miss an Ibsen play.

I have taken to sculpture. Began last week, on Soveral[3] and Pinero.
Tomorrow I am going to do you. Have taken to it like a duck to the
water. "Plasticine – the Child's Delight" is what I am working in at
present. The block of marble and the chisel may come in handy later on.[4]

## To Laurence Housman[5]
MS. Street

*Wednesday [Late March 1908]*          *48 Upper Berkeley Street, W.*

Dear Laurence Housman, If, in your new play, there is an important
woman's part that has not been filled provisionally – if, that is, you are
in need of a really poetic actress – do give your attention to the idea of
Miss Florence Kahn. I saw her the other day, and she said she was
going to write to you. And, as you may not have seen her act, and as
you may credit me with being a more or less good judge, I write to tell

---

[1] Florence played the part of Rebecca West in the revival of Ibsen's *Rosmersholm*, which
opened at Terry's Theatre on 10 February 1908. Max praised her acting extravagantly
in the *Saturday Review* of 15 February.

[2] American publicist and reformer (1868–1937). Editor of *Collier's Weekly* 1902–12.

[3] Marquis Luis de Soveral, GCMG, GCVO (1862–1922). Portuguese Ambassador in
London 1897–1910, friend of King Edward VII and nicknamed the Blue Monkey, was
a favourite subject of Max's caricatures.

[4] Max told Robbie Ross that he had also made Plasticine caricatures of himself, the
King, and Shaw, "which, at any rate, is better than Rodin's."

[5] Prolific novelist, poet and playwright (1865–1959).

you that I am sure she is a person who is "worth while". I have seen her in *Rosmersholm*, also in a short play of Alfred Sutro's:[1] her acting, in both these things, was of a quite extraordinary beauty and power.

With the possible exception of Mrs Patrick Campbell, there is no actress to touch her in sense of poetry, in *style* for poetry. (She is an American, of course; but with nothing American in her voice or ways.) I do hope she will, now that she is over here, have a chance of appearing in an *explicitly* poetic play. And, if you have it in your power to give her that chance, I am sure you would ever after be glad that you gave it to her.     Yours sincerely   MAX BEERBOHM

## To Rupert Brooke
MS. King's

[?*May–June 1908*][2]                    *48 Upper Berkeley Street, W.*

Dear Mr Brooke, It would be a very great pleasure to come to Cambridge and open a discussion or read a paper. But alas, I am absolutely no good at the platform or quasi-platform business: I can't do it tolerably well, and hate it. I can *write*, but not read nor speak. It is my misfortune that I can't; and I feel the misfortune particularly in the light of your very kind invitation.

Hoping we shall meet again soon,

Yours sincerely   MAX BEERBOHM

## To Kathleen Bruce
MS. Cambridge

*4 July 1908*                    *48 Upper Berkeley Street*

My dear Kathleen, Independence Day doesn't seem quite the most appropriate day on which to write and congratulate you on your coming marriage.[3] And I think I "conveyed" to you yesterday by word of mouth

---

[1] *The Man on the Kerb*, a one-act play by Alfred Sutro (1863–1933), performed at the Aldwych Theatre on 24 March 1908, with Seymour Hicks in the main part.

[2] It is impossible to date this letter exactly. Max and Brooke first met at Cambridge, where Brooke was an undergraduate, on 24 May 1908. In a letter to his mother he described Max as "a quaint little person". Assuming that this was their only meeting, I have dated this letter accordingly.

[3] Later in 1908 Kathleen Bruce married Captain Robert Falcon Scott R.N. (born 1868), who died in 1912 during his return from the disastrous expedition to the South Pole. In 1922 she married Edward Hilton Young (1879–1960), who was created Baron Kennet in 1935.

how very congratulable a matter this marriage seemed to me for you not less than for *him*.

But the more I think it over the more congratulable it seems, and the happier you both seem likely to be. Therefore I write

Yours ever    MAX

## To Florence Kahn
MS. Reichmann

*Friday [Mid-November 1908]*[1]                    *48 Upper Berkeley Street, W.*

Very dear little friend, Your letter of this morning, saying that you expect to sail on the 30th, makes me very sad. I had so hoped you were going to act. Perhaps the chance which you say is too remote to wait for will yet come off. If you *do* sail, they might yet in due time want you to sail back. I hate the probability, meanwhile, of not seeing you when I come back. I had so thought you would still be there. However, I mustn't be selfish. And indeed in our great friendship I do think more of you than of myself. And I constantly reproach myself with what has so often seemed evident: that I tend to make you unhappy. It rather seems that making people unhappy is my métier. I like you better than any person in the world. But the other sort of caring is beyond me. I realise quite surely now that I shall never be able to care in that way for any one. It is a defect in my nature. It can't be remedied. Dear, you have brought *so much* happiness to me. I can't bear to think of being the cause of unhappiness to you. It is difficult to express myself. Whether or not you will have sailed on the thirtieth, nothing can alter our friendship, dear, can it?                                        MAX

## To Florence Kahn
MS. Reichmann

*Monday [Early December 1908]*[2]                  *48 Upper Berkeley Street, W.*

*Darling* love, Goodnight again, sweet. And I love you, and wish I could say it in heaps of different ways. If only you were a hat-box or a rocking-

---

[1] It is impossible to date this letter more accurately. Two liners sailed for New York on 30 November 1908, and Florence must have planned to travel in one of them. In fact she sailed from Liverpool in the *S.S. Campania* on 12 December. For the difference between this letter and the ones that follow, see introduction p. xii.

[2] The dating of this letter is problematic, but it must have been written before Florence sailed for America.

horse or something of that sort, I could evolve a lot about you. But literary talent flies out of the window when real feeling comes in at the door – *my* door, at least. However, you don't need me to tell you in words how much I love you, darling.

I forgot I promised to lunch tomorrow at Herbert Vivian's.[1] I will get away as early as I can, in a taxi.      Your own loving   MAX
  Kisses

## To Florence Kahn
### MS. Reichmann

*Tuesday* [*15 December 1908*]                    *48 Upper Berkeley Street, W.*

Darling love, Thank you. I was so delighted to have your Queenstown letter.[2] Very glad to hear of the Inspector's "fair promise" about weather, which I hope is being fulfilled to the letter. You wrote overnight and did not add anything in the morning – and I hope this meant simply that there was no opportunity, and *not* that you weren't feeling well. I wonder if you are at a *long* table. By this time I suppose you are nearly half way across the Atlantic. How nice it will be for you to see Maurice! Today, on the red sofa in my room – on the bolster of it – I found Baedeker's *Italy* just where you had left it one day when you had been reading it lying down; and it did so remind me of you – not that any reminder is needed! – reminded me of all the times you had spent there, protesting that the time was wasted if you were not reading; and reminded me of all the times we shall spend together in the place named on the book's cover. Dear darling, how lovely it will be, won't it? I feel so happy in the thought of it, in the thought of you. I love you so much, dear, and think of you all the time, and wish I could project myself through space on to the upper deck of the *Campania*, at the risk of startling you.

Tonight I go to the performance of *Samson Agonistes*.[3] I have been reading part of it, and find it *very* dull. I think I shall be able to write something amusing about it, especially if the performance is bad – and poor William Poel's honoured name is a guarantee of badness.[4] Yesterday

[1] Journalist and author (1865–1940).

[2] The *Campania* called at Queenstown (Cork) on 13 December.

[3] William Poel's production of Milton's poem was given in the Lecture Theatre of Burlington House on 15 December 1908.

[4] William Poel (1852–1934) produced many Shakespearean and other early plays in his own style. Max's review in the *Saturday Review* of 19 December began "For good downright boredom, mingled with acute irritation, commend me to the evening I spent last Tuesday in the Theatre of Burlington House".

I supped with the Rothensteins. Many inquiries from Alice after you. She was so sorry to miss you when you called, and is going to write to you. The Tube was another reminder of you. It seemed so strange not to be going up Heath Street, and sad, and yet not altogether sad, because things are so much happier now than they were then; though there was a very great deal of happiness then too, wasn't there, dear sweet? Let me know how long you will be in Brooklyn, because of the address I am to put on the envelopes. And write to me, dearest, and don't tear the letters up: there is no need to do that now, surely, and try to read into my letters all the things I cannot express in letter-writing. And take all my love, because it is all yours. And take care of yourself in the different climate, and wrap yourself up well whenever you go out, and think of your own                                                    MAX

## To Arnold Bennett[1]
MS. Berg

*9 May 1909*                                          *48 Upper Berkeley Street, W.*

Dear Mr Arnold Bennett, I was much pleased at having your letter – much gratified, as you may well imagine, that my praise of your play had given pleasure to you.[2] I rejoice in the notion that you had "a particular curiosity" about my "views", and that the milkman had been instructed to bring the *Saturday* along. And I do wish I could share that curiosity. I can't. I write about plays – for, as you say, one must live; and I write about them to the best of my ability, and always correct the proof carefully, substituting colons for semi-colons, and so on. But, once that is done, it never occurs to me to do more. I never read my article on Saturday or thereafter. And I am touched and excited when I hear of any one not following my example. Especially am I excited and touched by the knowedge that the writer of *The Old Wives' Tale*[3] had been reading me with interest. So fine that book is that I daresay I under-rated the other books that I read after it – such as the *Tales of the Five Towns*, and *The Grim Smile of the Five Towns*.[4] Reading them after I had read that large masterpiece, these things seemed to me, for

[1] Prolific novelist, playwright and journalist (1867–1931).

[2] *What the Public Wants*, first produced at the Aldwych Theatre on 2 May 1909 and favourably reviewed at length by Max in the *Saturday Review* of 8 May.

[3] Published in 1908.

[4] Published in 1905 and 1907 respectively. Bennett's first two volumes of short stories.

the most part, cheap (barring the Simon Fuge[1] story): I could imagine the illustrations of them in the magazines for which they were written; and could imagine these illustrations without recoiling. But not Arthur Boyd Houghton[2] nor Keene[3] nor Millais[4] nor any man of the great little decade of illustration have portrayed for me Constance or Sophia,[5] or any of the people connected with those young-and-old ladies, without insulting my inward intelligence.

When I had finished *The Old Wives' Tale* (having gone slow in the later parts of it, being so loth to have no more to read of it) I felt a real void in my life; and this void I instinctively tried to fill a little by writing a letter to the man who had laid so large an aesthetic debt on me. I wrote the letter – and meant to send it – but said "Why?" I am always saying "Why?" That is the curse of the twentieth-century (and metropolitan and non-Bursley) nature. Happily, by some throw-back, I do occasionally say "Why not?" And to you I say "why not" give me the very great pleasure it would be to me if you would have luncheon with me at the Savile Club (107 Piccadilly) next Tuesday or Wednesday, at 1 o'clock (if you wouldn't mind so early an hour). Do come. I know I should like you, in my humble way; and you'd probably like me – *c'est mon métier* to be liked by the gifted: I somehow understand them.

Yours sincerely   MAX BEERBOHM

Are you, by the way, an intimate friend of Sargent, or is *Buried Alive*[6] sheer intuition?

---

[1] "The Death of Simon Fuge" in *The Grim Smile of the Five Towns*.

[2] 1836–75, illustrator of many books, including Dalziel's *Arabian Nights* (1865).

[3] Charles Keene (1823–91), *Punch* artist and illustrator of works by George Meredith and Charles Reade.

[4] John Everett Millais (1829–96) illustrated novels by Trollope and others.

[5] The twin heroines of *The Old Wives' Tale*, natives of Bursley.

[6] Bennett's novel (1908), which he later very successfully dramatised as *The Great Adventure*. It tells of a famous painter who changes places with his valet and watches his own supposed funeral in Westminster Abbey. This was not done by the American painter John Singer Sargent (1856–1925), but Bennett may have borrowed some of his characteristics for the story.

## To Edmund Gosse
MS. Berg

*48 Upper Berkeley Street, W.*

My dear Gosse, Please let me thank you for what I have just been reading – your wonderful essay about Swinburne.[1] I had so hoped you would write one, knowing how vivid it would be – no, not knowing *how* vivid it would be: that knowledge was withheld till I read the essay.

I, knowing *"les beaux restes"* of Swinburne – and very beautiful they were – had constructed from them a shadowy figure of him as he must have been in his prime; and it is a great joy to have this same figure set before me now in panoply of flesh and blood, all alive and alert and complete – set before me with such exquisite art and insight, from the fulness of your memory.

The passage that fascinates me most of all in your essay is that in which you describe Swinburne reciting "The Triumph of Time." I would give anything to have been there! That poem has always seemed to me the most profoundly magical of all his poems – the most *Swinburnian*. I was reading it again a few days after his death; and, oddly enough, read certain stanzas of it aloud to myself with such of Swinburne's manner and inflections as I could reproduce: that manner and those inflections seemed to be inherent in the words, though, in another way, so unsuited to them. I suppose it was by reason of the "personal experience", which you tell us he told you had inspired the poem, that Swinburne himself shone out so clearly to me through the verses. The contrast between the pathos of his own oddity and the splendid classic pathos of the actual phrases and cadences gives the poem an extraordinary added quality. I wonder how deep the "personal experience" had gone. Meredith (whom I saw less than a fortnight before he died)[2]

---

[1] "Swinburne: Personal Recollections" in the *Fortnightly Review* of 1 June 1909. The poet died on 10 April 1909.

[2] George Meredith, poet and novelist, died on 18 May 1909. Max's notes after two visits to him read:

> Grey dressing-gown – Olympian – Battered statue of Jupiter. Blurred outlines – eyes dim but magnificent ... The drawl of the swell of the 'sixties. "Leisah!" His chaff of the nurse – "no idea of poetry. Excellent creechah! Make a good wife for a soldier – some regular cut-and-thrust fellah!" Meredith's pre-occupation with women. No Puritanism or hypocrisy. The way German women love. About old men. Most of them envious. Not he. Read the reports of divorce cases with interest, envying the co-respondent, but not grudging him anything ... Pathos of his tears at Swinburne's death. He could not keep up his panache. Splendid old age. Serene – And yet sad – lonely.

was describing how one little chance spark in conversation was enough to set Swinburne in a blaze – one hint of drama, and there was Swinburne in the midst of a drama instantly completed by himself.

But, as regards "The Triumph of Time," however much there may be in it of sheerly *artistic* emotion, I feel the impact of that real *personal* emotion, too.

Do forgive this long rigmarole, and don't answer it.

With affectionate remembrances to Mrs Gosse,

Yours ever most sincerely    MAX

## *To Florence Kahn*[1]
MS. Reichmann

*Wednesday night [29 September 1909]*          *Savile Club*

My own *darling,* Smoke the cigarette, please, as much of it as gives you pleasure, and think of me while you smoke it. Do keep it unsmoked if you think Miss Webb might be shocked. I am finishing this letter at Upper Berkeley Street. Alec Ross[2] came and began talking to me at the Savile, and I could not resume my writing, for fear of making him think I thought him a bore. One is so at the mercy of things!

I was very glad to have your wire, darling. And your beautiful letter this morning. Have you been out riding today? You were going to. But perhaps it was too rainy? You look a great darling on horseback. I have seen *The Bells*[3] tonight, and have vaguely an amusing scheme for an article. I visited Arthur Waugh[4] this morning. The book had only just gone to the binders; and so, as it is important that the reviewers should have copies well in advance, we decided to postpone publication to October *12th* – Tuesday week, instead of next Tuesday. Shall you still be in Bognor then? I have to go to the Walkleys on the 9th. I could come to Bognor on the 11th for some days, if you were still there. *Darling,* you are all the world to me, now and always, and though I couldn't love you more than I did before my last visit to Bognor, I think I realise more than ever *how* much I love you.     Your own    MAX

[1] Who was now back in England.

[2] 1860–1927. Elder brother of Robbie. One of the founders of the Society of Authors.

[3] The revival of *The Bells*, Leopold Lewis's adaptation of *Le Juif Polonais* by Erckmann-Chatrian, opened at the Queen's Theatre on 22 September 1909, with H.B. Irving in his father's old part. Max's review appeared in the *Saturday Review* on 2 October.

[4] The chairman of Chapman & Hall, who were publishing Max's third book of essays, *Yet Again*. Father of Evelyn Waugh.

## To Florence Kahn

MS. Reichmann

[*12 December 1909*]                    *48 Upper Berkeley Street, W.*

My own *darling* love, I wonder how you are feeling today, and I *long* for your letter in the morning. I am going to the Actors' Benevolent Fund dinner, at which Herbert is presiding, tonight. Viola[1] is going to be one of the singers after dinner; but I doubt if I shall hear her as I have promised to go to a "studio warming" at the Walter Russells' afterwards. Walter R. has now a studio of his own near his house. Today I have been Zuleika-ising. I have now introduced, besides the Rhodes Scholar, the ghost of the founder of the Junta (who does not at all understand the Scholar), and much resents the presence of a "rebel" at dinner at the Junta! The Scholar, hearing from the Duke, how the founder broke Nellie O'Mora's heart, declares him to have been a scoundrel and "not a white man" – whereat the founder draws his sword and runs the Scholar through his ample chest. But as he is an invisible and intangible ghost, no one is any the wiser. I haven't done all this part yet: it is just what I am in the middle of.[2] Do you think it sounds all right? Tomorrow I go to see Alexander, and will let you know just what happens.[3]

Darling, good night, Your own always and always loving   MAX


## To Florence Kahn

MS. Reichmann

*Friday* [*17 December 1909*]                    *48 Upper Berkeley Street, W.*

My own *darling* love, I have just had your wire, and am so pleased, first at "much better" and next at "article splendid" (is it really? It is one of the articles that I didn't really feel able to judge in the proof). It is foggy and wet here; but I hope Rye may be better. I had heard of Henry James being in London – heard he was in the stage-box on the first night of the Haymarket, talking with great animation to Georgette

[1] Viola Tree, eldest daughter of Max's brother Herbert, actress and singer (1884–1938).

[2] This scene occurs in Chapter viii.

[3] George Alexander, the actor-manager, had asked Max to write a play for him, and had given him £100 as an initial payment.

Leblanc, who wore a yellow turban.[1] So evidently he *is* having "great fun". I have roamed around my library, wondering what of my books you hadn't read *and* would not disdain. The result (an unsatisfactory one) is that I am sending you a parcel of *Men and Books* by Herbert Paul, a volume of *Cornhill Magazine*, Volume I of Horace Walpole's *Memoirs of George III*, and Volume I of *Don Quixote* – which I think you would like best – and you may not know this particular translation, the language of which, as I told you, seems to me rather noble and quaint. I think I must have forgotten to tell you (in the excitement about Alexander) that I heard from Winter of the N.E.A.C. on Monday night that "The Horny Hand" and "Shaw's Sortie"[2] are both sold – to whom I know not. This brings up my sales to £84 – not deducting discount. Rather good to sell six out of nine. I am surprised at "Shaw's Sortie" selling, aren't you? Hugh Lane[3] is presenting his own caricature to Dublin.

Darling love, I long to see you, and it will be so lovely, won't it? And we shall be so happy.                                Your very own    M A X

## To Lady Desborough
MS. Hertford

*15 May 1910*[4]                                *The White Cottage, Hythe*

My dear Lady Desborough, Thank you for your charming letter – though this epithet is otiose, for any letter of yours always *is* charming. My wife and I are here for a week or so; after which we shall be in Italy for a while – probably quite a long while: it all depends on whether my wife likes Italy as much as I do. Whether it be Italy or elsewhere doesn't really seem to me to matter: I should be happy anywhere with this lady – even in her native America, if a sudden loyalty to that land befell her!
                                Yours ever sincerely    M A X   B E E R B O H M

[1] Hugh Walpole was also in the box with Henry James, Maeterlinck and his mistress Georgette Leblanc on the first night of Maeterlinck's *The Blue Bird* at the Haymarket Theatre on 8 December 1909. In the interval Herbert Trench, the manager of the theatre, invited them behind the scenes. Through the open door of a dressing-room Hugh caught sight of a number of middle-aged and elderly dwarfs busily shaving. He asked who they were and Trench answered: "Oh, they're the unborn babies in the next act."

[2] Two of Max's caricatures which had been shown in the Winter 1909 Exhibition of the New English Art Club.

[3] Irish art expert and collector (1875–1915). Knighted 1909. Drowned in the *Lusitania*.

[4] Max and Florence had been married on 4 May.

## To Arnold Bennett
MS. Berg

*Sunday, 12 March 1911*                                    *Villino Chiaro*

My dear Arnold Bennett, Help! Help! Where are you? I cannot remember your Fontainebleau address. Also, you may not be at it just now. So I send my cry to you through Methuen, who is likely to know your whereabouts. If you are going to be in London a week hence, please will you lunch with me there – say on Thursday, 23rd – at the Savile? But if you are by way of being in Paris on Wednesday, 22nd, will you lunch with me *there* – say at one o'clock, and at the Café de la Paix (the restaurant part of the place, *not* the grill-room, because I have an abiding horror of grill-rooms as they are death to anything I have of dignity in my nature). And if Mrs Bennett could be induced to come with you I should be doubly delighted.

Meanwhile you are asking what in reason all this urgent fuss is about – and this brings me to the dangerous part of my letter. I want to do a caricature of you for an exhibition at the Leicester Galleries, due in April.[1] And for this purpose I want to verify my remembrance – or rather to find some way of bringing my remembrance within the rubric of my art; for, in the rough sketches I have done, you come out looking exactly like Apollo's long-lost twin-brother, and though I am sure my memory doesn't deceive me I want to get a different sort of effect. In fact I want to make a "distortion", and only by seeing you with my eyes can I hope to find some way of making this distortion without altogether losing the likeness. So please don't leave me in the lurch. I shall be *here* till tomorrow week (Monday, 20th). Please send me word. You need not be afraid that I shall ask you to divulge the secrets of Hilda Lessways: I enjoy the agony of these tenterhooks.[2]

Yours very sincerely   MAX BEERBOHM

In case there isn't time to send word to this address, my Paris address will be Hotel de Castille, Rue Cambon. I arrive there on Tuesday night, and leave Paris on Wednesday night; and I do hope that in the midst of my day of horrible rushing around there will be this oasis at the Café de la Paix.

---

[1] This was entitled "Mr Arnold Bennett – Personally conducted tours from the cradle, through Bursley, to the grave". The *Daily News* of 22 April 1911 described it as having the cradle on the left, the smoking chimneys of Bursley rear-centre, and on the right a tombstone reading "*Hic Jacet Persona Bennettiana*, Aged 97, or thereabouts".

[2] *Hilda Lessways*, the second volume of Bennett's Clayhanger trilogy, was published in 1911, but the final volume *These Twain* not until 1916.

## To Edmund Gosse

48, UPPER BERKELEY STREET. W.

DAWN
The Viscount Haldene of Cloan

My dear Gosse, Very many thanks: I will entrust myself to you, for that great delight, at 3.45, on Thursday.

Yours affectionately   MAX BEERBOHM

¹ Haldane's peerage and title were gazetted in *The Times* on this day.

## To Lady Desborough
MS. Hertford

*12 May 1911*                                                    *Villino Chiaro*

My dear Lady Desborough, Your very delightful letter has arrived, and
has been, step by step, collated with the catalogue of the exhibition, so
that I feel as if I had really conducted you round the place and heard
your comments with my own ears (as Vergil wrote to Dante, on receiving
an inscribed copy of the *Divina Commedia*).

I rejoice that you like the things so much. But you are mistaken in
envying me the "fun" I had in doing them. They were born in travail,
for the most part, really – are the protests of a too-thin-skinned nature
against the coarseness and stupidities and pretentiousnesses of mankind
at large. That picture of the Tariff-Reformer, for example, came of
prolonged writhings against the wretched propaganda that has for the
present wrecked the Tory party. (I wonder, by the way, *when* the Tories
will begin to realise that the reason why the country won't have anything
to do with them is quite simply that they still feel it their duty to go on
hawking around that dismal and so quickly-seen-through and rejected
imposture for the benefit of some few rich people.) And the Roosevelt
drawing,[1] as another instance of my lack of joyousness: for weeks I could
not open a newspaper without being confronted by the volleyed-out
platitudes of that appalling bounder. I suffered and suffered. "Number
117" was but one of the cries that I could not suppress while Roosevelt
was in our midst.

Sargent's pictures of Venice, Shaw's megalomania, the life and works
of C. P. Little[2] – these are further instances of the agonies that wrack
me, and that compel me to cry out to all who pass by. And the worst of
it is that my groans sound just like ripples of rather good-humoured
laughter. By some kink in my endowment, I can't express pain and
abhorrence. Nor can I express reverence and joy. I revere and rejoice
in Henry James, very truly and deeply. But this I can't express at all in
drawing: Henry James comes out just as ludicrous as C. P. Little or

---

[1] Theodore Roosevelt (1858–1919). President of the United States 1901–9. This caricature of him, No 117 in the catalogue, entitled "Mr Roosevelt's visit to Europe – a
Souvenir," shows him saying to a robed and spectacled Europa: "2 plus 2 makes 4!!"

[2] Actor and journalist (1856–1914). This caricature is entitled "Mr C. P. Little, noting
zealously, for the benefit of readers of the Paris edition of the *New York Herald*, and
for the delectation of Thackeray in Elysium, the fact that Lord So-and-So was among
those who were out and about in the neighbourhood of Piccadilly this morning, and
that he was looking the picture of health".

Roosevelt. In fine, my talent is a horribly limited one. I want to bless and (more often) I can only giggle!

However – forgive this long and very German inquisition into myself.

I came back here the day after the exhibition was opened, as I was very home-sick, and sun-sick, and – I was going to say sea-sick; but that won't do at all.

I think we are going to Venice tomorrow for a week or so; but it is almost a pity to go away even there from here.

Yours ever sincerely   MAX BEERBOHM

## Postcard: Bernard Shaw to Max
### MS. Reichmann

[*Postmark 14 May 1911*]                    [*Ayot St Lawrence*]

Observe that I have had that snag tooth nipped off (there was only one, in spite of malicious exaggerations) and replaced by a symmetrical imposture. Your caricatures are now waste paper; and serve you right.

What's your address? and will your wife condescend to come and see us if we propose a lunch?                    G.B.S.

## To Bernard Shaw
### MS. Princeton

*23 May 1911*                    *Grand Hotel, Venice*

My dear G.B.S., Nothing would give my wife and me more delight than to come and lunch at Adelphi Terrace. But we are far away, for ever. I do not mean that we have decided never to leave the Grand Hotel, Venice: indeed, we are here for only a few days; after which we return to Villino Chiaro, Rapallo, our fixed abode; and there we shall be – well, not exactly for ever: we shall, once a year or so, come for a month or so to London. And on the first of these occasions I will write to warn you and Mrs Shaw that we stand waiting, hand in hand, for an invitation to lunch with you.

Meanwhile, yours to hand re change of tooth, and please note that our Mr Imagination has already waited on you, acting on advices as per picture post-card received.                    Yours ever   MAX BEERBOHM

Shaw Retoothed

LE GRAND HÔTEL
VENISE

*Where's Lily Elsie the noo?*

[Lily Elsie was then the reigning star of the West End musical theatre, following huge successes in *The Merry Widow*, *The Dollar Princess*, and *A Waltz Dream*.]

# To W.B. Yeats[1]

TS. Merton

*11 July 1911*                                         *Villino Chiaro*

Dear Yeats, How I wish I could be at the dinner next Sunday! When I lived in London it was one of my standing grievances that Gordon Craig[2] was in Italy. And now that I live in Italy, it is so like him to be in London. I won't go so far as to say that he never is where he is wanted; for he must always be *somewhere*, and wherever he is he is wanted. But he is wanted also wherever he *isn't*. Men of genius are so few that they ought to atone for their fewness by being at any rate ubiquitous. Craig's influence is ubiquitous, certainly – festooned from point to point around Europe. But the charming fellow himself – ever as gay as he is earnest, and as inspiriting as he is inspired – *he* is confined to one place at a time. I resent that. However, I don't want to spoil your evening, and with a forced cheerfulness but a full heart I raise my glass from afar.                    Yours ever sincerely   MAX BEERBOHM

# To William Heinemann[3]

MS. Princeton

*13 October 1911*                                         *Villino Chiaro*

My dear Heinemann, Many thanks for your amusing and reassuring letter. I illustrate this herewith, and meanwhile await the printed book in placid confidence that Ballantyne's proof-readers will have taken care of the typography. You will have had my telegram expressing my delight

---

[1] The Irish poet (1865–1939) was one of a band of Gordon Craig's friends who organised a dinner in his honour at the Café Royal on 16 July 1911.

[2] Son of Ellen Terry. Actor, stage designer, author and woodcut artist (1872–1966). He and his family lived outside Rapallo from 1917 to 1924.

[3] 1863–1920. Founded his publishing firm in 1890 and soon became a leading figure in the profession. He and his firm published *Zuleika Dobson* and all Max's subsequent prose works. Max had written to him, complaining about the state of the proofs of *Zuleika*, and Heinemann sent the letter on to Messrs Ballantyne & Co, the printers of the book. Their Managing Director Charles Howe McCall sent a long, amused and amusing letter to Heinemann, which turned aside Max's wrath. For the almost full correspondence (Max's original letter is missing) see "Max and Mr McCall" by Lawrence Danson in the *Princeton University Library Chronicle*, winter 1986.

at the binding. Superficially, at any rate, the book is as distinguished as a book can be. And my first impulse at sight of the binding was to wire to you "Stop publication, must write novel all over again, to make it worthy of the outside of it". But this might have tried your patience too far.

I haven't yet heard from Sutro about his article; and, as he is always a prompt correspondent, I rather fear he must be out of England; but I expect he will do the article anyhow.

As to the reviewer-friends to whom it was agreed that some copies should be sent . . . but this means the drawing up of a list, and a detailed explanation: I must spread myself on to larger paper.

Before I do that I sign myself here, with very many thanks for all your kindness and courtesy throughout the preparations for *Zuleika*, and with all hopes that she won't round on you and be a failure.

Yours very sincerely   MAX BEERBOHM

Mr Heinemann reading the Riot Act to
the Ballantyne Company
(The portrait of the latter is purely conjectural – the
clothes and the chevelure being symbolic of unrevised
Ballantynean typography.)

<h1 align="center">To Robert Ross</h1>
MS. Hyde

*15 October 1911*                                   *Villino Chiaro*

My dear Bobbie, Poor old Zuleika! She is at length to be dragged out, blinking and staggering, into the light of day.[1] And Heinemann will be sending her to the Reform Club, to wait for you there. Be kind, be courteous, to the hag. Incline your ear to her mumblings. Pretend not the hear the horrid creakings of her joints. Tell her she does not look a day older than when you saw her or at any rate her head and shoulders all those years ago. Don't hint to her that she makes a goblin of the sun.[2]

Yours affectionately    MAX

Zuleika being introduced to the public<br>by William Heinemann

---

[1] *Zuleika Dobson* was published on 26 October 1911.
[2] D.G. Rossetti, "Jenny".

78

## To William Heinemann
MS. Princeton

21 October 1911

*Villino Chiaro*

My dear Heinemann, Very many thanks for your letter. I didn't wire
to ask you to send out any of those copies before eve of publication. I
had already written to Tom and Dick and Harry, saying vaguely that
they *would be* receiving copies; and this announcement will, I think,
have served my mild diplomatic purpose well enough, by putting the
recipients on the alert.

By the way, as *Zuleika* would be by way of making a special *local*
appeal, it might be well to send copies for review to *The Oxford Magazine*
and to *The Isis* – both of which, as it is term-time, are now appearing
weekly.

Just as you think fit.     Yours very sincerely     MAX BEERBOHM

Ballantyne Reclaimed

79

## To Edmund Gosse
### MS. Princeton

*15 October 1911*[1]                                        *Villino Chiaro*

My dear Gosse, In a week or so, Heinemann will have published a book called *Zuleika Dobson*. I am the author of it, and I very much hope you will be one of the readers of it – or at any rate one of the skimmers. As I am so far away, a copy will be sent to you direct from Bedford Street, at my request; and this letter is to project, as it were, on to the fly-leaf of that copy an inscription in terms of the admiration and affection in which I hold you.

With all best remembrances to Mrs Gosse and to your daughters,

I am yours ever    MAX

P.S. The faults of my book as a work of art are as many as the sands of the sea, or as the works of Hilaire Belloc. But I claim to have given a truer picture of undergraduate life than is to be found in most of the other novels about Oxford!


## To Edmund Gosse
### MS. B.L.

*11 November 1911*                                          *Villino Chiaro*

My dear Gosse, Very many thanks for your most interesting and delightful letter. But I don't think I quite agree with you about the *ending* of *Zuleika Dobson*. You ask "How could an event so amazing as the conglomerated suicide be taken so tamely in the University?" But, if it comes to that, how could those (*circa*) 2500 young men have drowned themselves for love of a lady? How could the Duke have been, while he was yet *in statu pupillari*, a Knight of the Garter? And how – but innumerable are the questions that arise unless the claimed licence of fantasy be granted! Having granted to myself the licence claimed implicitly in the opening sentences of the book – the licence to be utterly fantastic – why should I have contrived a verisimilar outcome for things made in calmest defiance of verisimilitude? Of course, fantasy has – or

---

[1] The fact that Max clearly wrote this date as 1901 suggests a return to the early days of the book's writing, or perhaps to the dating of its story.

should have – a logic of its own, not less than realism or any other form. Without actual violence to such logic, I *might* have made a verisimilar ending.

I did consider that course. But I found it would not do. The grief and rage of the bereaved parents and sisters would have struck altogether too painful a note. It would have jarred. And then, to satisfy realism, the prospect of (*circa*) 2500 inquests, and Zuleika necessarily subpoena'd for every one of them … It would have been a violent, chaotic, inconclusive muddle, not an *ending* at all. (I know of no right ending to a piece of literature – poem or novel or essay or what not – that is not definitely in the minor key: tranquillity; "no more to be said"; but a hint that the world at large, despite these pothers that have been described, won't cease to go on.) And so I fell back on the first-conceived (and more natural and truly logical) scheme of letting my bland impossibilities be accepted in an impossibly bland, an impossibly and appropriately "Oxford" manner. Of course, if I were George Moore … Yet I, too, have a sort of "coral insect patience". Only, this patience is exercised by me for the scheme of my work, before I sit down to write; and thereafter, for details, while I am writing. When the work is at length done, it is immutable – oh, so very immutable! as having been done not as well as it could be done, but as having been done as well as I ever could do it. To reconstruct things? I could as easily be born again! I would as willingly introduce new steps into the Minuet!!!

Talking of Moore: do read, if you have not read yet, *Hail and Farewell, Vol I.*[1] The picture therein of Edward Martyn,[2] built up touch by absurd touch, until … but no, this isn't the right image for that masterpiece. I see Martyn rather as a vast feather-bed on which Moore, luxuriously rolling and pommeling and crowing and (it goes without saying) stark naked, is borne towards immortality.

With fond remembrances to you all,

Yours ever affectionately   MAX

---

[1] *Ave* (1911), to be followed by *Salve* (1912) and *Vale* (1914).

[2] Edward Martyn, Irish Catholic dramatist (1859–1923). President of Sinn Fein 1904–8, promoter of the Gaelic League. Friend and butt of George Moore.

From "The Daily Mirror" – 1915 or so
"Yesterday in Broad Street, Oxford, Lord Curzon, the Chancellor of
the University, made an eloquent speech before unveiling the colossal
bronze statute of Zuleika Dobson, executed by Mrs Scott. (Mrs Scott is
marked with a X.)"

## To Kathleen Scott
MS. Cambridge

*Saturday* [*Late 1911*]                                      *Villino Chiaro*

My dear Kathleen, I am delighted indeed by your letter. Very many
thanks. The book isn't of a kind to please many people, I fancy; but I
did fancy all along that it was of a kind to give a great deal of pleasure
to just a few people; and I am proud that you are one of those few.

Yours ever   MAX BEERBOHM

P.T.O. to inner [here opposite] page!


## To Arnold Bennett
MS. Fales

*10 January 1912*                                      *Villino Chiaro*
                                                  *Rapallo, Italy*

My dear Arnold, I dimly remember your surname, but take leave to
drop it now: so very delightful and friendshipful is the letter I have just
had from you. But you mustn't expect from me "a diabolically ingenious
defence" of *Zuleika*, any more than you would expect a woman who has
just borne a child to be diabolically ingenious in defence of that child
... "Madam, this baby is in many respects a very fine baby. I observe
many inimitable touches of *you* in it. But, Madam, I am bound to say
that its screams are more penetrating than a baby's screams ought to be.
I notice in its complexion a mottled quality which jars my colour-sense.
And I cannot help wishing it were" etc. etc... Will the young mother
floor you in well-chosen words? With a rapt beatific smile she does but
turn on her pillow, very sure that this baby is as perfect as a baby can
be ... Or perhaps, raising herself on one elbow, she gazes at you with
an exquisite forgiveness and murmurs (*mutatis mutandis*) some such
faltering words as these: "I admit that a humorous work cannot end
with propriety on a tragic note. But I don't think *Zuleika* really has that
kind of ending. Nothing is *in itself* tragic – not even death. Death in
fiction is tragic or otherwise according to who it is that dies, against
what manner of background, in what way described. Suppose I were
destined to read next autumn that all the young men in the Five Towns[1]

---

[1] Bennett's trilogy – *Clayhanger*, *Hilda Lessways* and *These Twain* – was set in his native
Five Towns, the Potteries of Staffordshire.

did with one accord throw themselves into the Knype and Mersey Canal, and were all of them without a single exception drowned, for love of Hilda Clayhanger, née Lessways – why then I should feel I must take my own life, into the bargain: I should never be able to shake off the horror of that disaster. Why? Because Hilda is a creature of flesh and blood, and because all those young men as described by you would be doubtless as actual to me as she is. Zuleika, on the other hand, in so far as she is anything more than a symbol, has a purely *fantastical* reality; likewise the Duke of Dorset; likewise that shadowy ballet-chorus of other undergraduates. The *Spectator* in its review of the book agreed with you (I see you start and turn deadly pale) that I ought not to have let the general suicide be achieved; but it added that "of course the catastrophe moves us no more than the cutting-in-half of a property policeman in a harlequinade". That remark seems to me very exactly right, though it knocks the bottom out of the previous objection which you share ... Oh Arnold, dry your eyes. Be brave. There's work to be done in the world, lad! Let the Dorsets bury their Dorsets!

as Arnold Bennett almost undone by the death of the Duke of Dorset,

As to my not having dealt with the consternation of the outer world after the death of the undergraduates ... well, had I done this it would have queered the whole compact little form of the book: it would have been a large and violent and new matter, impossible as an appropriate *ending* to what was written. Just imagine the 3000 inquests! And moreover the thing couldn't have been done without just that trenching on realism that would have made the absurd catastrophe truly painful. It *had* to be skipped – or (say) to be merely *suggested,* as suggested it was parenthetically at the beginning of the chapter about Clio.[1] Stillmoreover, it was none of my business: Clio's injunction was that I should record "Miss Dobson's visit to Oxford". Those three days in that place I faithfully recorded. What happened afterwards and elsewhere, I was justified in leaving to the recollection of the newspaper-reading public.

Stillmoreover yet – but at this moment the door of the young mother's bedroom is flung open. In rush the young mother's husband, and her physician, and her two trained (though temporarily neglectful) nurses. They dart to the bedside. It is found that the young mother's temperature has been sent up two degrees – by *you* – all by *you* – the fault all *yours.* Glared at, you beat a hasty though not ungraceful retreat, murmuring something or other about the restorative air of Cannes ... Well, it would be a joy indeed to come to Cannes. But this is, alas, impossible. I simply can't do a stroke of work away from my own premises; and during the next three months I am compelled to do a great many strokes of work; and, as I am a lamentably slow worker, here must my wife and I abide. But we shall afterwards be going to London for a little while; and there, or in Paris, or in both places, it will be a delight indeed for us to foregather with you both.

Meanwhile, William Heinemann, who was here last night, will be calling on you in Cannes and delivering to you and to Madame the best messages of                              Yours ever   MAX BEERBOHM

---

[1] The Muse of History, who accompanies Max in the recital of his story.

# To John Galsworthy
TS. Merton

*14 December 1912*                                    *48 Upper Berkeley Street, W.*

My dear Galsworthy, In the stress and rattle and frittering botheration of London, I have done my best to enjoy your beautiful book in a way worthy of it.[1] I have devoted to it such clear intervals and respites as I have been able to get in the course of a visit congested in proportion to the visit's brevity. And, even in this inauspicious way, I have been much illuminated, touched, harrowed, quickened, refined, made more human, made to admire you more than ever. Many thanks for all this. And now that we are near to the time of going home to Rapallo, how I look forward to reading your *Inn* there – in that lucid air where everything that is good can be tasted so much more keenly than here.

Tasted and, I grant you, *smelt*!! In London my nostrils are conscious of nothing but the smoke and the petrol; and what I wrote about scents in my parody of you[2] was but an expression of envy: it must be lovely to be able to distinguish pretty scents in London. (I myself hardly know which is petrol, which smoke.)

As to that phrase about which you ask me: "Because it takes more out of us". I think I may claim that I "divined" it. I don't think it is in any of your books; and I don't think you ever said it to me: you would have adjudged me too frivolous for such a confidence. I must have read it in your eyes – particularly in the unmonocled eye!

With best remembrances to Mrs Galsworthy.

Yours ever    MAX BEERBOHM

---

[1] *The Inn of Tranquillity*, studies and essays, published in October 1912.

[2] "Endeavour" in *A Christmas Garland* (published in October 1912). In the parody Adrian Berridge, coming down to breakfast, perceives "the immediate scents of dry toast, of China tea, of napery fresh from the wash, together with that vague, super-subtle scent which boiled eggs give out through their unbroken shells. And as a permanent base to these there was the scent of much-polished Chippendale, and of bees'-waxed parquet, and of Persian rugs. To-day, moreover, crowning the composition, there was the delicate pungency of the holly that topped the Queen Anne mirror and the Mantegna prints."

## Edmund Gosse to Max[1]

MS. Reichmann

*Christmas night 1912*          *17 Hanover Terrace, Regent's Park, N.W.*

My dear Max, Henry James has been eating his Christmas dinner here with us, and I am anxious to let you know that he started the subject of your *Christmas Garland*, and discussed it with the most extraordinary vivacity and appreciation. I told him that you had a certain nervousness about his acceptance of your parody of him and he desired me to let you know at once that no one can have read it with more wonder and delight than he. He expressed himself in superlatives. He called the book "the most intelligent that has been produced in England for many a long day". But he says you have destroyed the trade of writing. No one, now, can write without incurring the reproach of somewhat ineffectively imitating – *you*! What could be more handsome? And, alas! my dear Max, what can be more true? I, for instance, shall never be able to draw another portrait without calling down upon me the sneer, "Not half so amusing as your dinner with Ibsen and Browning!" You are our Conqueror. And I am your affectionate and ever-amused admirer

EDMUND GOSSE

If you had time to call on Henry James, I think he would greatly like it. He is staying at Garland's Hotel, Suffolk Street. E.G.


## To Edmund Gosse

MS. Brotherton

*26 December 1912*                    *48 Upper Berkeley Street*

My dear Gosse, That is a Christmas letter indeed. And I know not which has delighted me the more: the thought of your thoughtfulness in sitting down then and there to send me the good news, or the good news itself that Henry James had not been displeased and was pleased so positively. Ever so many thanks. And I will certainly, before our imminent departure to Rapallo, ask Garland's hall-porter whether Mr James be – down, pedantry! – *is* – at home. I should much love to see him again.          Yours ever affectionately   MAX BEERBOHM

---

[1] Max had been worried lest Henry James might be upset by the parody of him, "The Mote in the Middle Distance", in *A Christmas Garland*.

## To Edmund Gosse
### MS. B.L.

*15 June 1913*                                                    *Villino Chiaro*

My dear Gosse, Many thanks for your delightful letter. My great pleasure in the distinction of belonging to the Academic Committee is all the greater for my knowing now that you wished me to belong.[1] I hope I shall not disgrace you. It is perhaps well that, living here, I shall so seldom be able to attend meetings. Some years ago I did serve on a committee (of a trivial and debased kind); and this service quickly formed in me an opinion, still held, that I am not wise in council – or at any rate that my wisdom is of so taciturn a kind that no one is a penny the better for it.

Out here, my silence and my probable folly will not matter. And, for the rest, let us hope that I shall not write less well than heretofore. Honour having come to me through (what you charmingly call) the beautiful purity of my prose style, I must set my face against the not unnatural impulse to say "*Nunc dimittis*; it is enough; henceforth I shall take the line of less resistance and wield the pen of that ready writer, that fluent old Adam, which is in all of us".

Flesh is weak, and strong now is the temptation to show myself, after all these years, in my true colours – a splitter of infinitives and a reckless and-which-er, a verb-sap-er and *caeteris paribuster*, a reliable *pro-tempster* and a *vae victist à outrance*, a temperamental milieuist with a welcome touch of sincerity (to say nothing of undeniable gifts and undoubted promise), a scarcely-too-much-to-sayer and a dare-we-adder, a haver of little hesitation in averring, and pre-eminently a ventilator of Britishers' grievances, and a voicer – a no uncertain voicer – of their most cherished aspirations, on which the sun never sets.

But this horrid temptation I shall fight and beat, made strong by your faith in me.

You say I must "continue to caricature the members". And this

---

[1] The Royal Society of Literature had instituted an Academic Committee of not more than forty members, "to maintain the purity of the English language" and in general act like the Académie Française. Max had recently exhibited a caricature entitled "Members of the Academic Committee [all crowned with laurel wreaths] discussing whether at future meetings an Agenda Paper shall be provided, and, if so, what on earth to put into it". When Max was formally received into the Committee on 28 November 1913 the poet Laurence Binyon (1869–1943) delivered an address in his honour, which was published in *A Laurence Binyon Anthology* (1927). The Committee expired in 1939.

licence has a particular application at this moment. The Eternal Volatile[1] is publishing in the autumn a book of reproductions of fifty or so of my drawings. And among the drawings which he has caused to be photographed for the book is the group, which you may remember, of the Academic Committee. This could, doubtless, be withdrawn, on the argument that chaff from without is one thing, chaff from within another. Personally I think the drawing had better go into the book with the others; but if you were to think otherwise (as I deduce, from your remark, that you would *not*), then I would be guided by you, and ask the Eternal Volatile to suppress the drawing.[2] I am glad, by the way, to see that he is going to produce a new and grandiose edition of *Father and Son*,[3] in regard to which I shall say to him, as Pilgrim said to the Angel, "Put down my name, Sir". With best regards from us both to Mrs Gosse and to you all,

Yours sincerely and affectionately   MAX BEERBOHM

I *must* try to draw the Public Orator of Cambridge, flushed with oratory, sitting down to read Mr Thomas Hardy's "great epic drama ON THE VICTORIES OF NELSON AND WELLINGTON!"[4]

## To A.G. Gardiner[5]
TS. Merton

*21 July 1913*  *Villino Chiaro*

*Very Confidential*

Dear Mr Gardiner, Many years ago I wrote to congratulate you on your fine series of studies of well-known men.[6] You won't remember that letter. But well do I remember the charming reply I had from you. And by that reply I am emboldened to write to you again – this time to suggest to you a few points in which, as I think, the *Daily News and Leader* might be improved. The matter is near to my heart because the *D.N. and L.* is the one daily paper that I take in. And, conversely, I

---

[1] Presumably William Heinemann.

[2] It duly appeared in *Fifty Caricatures* in October 1913.

[3] Gosse's account of his early life, originally published in 1907.

[4] At Cambridge on 11 June 1913 the Public Orator, Sir John Edwin Sandys, presented Hardy for his honorary degree with a long encomium in Latin. Its penultimate sentence can be translated: "Finally, attempting an enormous subject in the victories of Nelson and Wellington, he has constructed a tragic poem, an epic poem, perfected with every kind of metre," i.e. *The Dynasts*.

[5] Author and journalist (1865–1946). Editor of the Liberal *Daily News* 1902–19.

[6] *Prophets, Priests and Kings* (1908).

take in the *D.N. and L.* because it is near to my heart. I admire your writing; I like your political views.

Also, your P.W.W.[1] seems to me to do the partisan-graphic business excellently – as well as Massingham[2] used to do it for the *Daily Chronicle*. Also, James Douglas[3] and William Archer and (again) Massingham are writers whose work is necessary to my pleasure in studying London from the blest distance at which my abode is. All three are very good.

Also, I am prepared to believe that your S.L.H.[4] is a valuable asset. I seem to have seen and heard him often, in past days, on the stage of this and that music hall – the tired, earnest, perspiring "Comedian," of the second rank, driving his points hoarsely home either very late or very early in the programme of "turns": not a "star", but much liked by much of the audience. The fact that he didn't appeal to me personally in those music halls, the fact that I carefully avoid his column in the *D.N. and L.*, is not offered to you as an important fact. The gentleman is worthy of his hire. Keep him on.

Keep E.A.B.,[5] also, because he has done you long service, and is an honest and industrious man who would find great difficulty, I imagine, in finding a job elsewhere. He is quite the dreariest of all dramatic critics – the most arid and pettifogging and theatre-detesting. As an attorney in a provincial county-court he might shine: that was what Nature meant him to be. But Fate stepped in and made him a dramatic critic. And, as Fate gave him also a wife and children, I hope you will keep him to the bitter end.

The few points I have to suggest are mere points of detail. For example: your photographs are seldom interesting; and the designed lines and emblems placed around the more important ones (such as those of Princesses) are of a hideousness and vulgarity which would disgrace the least and remotest of provincial papers. The man who (signing himself, I think, W.M.) does occasional pictures of Cabinet Ministers orating in the House of Commons – sodden men with waxwork hands, mysterious sodden men disclaiming all connexion with the men whose names are solemnly printed underneath them – ought not merely to be dropped by you, but ought to be dropped off the face of the globe.

---

[1] Philip Whitwell Wilson, Parliamentary sketch-writer and author of books (1875–1956).
[2] H.W. Massingham (1860–1924), editor of the *Daily Chronicle* (1895–99), and of the *Nation* (1907–23).  [3] (1867–1940). Sometime editor of the *Star*.
[4] Spencer Leigh Hughes, Liberal M.P. and humorous Parliamentary commentator as "Sub Rosa" (1858–1920).  [5] E.A. Baughan, drama and music critic (1865–1948).

Your cartoonist, too, is a feeble (though inoffensive) fellow. If you can't get a better one, you had surely better not have any cartoons at all. The drawings on the back page are, also, deplorable, for the most part. You could very easily get better drawings there. And why should the harmless, necessary little column of Publishers' puffs be signed with the absurdly pretentious and affected signature *Moi Qui Passe?*

Also, if you do have "social news" of any sort (and I imagine that such news is commercially a needed thing, a popular thing), why not have it done thoroughly and well? What the public (I fancy) wants, in this kind, is to read the names of those persons who *have* a "social" significance. What some pretty Duchess was wearing at such-and-such a party is a matter in which Britannia, with her fallen nature, really is interested. But in the matter of whether Mrs Lloyd George was or wasn't attired in "grey charmeuse" at some reception given by someone to meet some Delegates, and in the matter of what Mrs Sydney Buxton was or wasn't wearing at Lady Mond's, the public is profoundly indifferent. And the attempt to edify them, and to direct their minds to a higher, more austere plane by describing the dresses of only those ladies whose husbands are politically on the right side,[1] is foredoomed to failure, I am sure.

One more point (and this is a large, revolutionary suggestion). If a speech is worth reporting at all, why not report it in the actual words of the speaker? When newspapers report an important speech by an important person, from end to end, the absence of *oratio obliqua* makes that (probably uninteresting) speech quite readable, by reason of the reader's relief at reading (for example) "Is the country ripe for the change which is proposed?" instead of "He asked whether the country was ripe for the change which had been proposed". All the pungency and brilliancy of the speaker (as here exemplified) evaporates through *oratio obliqua.* In the case of unimportant speakers, reported in a few lines, why not give the actual words uttered? – just a few sentences, either in separate lines or with intervening dots to mark the transitions? I know that this *oratio obliqua* is a sacred tradition of Fleet Street, but I know it is also an absurd superstition. And I do believe that any newspaper that "chucked" it would endear itself to everybody.

And now, please, dear Mr Gardiner, "chuck" this letter into your waste-paper basket. I wanted to write, but I do *not* need a reply from a man so much busier as you are than am I.

Yours sincerely   MAX BEERBOHM

[1] i.e. the left or Liberal.

## To Compton Mackenzie[1]
MS. Texas

*13 October 1913* *Villino Chiaro*

Dear Mackenzie, Your works are having here, as everywhere else, a great vogue: my wife is sunning herself in Curtain Wells,[2] as she will have told you; and I am in the thick of *Sinister Street*[3] – a truly fine work, as well you know and don't need to be told by me. In spite of the needlessness I should like to write my reasons for admiration, but I refrain because I am no letter-writer and no critic: no critic, in the sense that I am in praising so deadly dull that I dishearten my praise's object and myself into the bargain. In writing, that is. By word of mouth I can praise all right. So to our next meeting.

There meanwhile is that ballade. Also here are some photographs of you – including one of myself – myself a choleric Colonel of Volunteers, entertaining a Faun ... But haven't the Volunteers ceased to exist? I dwell in the past ... Fauns, too worn down by the persistency of Maurice Hewlett[4] in writing them up, they have in self-defence abolished themselves, I believe.

It was a great delight to us both, your coming here, and we hope the same sort of thing will recur soon.

Yours very sincerely    MAX BEERBOHM

## To Holbrook Jackson[5]
MS. Princeton

*30 October 1913* *Villino Chiaro*

My dear Mr Holbrook Jackson, I told you with what gratification I was filled by your intention of dedicating your new book to me. Now that here the book itself is, my gratification is all the greater. It is a fine book indeed – fresh and keen from first to last, full of understanding and of the generosity that comes of understanding. To me, of course, as a survivor from the thick of that by-gone period, it is of special interest. I don't say that it plucks any particular chords of sentiment in me.

[1] Novelist and autobiographer (1883–1972).

[2] The scene of Mackenzie's first novel *The Passionate Elopement* (1911).

[3] The first volume of *Sinister Street* was published on 1 September 1913. Volume Two followed in 1914.      [4] Novelist, poet and essayist (1861–1923).

[5] Author and editor (1874–1948). His book *The Eighteen Nineties* appeared in 1913.

Choleric Colonel of Volunteers entertaining a Faun

Somehow one doesn't feel sentimental about a period in which oneself has footed it. It is the period that one *didn't* quite know, the period just before oneself, the period of which in earliest days one knew the actual survivors, that lays a really strong hold on one's heart. The magic of the past begins for me at the 'eighties and stretches back as far as the 'sixties. Thus the interest with which I have read every word of your book has been unblurred with tears.

I daresay the undergraduates of to-day will cry over your pages. *My* withers (whatever they may be – I have never known – I really must look them up in the dictionary) are unwrung. Write a book about Trollope and the Pre-Raphaelites and John Stuart Mill and Martin Tupper and Carlyle, and then my heart as well as my head will be stirred profoundly ... This time it is only my head. This part of me I hold

93

higher since reading your book: I had no idea, before, that the 'nineties I lived through were so interesting and altogether remarkable. I wonder whether, twenty or thirty years hence, the 'noughts and the 'teens will be as fine material for the literary historian. Probably that will just depend on the literary history. Probably it is just you, and not the 'nineties after all, that make this book of yours a thing of such high value.

I am glad you have as frontispiece that drawing of John Bull – quite the very best drawing, I think, Beardsley ever did, the most exquisitely simple (*and* ornate *and* witty) of all his designs (though perhaps "The Barber" is as beautiful a thing). It is amusing to see again the cover-designs for *The Yellow Book* and the *Savoy*. I remember meeting Oscar one afternoon in the domino room at the Café Royal and being told by him that Aubrey had just been showing him the drawing for the cover of *The Yellow Book*. I asked what it was like. "Oh," said Oscar, "you can imagine the sort of thing. A terrible naked harlot smiling through a mask – and with ELKIN MATHEWS written on one breast and JOHN LANE on the other." A perfect description of "the sort of thing", isn't it? By the way, that photograph of Oscar, dated 1895, ought to be dated some years earlier. It was done at about the time when *Lady Windermere's Fan* was produced.

This emendation sounds like the end of a dull review in a newspaper. As a matter of fact it isn't even the end of a dull letter. For I want to tell you – but no, what is the good of saying how thoroughly I agree with you about this, or how glad I am you said that, or how illuminating is what you say about the other? *Dis*agreement is all that might interest you. But is there any judgment of yours that I *do* disagree with? ... Kipling, yes, I think you much over-rate him. Of course I leave a very wide margin, for my own injustice to him. To me, who get the finest of all literary joy out of Henry James (his middle and later manners), the sort of person that Kipling is, and the sort of thing that Kipling does, cannot strongly appeal – quite the contrary. I carefully guard myself by granting you that Kipling is a genius. Indeed, even *I* can't help *knowing* him to be that. The schoolboy, the bounder, and the brute – these three types have surely never found a more brilliant expression of themselves than in R.K. (Nor, I will further grant, has the nursery-maid.) But as a poet and a seer R.K. seems to me not to exist, except for the purpose of contempt. All the ye-ing and the Lord-God-ing and the Law-ing side of him seems to me a very thin and trumpery assumption; and I have always thought it was a sound impulse by which he was driven to put his "Recessional" into the waste-paper basket, and a great pity that Mrs Kipling fished it out and made him send it to *The Times*. I think (absurd though it is to prophesy) that futurity will give him among poets a place corresponding exactly with the place reserved for Theodore Roosevelt among statesmen.

Morris, again – I think you greatly over-rate *him*. He is splendid, certainly, by reason of the bulk and variety of his work. But when it comes to the quality of any part of that work ...? I think that the Coleridge title-page[1] which you reproduce is a rather destructive sample and symbol. Here again I leave a wide margin (I am glad Morris isn't alive to fill in the margin with decorations) for my necessary injustice. I like, in visual objects, lightness and severity, blitheness and simplicity. A gloomy complexity is no doubt equally a noble thing to strive for. Morris achieved it in his wall-papers. He achieved it too in this Coleridge page. But how poorly! Compare the gloomy complexity of Aubrey Beardsley's border for the Morte d'Arthur, facing page 110 of your book. There (though of course it wasn't Beardsley's *own* work, but merely work done to order in immaturity) you have strength and rhythm. Then look back at the muddled and fuddled, tame, weak, aimless, invertebrate and stodgy page done by Morris. The only "sense of inevitability" it gives *me* is that I shall be sick if I look at it again! To me, the format of your bookling *Town*[2] is worth all the Kelmscott books heaped together – unless indeed there were a lit bonfire underneath them. They seem to me a monument of barren and lumbering affectation: not *books* at all, for books, to be alive and to deserve their title, must be printed in such wise that the contemporary reader can forget the printing and be in direct touch with the author's meaning. Morris's pseudo-mediaevalism utterly prevents ... but there, there! I am boring your head off, and my letter is so long that you will be sorry you ever dedicated your book to me. So no more. I will merely thank you again most heartily for that dedication, and for your praises of me – praises which in their now amplified form give me even more pleasure than they did before.　　　　　　　　　Yours sincerely　MAX BEERBOHM

---

[1] *Poems Chosen out of the Works of Samuel Taylor Coleridge*, designed and published by William Morris at his Kelmscott Press in 1896.
[2] *Town: an Essay* by Holbrook Jackson (1913).

## To Frank Harris[1]
MS. Sterling

*4 February 1914*                                      *48 Upper Berkeley Street*

My dear Frank, This isn't to "condole" with you on your adventure; for you have always enjoyed adventures of all kinds and come out of them smiling, and will very soon come out of this one, smiling more than ever perhaps, because this one will have had for you a special element of comedy; and meanwhile the Café Royal will have been allowed to minister to you as it has ministered to you for so many years; and as for the brief confinement of your actual body – you, with your intellect and imagination, will have been much more free and at large, really, than the rest of the population of Great Britain.

I fancy that all you are worrying about is Mrs Harris, who naturally cannot be expected to take the broad philosophic view of the matter taken by you and me. For her I am truly sorry. I am afraid she must be very unhappy, in being parted from you, as are you in being parted from her; and I am afraid she must be worrying about you all the time – whether the air of Brixton is really good, whether the food from the Café Royal is really well-served, and a thousand and one other things that a devoted wife *would* worry about. Will you please offer her my sincerest sympathy. I wonder if it would at all please her at any time to see an old friend who would talk about nothing except that ever-rich topic: Frank. If so, I should very much like to go and see her, at any time before I go back to Italy. I go back in about a fortnight. My wife is on a flying visit to America, and is on the eve of return. I am afraid she will have had an unpleasant shock in reading out there the cabled news of your imprisonment. She won't have understood that the hardship is a purely technical one; and I shall hasten to re-assure her that the brilliant man whose talk so delighted her last year at the Savoy is not really to be grieved over at all, and that he has but a topic the more for his incomparable conversation.

You didn't write to me again about those drawings. I hope this wasn't that you thought the price I asked unreasonably high? I expect it was merely that you decided not to take *Vanity Fair*[2] . . .

But I really must not write any more. Else will Brixton be penitential indeed.                                      Yours ever   MAX BEERBOHM

---

[1] Who was serving six weeks in Brixton Prison for contempt of Court.

[2] Of which Harris was editor.

Your two latest books are, I think, your best.[1] And to say this is to utter a dithyramb indeed.

## To Edmund Gosse[2]
MS. B.L.

*9 February 1914*                    *48 Upper Berkeley Street, W.*

My dear Gosse, Your second letter arrived within an hour of your first, to which I then wonderingly referred; and I found, sure enough, an *au* instead of an *oh*; and "*Oh!*" I ejaculated. But the fault wasn't yours at all: the fault is in the outlandish and irrational spelling of the name itself. Beerb*aum* is well enough; so was Beer*boom*, and in the earlier years of the nineteenth century – certainly as late as 1810 – Beer*boom* was still the decent, authorised, Batavian spelling of our name, which presently in Germany got itself corrupted into the form that eluded you just now. Some years ago I wanted to resume the name of Beer*boom*, in all its seemly and stolid charm; but this would have led to various legal and social complications, and wasn't worth-while.

I like *boom* better than *baum*, but I prefer *baum* to *bohm*; so that I am glad you did for once make that spelling of me.

Ever so many thanks for the "Sesame" enclosed in your first letter. I am on tip-toe of excitement for tomorrow.

Yours affectionately    MAX

## To an Unidentified Lady
MS. Edinburgh

*20 March 1914*                    *Villino Chiaro*

Dear Madam, I have never read *Lovers' Vows*,[3] and was never even present at one of the rehearsals of it; for (I am ashamed to say) I have never read *Mansfield Park*. I have always been intending to read Jane Austen, and have several times tried one or another of her books; but

[1] Presumably *Great Days* and *The Yellow Ticket* (both 1914).

[2] Gosse had inadvertently addressed his letter to Max Beerbaum.

[3] An English translation of *Das Kind der Liebe*, a play by the German dramatist A.F.V. von Kotzebue (1761–1819). In Chapter xviii of *Mansfield Park* the young people are busily rehearsing this play all over the house, until the unexpected return of Sir Thomas Bertram from Antigua puts a stop to their exertions.

she has always left me cold – or, rather, hot with shame at not being able to read her.

As confession is good for the soul, I make this confession to you.

Yours truly   MAX BEERBOHM


## To Edmund Gosse
MS. B.L.

*30 June 1914*                                                              *Villino Chiaro*

My dear Gosse, You may remember that when I was in London you said to me that you hoped George Moore might soon be elected to the Academic Committee. I certainly think he ought to be there; but his name isn't in the type-written list of candidates that has just been sent to me. Perhaps you orally "sounded" the Committee at its latest meeting and found that Moore would stand no chance of election. I am sorry if this is so, for, though reasonable objections may be made to parts of his work, his art is such – has in recent years become such – that a Committee of this kind is surely not complete without him. Personally I should be very glad to see Bennett elected, and shall certainly vote for him. But is it known that he would join? When I was in London I heard – though only at third or fourth hand – that H.G. Wells, before refusing to join, had taken Bennett, Chesterton, and one or two others, into his confidence, and had got from them an informal understanding that they too, if they were elected, would remain outside. This may not have been true; but, on the chance that it *is* true, hadn't it better be verified by some discreet means? It would be a pity if the Wells episode were repeated.

With all best messages to Mrs Gosse and to you and to you all, from us both,            Yours ever affectionately   MAX BEERBOHM

P.S. I shall vote against Miss May Sinclair[1] (making the X with a thick quill dipped in red ink), clever and accomplished writer though she is. I think two women on the Committee are quite enough. If George Sand came to life again and were English this time, I should vote for her. If Mrs Craigie were re-incarnate, I should *not* vote for her. I think genius, or at any rate a magnificent distinction, is needed to enable a woman to add lustre to the Committee and to prevent her from making it slightly ridiculous. I don't say that Miss Sinclair isn't much more remarkable

[1] Novelist (1865–1946).

98

than (for example) *I* am. But the question is not of deserts, but of policy. The election of women to the Committee – unless they are quite transcendently gifted – is bad policy.


## To Edmund Gosse
MS. B.L.

*6 July 1914*                                                      *Villino Chiaro*

My dear Gosse, I am most glad that my sentiments are the same as yours. I have just written to the Secretary, urging the election of George Moore.

If Miss May Sinclair is (*absit omen*) elected, and if you resign, I shall promptly resign too. There would be no honour in belonging to a body belonged to by her – and presently to be belonged to by Mrs Belloc Lowndes, Miss Netta Syrett, Miss Evelyn Sharp, Mrs Annie S. Swan, and indeed, *ex officio*, by all the members of the Women Writers' Club, the Lyceum Club, etc.   Yours ever affectionately   MAX BEERBOHM

P.S. When I wrote to you the other day, I wrote more respectfully than I would now of Miss Sinclair; for I confused her with a tall, sad, nice woman, author of *Red Pottage*. This, I have since remembered, is Miss Mary Cholmondeley, *not* Miss Sinclair. The latter I have looked up in *Who's Who*, and she doesn't prepossess me.


## To Edmund Gosse[1]
MS. Brotherton

*26 July 1914*                                                     *Villino Chiaro*

My dear Gosse, Very many thanks for your letter – so vivid a letter that I almost feel I was present at that meeting. I am very sorry that your desire for Moore's election involved you in so unpleasant a to-do. I had supposed there would certainly be some opposition to Moore; but, oddly, I hadn't supposed it would come from that quarter from which it might most reasonably have been expected. Yeats is one of many people whom Moore has treated ill. But I never can help thinking of Yeats as an ethereal creature immune from all ordinary human emotions;

[1] Gosse had proposed George Moore as a member of the Academic Committee, but had been obliged to withdraw his name owing to the objection of W. B. Yeats, whom Moore had lampooned in his *Ave*, *Salve*, and *Vale*.

and I had not thought he would feel the resentment which any one else, in his case, would feel against Moore; still less had I foreseen in him the natural instinct for vengeance – I should as soon have been able to imagine his lips forming the words "getting a bit of my own back". (This shows how superficial I am in my judgments.) As Yeats took the very human line that he did take, of course there was no more to be said: not you nor the Archangel Gabriel could have undone the effect made. Once the question of Moore's general *behaviour* was raised, the game was up. Let us be glad of the point you scored in preventing from being black-balled one who, in his art, is so very much to be respected.

Further consolation is in the withdrawal of the on-coming shadow of Miss Sinclair, that great and good woman.

Yours ever affectionately  MAX BEERBOHM


## To Edith Wharton[1]
MS. Yale

*11 August 1915*                    *26 Oxford Terrace, London, W.*

Dear Mrs Wharton, I have just heard from Mr Sargent; and it goes without saying that I am much pleased by your invitation and by the idea of doing something for your hospital; or rather this *would* go without saying were I not, naturally, a trifle appalled by the thought of my work being foisted in amidst works of the hierarchic and august men named to me by Mr Sargent.

I will do what I can – but on the strict condition that if you don't like it you will not hesitate to say so and to put it aside. Just what shall I do? In times of peace I am by way of being a cartoonist – a dealer in symbolic groups with reference to current events. But now there is only one current event; and it, the war, is so impossible a theme for comedy that one cannot (unless one is on the staff of a comic paper, and *has* to) do a cartoon touching the remotest fringe of it. My cartooning days are thus over, for the present. I must fall back, for your purpose, on caricature of some single figure, I think; just a caricature, pure and simple, of someone or other. Of whom? I wonder if you could suggest a few names to me? That would be something to go on.

I am sincerely yours  MAX BEERBOHM

[1] Wealthy American novelist (1862–1937), who lived a great deal in France. Sargent had passed on to Max an invitation from Mrs Wharton to contribute to her *Book of the Homeless* for the benefit of war-refugees.

## To Edith Wharton
MS. Yale

*25 August 1915*                                    *26 Oxford Terrace, London, W.*

Dear Mrs Wharton, Thank you for your very kind and delightful letter.
I wish I could have done the *Kipling* theme: a beautiful opportunity,
but one not to be taken by me. For several reasons – too complicated
and tedious to be explained in a letter – I would rather not have a fling
at Kipling. I must leave his behaviour to be punished in the next world.
Meanwhile I have done a drawing which I shall entitle either *A Gracious
Act* or *My strength will I ascribe unto thee.* The legend written on it is
*Lord Curzon reading to M. Cammaerts a translation (signed with his own
hand) of a poem by M. Cammaerts.*[1] And I enclose a sort of rough draft
to show you what the scheme of the drawing is. Need I send the actual
drawing? Mr Sargent told me that the book was to be published in
London and New York. I deduce that the reproductions will be made
in one of those cities. And I would rather send it straight to the
reproducer. For I am told that practically all unofficial packages sent
from England to France are opened on the way; and it would be very
difficult to pack this drawing in such a way that it would be sure not to
be injured by the frantic fingers of the openers and shutters. The
slightest crease made in it would spoil it for reproduction. Please let me
know, therefore, whether you are willing to take the drawing on trust,
in the light of the enclosed sketch; and to what reproducer, if you *are*
willing, I should post or take the drawing.

Yours sincerely   MAX BEERBOHM

## To Edmund Gosse
MS. B.L.

*16 February 1916*                                    *26 Oxford Terrace, W.*

My dear Gosse, I have posted to you – at Room 97, etc – the illustrated
copy of the *Christmas Garland.* I do so hope you will think it is all right.[2]
    I would have posted it sooner, but for the difficulty of solving the

---

[1] Emile Cammaerts, Belgian poet (1878–1953). The finished drawing duly appeared in
*The Book of the Homeless* (1916), with "A Gracious Act" and then the legend beneath
it. For this rough draft see overleaf.

[2] For the Red Cross Sale at Christie's, where it fetched seventy guineas. But where is
it now?

A Gracious Act

problem of how to illustrate the first of the parodies (Henry James) without "jarring". This problem I have had to give up finally. There are therefore only sixteen drawings – some of them plain caricatures of the writers' own faces; others by way of being illustrations of the themes.

I have used no ink for the drawings – only wash and pencil. The pencil was not a soft one; but the paper *is* of a queerly soft texture, and thus it would be very easy for the lines to be blurred by the indicative fingers of Christie's young men, or by the questioning fingers of possible purchasers. Would you, therefore, when the time comes, warn somebody at Christie's about the sensitiveness of the paper, so that the book may be gingerly treated? Not *too* gingerly, however. I don't want it to be thought that the book is as those flowers which fade at human touch. Nobody, in that case, would pay twopence to possess it. I merely mean that the drawings might suffer if they were handled harshly.

Yours ever affectionately   MAX BEERBOHM

## *To the Editor of the* Century Magazine
MS. Princeton

*6 March 1916*                                        *48 Upper Berkeley Street, W.*

Dear Sir, I send in another envelope the corrected proofs of my two stories – "Enoch Soames" and "A.V. Laider". Every page of these is scored all over with corrections. But I am not to blame: I am not giving any unnecessary trouble. On the contrary, I am to be pitied for the great amount of unnecessary trouble that has been imposed on me. I have not added anything that wasn't in my manuscript; nor have I subtracted anything that was there. I have readily fallen in with your wish that I shouldn't alter the Century Dictionary spelling – "envelop" (instead of envelop*e*), "honor", "defense", and so forth. (Indeed your wishes in this matter are mine. The one important thing in spelling is not to give the reader a "jump". In writing for an American magazine, one prefers the spelling that is most familiar to Americans.) Furthermore, the number of my corrections in these proofs is not due to any *carelessness* on the part of your printers and proof-readers. It is due merely to their crude and asinine interference with my punctuation, with my division of paragraphs, and with other details ... Details? No, these are not details to me. My choice of stops is as important to me – as important for the purpose of conveying easily to the reader my exact shades of meaning – as my choice of words.

Please don't think I am taking up a "high-and-mighty" attitude. I am very well aware that I am not a great or heaven-inspired writer. But I am equally well aware that I am a very careful, conscientious, skilled craftsman in literature. And it is most annoying for me to find my well-planned effects repeatedly destroyed by the rough-and-ready, *standardising* methods of your proof-readers. These methods are, no doubt, very salutary, and necessary, in the case of gifted but illiterate or careless contributors to your magazine. But I, personally, will none of them. And if, at any future date, you do me the honour to accept any other piece of my writing, please let it be understood that my manuscript must be respected, not pulled about and put into shape in accordance to any schoolmasterly notion of how authors ought to write.

Meanwhile, the corrections in these two proofs will necessitate a good deal of rearrangement of the type. In a vast number of cases, my "strokes" were replaced by commas. These "strokes" I have religiously restored. "Strokes" occupy far more space than do commas; and therefore, unless the lines are to be unpleasantly congested with words, there will have to be plenty of translineation. I don't know whether there is such a word as "translineation" in the *Century Dictionary*. (My volumes of that very admirable work are at my home in Italy, and therefore not available for reference at this moment.) I fancy I have just coined the word. In case its meaning is obscure, let me say that I mean the carrying-down of the last word in a line into the next line, and, of the last word in the next line into the next-but-one, and so on, to the end of the paragraph.

Please give instructions to the printers that all this shall be done carefully. I am, dear Sir    Yours very truly    MAX BEERBOHM[1]

## To Robert Ross
MS. Hyde

*10 June 1916*                                        *21 Southwick Street*

My dear Bobbie, "*Poète devenu critique*" is certainly good Enochese;[2] many thanks for drawing my attention to it.

The waterproof cape worn by Enoch was itself suggested, I think, by

[1] "Enoch Soames" appeared in the May issue of *Century Magazine*, "A.V. Laider" in the June issue.

[2] "Enoch Soames" appeared in the *Cornhill* for June 1916. Republished in *Seven Men* (1919).

memory of one worn by Arthur Symons. Otherwise Enoch, as drawn by me, owes nothing to Symons, but much to my imagination of what Ernest Dowson (whom I never saw) might have been if he had been rather like Victor Plarr (whom I never had the pleasure of meeting) with a dash of Theodore Wratislaw and others.[1]

We have been staying at Bognor. You will be sorry to hear that the unassuming music-hall, dear to you and to Mrs Clifton,[2] has been superseded by a vast Kursaal.★          Yours ever   MAX BEERBOHM

★ of which the name will be changed to Casino as soon as the Bognorians thoroughly realise that we are at war.


## To D.S. MacColl
MS. Glasgow

*28 June 1916*                                    *21 Southwick Street, W.*

My dear MacColl, I hoped to come round to see you this morning, but had to go to the other end of London. I am immensely flattered by your wishing me to do some illustrations, and I shall always remember with pleasure the suggestion; and I wish I could come up to the scratch – but alas I can't. Soon after the beginning of the war, and after I had made some attempts at drawings in connexion with it, I registered a vow that I would utterly abstain from any further attempts at any drawings howsoever remotely connected with it. My way of drawing is so merely funny at best; whereas the times we live in do absolutely need and demand that one should be able to draw *savagely* if at all: mere fun is beside the point, and it jars. Your written satires are funny *and* savage; and you ought to have an illustrator who can express both these elements. Such am not I – more's the pity; and therefore I must refrain. We had a very pleasant time at Mrs Hunter's,[3] and it would have been pleasanter still but for the knowledge that Mrs MacColl and you had been asked and were not there.                    Yours ever   MAX BEERBOHM


[1] Poets of the Eighteen-Nineties.

[2] Wife of Arthur Clifton, who had been a partner of Robbie Ross in the Carfax Gallery. Oscar Wilde described Mrs Clifton as "so like Rossetti's wife – the same lovely hair – but of course a sweeter nature".

[3] Mary (1857–1931), wife of Charles Hunter. Sister of Dame Ethel Smyth. She entertained a lot at her country home, Hill Hall in Essex.

## To Lady Lewis[1]
### TS. Merton

*28 March 1918*              *12 Well Walk, Hampstead*

My dear Lady Lewis, I was deeply touched by your letter, for which I send you my sincerest thanks.[2]

It has been a sad and sorrowful time for my sisters and for Florence and me. We were all with my dear Mother when the end came: and it is some comfort that she died very peacefully, without any pain.

She had no ailment of any kind. Her heart gradually ceased to beat, merely by reason of her great age. Her memory, and her power to realise things, had been failing during the past three years. But in such years as these have been, in a world so full of horror, one cannot say that this was not a blessing. And, though her memory went, her sweetness and charm of nature was as ever; and a great blank is left in our lives by her going. Letters such as yours and Katie's are, nevertheless, really helpful. Florence and I are going away for a week. As soon as we come back, we should so love to see you, if we may.

I am always yours    MAX BEERBOHM

## To Lytton Strachey[3]
### MS. B.L.

*28 July 1918*              *12 Well Walk*

Dear Mr Strachey, I have just been reading *Eminent Victorians*, and – having the excuse that we did meet at Mme Vandervelde's last year – I simply cannot repress the impulse to thank you for the immense pleasure your book has given me, and also for the immense pleasure it will often give me again (for unless I am cut off in the flower of my middle-age I shall read it again often). There are so many qualities in it that excite me to reverence, and of these I would, for two pins, draw up a list – (a) (b) (c) etc, in the regular Victorian manner. But I restrain myself. You are no doubt already satiated with praises from people whose opinion is

[1] Widow of Sir George Lewis (1833–1911), the most successful solicitor of the age. Katie was their daughter.

[2] Max's mother had died on 13 March, aged 87.

[3] Biographer and essayist (1880–1932). His second book, *Eminent Victorians*, was published on 9 May 1918. For Max's description of his first sight of Strachey in 1912, and final appreciation of his work, see his Rede Lecture *Lytton Strachey* (1943).

more valuable than mine. Only I must say how greatly I admire, for example, your *construction* of each essay – the beautiful solidity of it, everything calculated, nothing left to chance – in these days of blithe improvisation!

I think it was Goldsmith who said of Burke that he loved "to watch him winding himself into his subject like a serpent". That is the sort of pleasure I too have in studying your method. You wind yourself so smoothly and strongly in. Most writers – especially the most brilliant ones – leave so much to the good-will of the reader: they are so cursory and casual: the reader has to lend a hand, all the time, and is always in a state of agitated misgiving as to whether the writer and he won't break down ignominiously. You are finely considerate of your reader and of your art. One can sit comfortably back and just watch you with perfect confidence, knowing that the end of each essay will be as perfect as its outset ... But it doesn't seem right to talk about your beginnings and your endings. Each of your essays is *globular* in effect – no angles, no points out-sticking; a lovely rotund unity, shining and unyielding.

I don't express well my meaning. But you know what I mean. Your endings are implicit in your beginnings. You finish, as a writer should, at the starting-point, however long the journey. And while I love the firmness of your grasp of a whole, I get no less a delight from the minute workmanship of your sentences. It is wonderful that English so pure as yours, so laboriously filtered, should be so full of animation. (Wonderful also that with its rejection of anything like affectation or eccentricity it should be so clearly personal and your own.) To write good and lucid English does involve a great deal of laborious filtration, surely. And that process is so miserably apt to rob the language of its life, its sparkle and strength. The all-important *vocal* quality – how rare that is among careful writers! But in you it is never lost. You keep it against all odds. In fact you are wonderful!

This is my third page, and – but it seems absurd to have said so much about your vehicle and nothing at all about what rides in it. One really can't say nothing about your exquisitely keen sense of human character – your quite wanton *joy* in the variations and recesses of human character; nothing about your strong specific gift for narrative, always dramatic narrative, and your constant power of *visualising* a scene, great or small, essential or by-the-way – Rome in 1870, or Gordon at Khartoum, or the Archdeacon of Chichester speeding in his phaeton "between the hedges" at night. And above all one can't say nothing of all the loud laughter, not mere smiles but thorough bursts of laughter, that you again and again in every essay make inevitable. I think perhaps my favourite passage in all the book is the Clough passage, page 154 – the repeated-Certainly passage – where laughter rings out at the end of every single sentence into the middle of the next. This is a passage of which one may well indeed doubt whether, as A.H.C. would have said, "there is better than it".[1]

I much wonder what you are going to do next. When a writer pleases the critics and the public with his treatment of some special theme, they all of them assume that he will stick to that theme for ever and ever. That is rash of them. I conceive it possible that you have said as much as you want to say about the Victorian times. All the same, I hope you haven't. Present times, obviously, don't provide you with good material; and the immediate past – the past that one can all but touch – is (to me) so much more enchanting than any other past. And there are so many great and little Victorians whom I positively hear clamouring from beneath their marble slabs that you should write about them – a nobly disinterested wish that does them credit, I think. There is, for example ... but I won't be so impertinent as to suggest subjects.

A letter of this kind isn't complete without some pettifogging objection or another. Let us turn, therefore, to page 286. A beautiful presentment of Lord Hartington, yes; but surely that nobleman never "confessed to two ambitions – to become Prime Minister and to win the Derby". I have often heard that Lord *Rosebery*, when he was at Eton, said that he meant to be Prime Minister, to win the Derby, and to marry a Roths-

---

[1] "Arthur Clough, the poet, also a connection by marriage, she [Florence Nightingale] used in other ways. Ever since he had lost his faith at the time of the Oxford Movement, Clough had passed his life in a condition of considerable uneasiness, which was increased rather than diminished by the practice of poetry. Unable to decide upon the purpose of an existence whose savour had fled together with his belief in the Resurrection, his spirits lowered still further by ill-health, and his income not all that it should be, he had determined to seek the solution of his difficulties in the United States of America. But, even there, the solution was not forthcoming; and when, a little later, he was offered a post in a government department at home, he accepted it, came to live in London, and immediately fell under the influence of Miss Nightingale. Though the purpose of existence might be still uncertain and its nature still unsavoury, here, at any rate, under the eye of this inspired woman, was something real, something earnest: his only doubt was – could he be of any use? Certainly he could. There were a great number of miscellaneous little jobs which there was nobody handy to do. For instance, when Miss Nightingale was travelling, there were the railway-tickets to be taken; and there were proof-sheets to be corrected; and then there were parcels to be done up in brown paper, and carried to the post. Certainly he could be useful. And so, upon such occupations as these, Arthur Clough set to work. 'This that I see, is not all,' he comforted himself by reflecting, 'and this that I do is but little; nevertheless it is good, though there is better than it.'"

child. The speech may have been – probably was – invented for him, but the sentiment is Roseberyan enough. Wholly un-Hartingtonian, on the other hand, are even the first two-thirds of the speech. Surely it was a cardinal point in H. that he never wanted anything greatly. He would have liked to win the Derby, no doubt, but he wouldn't have gone out of his way to win it, any more than he went out of his way to take the Premiership on either of the occasions when it was offered to him. Surely you have saddled the wrong horse. It is human, but it isn't Lytto-Stracheyan, to err. And it is very human to rejoice at catching you in what does seem to be an error.

Forgive this all-but-endless screed from yours sincerely

MAX BEERBOHM

And *don't* feel you need answer it. It is pleasant to sit down and write a long letter of one's own accord. But to feel that one must sooner or later sit down and *answer* a long letter is a disastrous and a deathly feeling, which I don't want to let you in for. Here your book is – an ample reward for any praises it may evoke.

### To Egan Mew[1]
TS. Merton

[*28 July 1918*]                                         *12 Well Walk*

Dear Egan Mew, You will not, I know, be able to read without emotion the last line on the page attached.

For my part, I have spent the day very quietly. Yours    M.B.

Let us hope there are camels in Heaven.

---

JULY
28
SUNDAY
In trickery, evasion, procrastination, spoliation, bother-ation, there are influences that can never come to good.

*Bleak House*

9th Sunday after Trinity.
Robespierre guillotined, 1794.
F. Goodall, R.A., died, 1904[2]

---

[1] *Bon vivant* and journalist (1862–1945). An expert on old china.

[2] Frederick Goodall, born 1822. Painted many pictures of Biblical and other Middle-Eastern scenes.

## To John Galsworthy
### TS. Merton

*8 November 1918*                                                    *12 Well Walk*

My dear Galsworthy, We are back from Wales, where we have made a long sojourn. I had wanted to see you before we went away, and consult you about my drawings for *Reveille*.[1] Now that we are neighbours in Hampstead I hope I may see you, for it has always seemed to me that "Artists at the Front" would be a good theme only so long as the war continued, and that as soon as peace came it would be well to start another series, and ... but I won't bother you with this now. Rather let me say how immensely I have enjoyed and admired *Five Tales*.[2] I have read them all twice, once in London and once in Wales – once for enjoyment of the narratives, and once for enjoyment of the technique. This second motive sounds rather cold-blooded perhaps. But I hasten to assure you that in re-reading I wasn't *merely* the curious student. I was thrilled and moved too, as before. I cannot remember that in any of your books there is finer or more beautiful work than in this one; and all of your books are remembered by me very vividly. I would tell you which of the five tales I love best, if I were at all able to make up my mind.

Please give my best regards to your wife.      Yours ever    MAX

## To William Archer
### MS. B.L.

*8 February 1919*                                                   *12 Well Walk*

My dear W.A., I am not sure about the justice of your claim to royalties on the production of "Savonarola".[3] I think the matter had better be submitted to arbitration. (Squire Bancroft,[4] I believe, is the person

---

[1] A quarterly edited by Galsworthy for the benefit of disabled servicemen. Only three numbers appeared, in August 1918, November 1918, and February 1919. Max contributed a caricature to each – of Orpen, Augustus John, and Sargent, at the Front.

[2] Published on 25 July 1918.

[3] In Max's "Savonarola Brown", published in *Seven Men*, Ladbroke Brown describes his method of writing: "All sorts of people appear," he would say rather helplessly. "They insist. I can't prevent them." I used to say it must be great fun to be a creative artist; but at this he always shook his head: "I don't create. *They* do. Savonarola especially, of course. I just look on and record. I never know what's going to happen next." [4] Actor-manager (1841–1926). Knighted 1897.

usually gone to on such occasions.) If you had ever told me the story about Hewlett (which I long to hear in full), I am sure I should have definitely remembered it. On the other hand, I do remember that while I was writing about Ladbroke Brown and his refusal to be regarded as a creator, there was floating in the back of my mind an idea that I had at some time *read an article* in which you sceptically dealt with the Nature-taking-the-pen theory. And I have no doubt that this article of yours – for surely there was such an article? – written perhaps just after Hewlett poured his golden words into your ears? – was the germ of my presentment of L. Brown's theory. Such, roughly, will be my evidence at Bancroft's tribunal. I hope you will insist on calling Hewlett as a witness. His flashing eye, his soldierly abruptness, and the mild foolishness of what he says, are always a joy. We did so greatly enjoy your visit to us, and we both send you our best messages.

Yours ever    M A X

## To Philip Guedalla[1]
MS.[2]

22 March 1919                                                    12 Well Walk

Dear Mr Guedalla, I never thought the name of Bernard Posno would be a name to conjure with. But, as I had quite forgotten it, you, by your sudden use of it, have wafted me back across a wide gulf of years; and I see clearly Bernard Posno seated at that particular table which was reserved for him every night at supper time by the manager of the Savoy Restaurant – a table for two, a table for him and Miss Helen Forsyth,[3] a pretty though too plump actress whose protector he was. I wish I could tell you all about him, but I know so little. I wasn't personally acquainted with him – only with this and that acquaintance of his, who seemed to have nothing to say about him except that Miss Forsyth really adored him. This adoration seemed to me, having regard to his age and appearance, odd. I doubt whether it existed. I saw in her no sign of a

---

[1] Historian (1889–1944), who formed the largest and best collection of Max's caricatures in private hands. After his death his widow gave sixty of them to the Ashmolean Museum at Oxford. Clearly he had just acquired the drawing of Bernard Posno.

[2] I have a beautiful photo-copy of the original letter, but I cannot remember where or from whom I obtained it. All I can do is to beg the forgiveness of the present owner.

[3] English actress (died 1901). She had been on the London stage for some ten years when in January 1895 she created the part of Mrs Marchmont in Oscar Wilde's *An Ideal Husband*.

broken heart, or even of a bruised one, when presently (in '96, I think) I went to stay in the country with Frank Lawson[1] and found her living under *his* protection. A year or two later, Bernard Posno, it would seem, decided that the time had come for him to marry and settle down. He induced (by what means I know not: I should think she and her family must have been starving) a respectable young woman to marry him. He settled down further than he had intended: into the grave. Miss Forsyth, too, has been dead this many a year. Perhaps she and he are once more united.

I cudgel my brains to remember more about him. Nothing recurs except that he was a member of the Orleans Club.[2] And this fact you could, I am sure, deduce from the drawing. At least, I hope so. I remember the drawing only dimly. If it doesn't proclaim "Orleans Club" it is a failure, and you had better throw it away!

Yours sincerely  MAX BEERBOHM

## To Edmund Gosse
MS. Berg

*19 September 1919*               *Glottenham, Robertsbridge*[3]

My dear Gosse, Here, there, and everywhere, at this moment, are (I conceive) people beginning their letters to you with the words: "It seems utterly impossible that the forthcoming birthday should be your seventieth" – or words to just this effect. And very much do I wish I could stand out from the crowd and start some utterance that you will not have heard over and over again. But ... well, it *does* seem so utterly impossible that etc. etc. and I simply can't help saying it. Nor, on reflection, can I help saying how splendid it is, and what fun it must be for you, to have lived seventy years and have achieved in them so many beautiful and enduring works *and* to be so young – so fresh and verdant, ever putting forth new leaves and bearing new fruits and offering shade and coolness and refreshment to new generations. Most heartily do I wish you, and wish to these new generations, very many happy returns of your birthday. Please tell dear Mrs Gosse and your daughters and

[1] A half-brother of Reggie Turner.

[2] A picturesque club in King Street, St James's Square, which was renowned for the excellence of its cooking. Members paid nothing at the time of eating, but were sent a bill every quarter or half year, reading "To food £268" or whatever. Checking was impossible. The club was destroyed by enemy action in the second world war.

[3] Where Lady Tree was living.

Philip that my heart is with them in their happiness on the auspicious day.

I have conceived a caricature which I shall send to you for your acceptance. I can't actually *do* it till I know the full list of subscribers to the bust. This list I shall have anon.[1]

I hope you didn't think my Hardy-Owl too irreverent to T.H.? I plead that I only illustrated *your* idea.[2] Also, I will mention that I have received from Mrs T.H. a letter asking where she can purchase a drawing by me of T.H. – of whom, says she, my portraits show greater insight than any other portraits of him. This is a great compliment; and I have sent her a drawing accordingly.

I have here two manuscripts – essays – which I should like to give you because I think you might approve of them. But I have to withstand the impulse to send them to you. I cannot forget those magnificent bindings in which two other manuscripts of mine so very unworthily are enshrined. I can give you no more manuscripts.

My wife has gone to Italy (leaving me here with my sister-in-law) to "prospect" – to decide from a housewifely standpoint whether we can live again in our Villino. The proprietor has raised the rent. And is there any coal to be had? And isn't even bread worth a king's ransom? All sorts of questions – which I couldn't decide, having no skill – have to be decided. Possibly we shall henceforth live in England. Possibly we can resume our Italian bliss. It remains to be seen.

But all this is a digression from the birthday. Very many happy returns again and always. Your affectionate MAX

---

[1] This caricature, entitled "The Birthday Surprise," shows Gosse, surrounded by a throng of his aristocratic and literary friends, receiving a bust of himself to celebrate his seventieth birthday. It was reproduced in *The Life and Letters of Edmund Gosse* by Evan Charteris (1931). Gosse is holding out his hands in feigned surprise at the sight of the bust, for which he had been patiently sitting to Sir William Goscombe John, R.A.

[2] "Nicholson's Owl – revised, under flashlight from Edmund Gosse, by Max". William Nicholson's cover for the first issue of a short-lived periodical, *The Owl*, in May 1919, consisted of a large owl in the centre, with seven smaller owls round it, looking outwards. For fun Max redrew the owls, giving them the faces of contributors to the magazine. The large owl is Thomas Hardy.

## To Bernard Shaw[1]
### MS. B.L.

*18 June 1920*                                                    *Villino Chiaro*

My dear G.B.S., I have just written to Curtis Brown, telling him that
he must without delay fix up definitely whether the N.Y. Macmillans
or some other publishers are to have the Herbert book in America.

And I have incidentally told him that he will probably hear from you,
asking that your exact position in the book – as to copyright and all
that – shall be regularised.

I do hope that in writing (or telephoning) to him you will do as I this
morning urged you to do: make some arrangement by which you shan't
be deprived of the proper proceeds of your work. You see, you aren't
at all in the same position as the majority of the contributors to the
book. You aren't a sentimental old friend of Herbert's, dying to pay a
tribute to Herbert's memory. You were, with great difficulty, roped in
by *me*. Moreover, you have a name to conjure with – a name that is
likely to make the book sell like hot cakes. In England the book will, I
suppose, have a pretty good sale because Herbert is still remembered
here. In America, I fancy, the book will sell only on the strength of your
name. And so, for heaven's sake, do be commercial. All the more
because, as I told you this morning, such cheques as will be paid to
Maud Tree and me by publishers shall *not* be devoted to any dismal
communal purposes, such as appeal to you. Every penny shall go to
some cosy charitable scheme (unless it go to some definitely personal
memorial of Herbert). Some ailing child or indigent spinster shall be
the beneficiary. No doubt this is very wicked. But *I* am awfully wicked.
I have no public spirit whatsoever. I am determined that the National
School of Dramatic Art (or whatever its name is) shall not get a red cent
from Maud Tree or from me. I am determined that you shall hold up
your hands in horror at my iniquity and shall bring your outstretched
right hand quickly down to snatch *some* of the gold for some noble non-
anti-social purpose.                                      Yours ever   MAX

P.S. Remembering your advice, I am keeping a *stamped* copy of this
letter and am sending it to Somerset House, and am asking that another
copy shall be made and offered to the Trustees of the British Museum.

---

[1] Max had collected tributes to his brother who had died in 1917, and *Herbert Beerbohm
Tree: Some Memories of Him and his Art* was published by Hutchinson in the summer
of 1920. The American rights were handled by Curtis Brown, the literary agents.

In the event of the aforesaid Trustees refusing it, I shan't quite know what to do . . . but shall doubtless think of something . . .

P.P.S. I meant, but forgot, to tell you how very greatly I had been interested in your manuscript corrections of the typescript of your essay on Herbert. It was delightful to see *in the making* the wonderful swiftness and slickness and bracing-ness of your style. The first script was so *you*, but the amended script so much *more* you.

And also (I have already mentioned that I am wicked) I had the pleasure of catching you in the act of a "howler". You had spoken of yourself and Herbert as doing something to "*each other*". And this you altered to "*one another*". Whereat my soul cried fie and hurrah!

You are such a precisian and a Zoilean[1] that it's a joy to catch you tripping. But of course the main joy, after all, is that after these many years you are as strong and as light and surprising as ever.

### To Lytton Strachey
MS. B.L.

*7 July 1920*                                          *Villino Chiaro*

Dear Lytton Strachey, Some time in 1913, at this address, my wife and I acquired a young fox-terrier. We debated as to what to call him, and, as Henry James had just been having his seventieth birthday, and as his books had given me more pleasure than those of any other living man, I, rather priggishly perhaps, insisted that the dog should be known as James. But this was a name which Italian peasants, who are the only neighbours we have, of course would not be able to pronounce at all. So we were phonetic and called the name of the dog *Yah-mès*. And this did very well. By this name he was known far and wide – but not long; for alas, he died of distemper.

Now that we are re-established here, we haven't another dog; dogs aren't so necessary to one as they seem to be in England, and they have an odd and tactless way of making one feel that one *is* in England – perhaps because they don't gesticulate and don't speak one word of Italian and seem to expect to find rabbits among the olive-groves and to have bones of Welsh mutton thrown to them from the luncheon table.

But the other day we were given a small kitten – charming in itself and somehow not destructive of local colour. The old question arose:

[1] A carping critic.

what shall we call it? Again I laid myself open to the charge of priggishness, perhaps. And again you will perhaps think I have taken a
liberty. But – well, there it is: no book by a living man has given me so
much pleasure – so much lasting pleasure in dipping and in re-reading
since I wrote to you – as your *Eminent Victorians*. And the name of that
kitten is, and the name of that cat will be, *Stré-chi* (or rather, *Stré-ici*).
I hope you don't mind. I am sure you would be amused if you heard
the passing-by peasants enticing it by your hardly-recognisable name.
We will re-christen it if you like.

You can't think what pleasure I had from the letter in which you told
me you liked my *Seven Men*. I hope you will like another book of mine
that will be out in the autumn – a selection of essays. I will send it to
you, anyway.[1]

But what most of all excites me is: Are you really doing (as you
proposed to do, and as I have heard that you *are* doing) a monograph
on Queen Victoria? And, if so, how far have you got? – how soon will
the book be? – what sort of length will it be? – what kind of scope have
you chosen?

Don't bother to answer. Excitement isn't a really good excuse for
inquisitiveness. Only – I do hope the book proceeds as quickly as your
carefulness will let it, and that it will be in my hands and on my shelf,
and down in my hands again, before *very* long.

I was reading last year, for the first time, the book of Q.V.'s letters;
in the course of which I thought many times of you, and of the
extraordinarily congenial problem that Q.V. offers to you in her tough
strength and ability and the delicious *personal* (never *positional*) silliness
in which she abounds. That series of letters stopped short at the death
of the remarkable Albert. I was much intrigued as to how she would
fare, in the State Documents, without him. Was the "grip" of things all
his? Was she a mere silly prattler when he had gone? Or did he, though
dead, speak in measured and stentorian tones through her veil of eternal
crêpe? Or had conscience and careful up-bringing and preparation, quite
apart from him, and in despite of her innate ninnyhood, endowed her
with a real professional virtuosity?

I haven't yet seen the new Disraeli volumes.[2] In these, I fancy, some
light will have been thrown. But it's *your* light that I'm impatient for.

Yours sincerely   MAX BEERBOHM

[1] *And Even Now*, published on 7 December 1920.
[2] The final volumes (V and VI) of Monypenny and Buckle's *Life of Disraeli* (1920).

117

P.S. I was glad you were glad that I admired most of all your *constructive* power in writing. I am inclined to rate now the "Gordon"[1] as your highest achievement, because the construction of that seems to me the most ingenious and monumental of all. I don't say the others don't equal it in the adjustment of their beginnings to their endings – or rather, in the lack of beginnings and endings as such. The serpent swallows its own tail every time admirably. My reason for plumping for the "Gordon" is my admiration for that to-and-fro method of narration towards the end: Khartoum – Downing Street, Downing Street – Khartoum; by which device of the steady pendulum we get *all* the tragic irony of the whole matter.

## To John Middleton Murry[2]
### MS. Merton

*7 August 1920*                                                    *Villino Chiaro*

Dear Mr Middleton Murry, Many thanks for the invitation; but I think I would rather not write about Frank Harris's book about Oscar Wilde.[3] I saw the book two years ago in London – a copy of an American edition of it; and it seemed to me remarkable, like all F.H.'s work, full of vivid touches and strength. But all that raking-up of the old Sodomitic cesspool – the cesspool that was opened in 1895, and re-opened in recent years by various law-suits – seemed to me a disservice (howsoever well-meant) to poor old O.W.'s memory. And if I wrote about the book I should have to say so. And, as F.H. is an old friend of mine, I don't want to say so. Why not have the book reviewed by one of your coaevals, or by yourself – taking the book simply as a peg on which to hang a criticism of O.W. as dramatist, essayist, etc? – and leaving O.W., the man, out of it? I am delighted that you liked my essay on "The Pines".[4] I was inclined to like it myself. But one never knows, until one is re-assured. At least, *I* never do.       Yours sincerely   MAX BEERBOHM

[1] In *Eminent Victorians*.

[2] Author, critic and journalist (1889–1957). Husband of Katherine Mansfield. Editor of the *Athenaeum* 1919–21.

[3] *Oscar Wilde, his Life and Confessions*, first published by the author in New York in 1916. The second edition (1918) contained "My Memories of Oscar Wilde" by Bernard Shaw.

[4] Max's essay "No. 2 The Pines", appeared first in the *Fortnightly Review* of August 1920, and then in his book *And Even Now* in December 1920.

## To Clement Shorter[1]
MS. B.L.

*14 September 1920*  *Villino Chiaro*

Caro Shorter, I saw only yesterday the *Sphere* of September 4th, in which, discoursing pleasantly on my essay about Swinburne and Watts-Dunton, entitled "No. 2 The Pines", you declared that there was "no such place as No. 2 The Pines". You are usually right in your facts; so that your positive denial of the "No. 2" made me suddenly wonder whether my memory had played me some queer trick – wonder whether I had actually not seen on that front-door the numeral which I still so clearly visualised there. Accordingly, I searched among some old letters; and there promptly forthcame a letter from Watts-Dunton (October 11th '01) stamped in large red capitals "2 The Pines, Putney Hill, S.W." I found also a letter from him (3 December 1903) stamped in large black capitals "The Pines, 11 Putney Hill, S.W." I presume that at some time between these two dates the address of the house was for some reason revised. You are, therefore, right in a minor sense, but entirely wrong in the major sense, and must stand up in a white sheet, holding a candle in the light of which your readers shall see that there is no reason to doubt my accuracy in more important matters.

Yours very sincerely   MAX BEERBOHM

P.S. Leaving facts apart, and coming to the thornier realm of psychology, let me insist that you are quite wrong in coupling Swinburne and Watts-Dunton as having "a peculiar inclination" to invite journalists to their home. Watts-Dunton was, I think, rather a prey to that perilous (though not peculiar) inclination. But Swinburne! Dear little proud old Swinburne! Utterly remote and indifferent Swinburne! O, Shorter! Come!

## To Bernard Shaw
MS. B.L.

*24 September 1920*  *Villino Chiaro*

My dear Micawber – or rather, as I have known and loved you for so many years, surely I may call you Wilkins? So that there should be no possible mistake, I posted your stamped document to Curtis Brown, who has submitted it to the dazzled eyes of Hutchinson. So *that* is

[1] Journalist and author (1857–1926). Editor of the *Sphere* 1900–26.

settled; and Hutchinson goeth not in terror of you. It seems that Curtis Brown's man in America has at length disposed of the book. I have had a wire to that effect, and am awaiting particulars. I had suggested to C.B., with great delicacy, that in consequence of the long delay, "another agent in America ought now to have an opportunity of" etc. He replied most cordially: "I suppose you mean Paul Reynolds. He is a capital fellow" – and agreed that, if the rights had not been disposed of already, P.R. should have a try. It seems that Maud Tree had already, on the spot, broached the matter; so that the shy old circumlocutor of Rapallo felt slightly foolish. However, C.B.'s man has now done the trick, and all's well.[1]

But – what on earth is all this about your Hearst money?[2] The money, my dear friend, is yours. It can't possibly be ours. Why should it be? I can see no reason whatsoever. I urged you to make with C.B. some arrangement by which you should derive from the book some monetary profit more or less commensurate with the value of your contribution. When you arranged that your contribution should be "serialised," it seemed to me, as you "do big" (American slang, invented on spur of moment; meaning: "command high prices for serial rights"), that you would probably want no fee from the proceeds of the book itself. But this notion of handing over your fee from Hearst to us is entirely monstrous – though beautiful, of course. Curb yourself. Or get somebody to curb you. Spend a week or two in some nice little private lunatic asylum. Why not come here? My wife and I would watch over you with the greatest care and unfailing presence of mind. I am meanwhile telling Maud about your sad case. And I think she will cure you by revealing to you that her idea of the best way to spend the profits of the book is to devote them all to the fund raised by General Haig for the relief of indigent officers. I myself have no radical objection at all to this idea. I have no inhibiting principles as to what the State ought to do and what private people oughtn't to do. I only have a feeling that the scheme is rather remote from Herbert. The idea of a "Tree Scholarship" at the Academy of Dramatic Art isn't remote from Herbert. But it seems to me unspeakably dreary. I cling to my idea of surprising and making happy some one single needy and deserving person. However, I am not trying to persuade Maud against her own inclinations. I am too far away.

[1] The American edition of the book on Tree was published by E. P. Dutton & Co.

[2] William Randolph Hearst (1863–1951), American newspaper tycoon, owned dozens of papers, including *Harper's Bazar*, in which Shaw's contribution to the Tree book was published in November 1920.

I am sure she will be much touched, as I am, by your generous idea. But – oh, my dear G.B.S., do come here and have a thorough rest.

Yours ever    MAX

P.S. I am asking Maud to write to you.

### To Gordon Craig
TS. Merton

*2 October 1920*                                              *Villino Chiaro*

Excuse this blot –
I don't know how it happened.


My dear Ted, I haven't the faintest notion who "St John Ervine" may be.[1] I infer that he is a Saint; and I infer also, from his manner of writing, that he is an Ass. And I am delighted to hear of him from you, for it is a sign that you are splendidly convalescing. Perhaps your annoyance at St John has quickened your recovery. If so, go on being annoyed till you feel *quite* well. But not a moment later. What do the St Johns of this world matter? I cast no aspersion on the memory of that charming singer, Florence;[2] nor on the memory of the rugged but gifted Baptist. But Ervine . . . no, I refuse to bother about Ervine. I am glad to see that the "correspondence is now closed"; otherwise perhaps you, in your unworldly way, would be rushing in and giving Ervine an advertisement that would waft him into the seventh heaven. Never take any notice of what Ervines say. That is a golden rule. I have been something of an Ervine myself, in my day. When I started writing, I delighted in being rude to eminent elder men. And oh, my delight when (as frequently happened) I "drew" them! Never be drawn, I repeat.

I certainly *shan't* tell you the name of anybody on the staff of *Punch* who might make fun of Ervine and thereby make him permanently happy and temporarily important. As for your own feelings in the matter – well, well! I remember Gosse told me years ago a pretty and touching little story about Hans Andersen, whom he met once in Copenhagen. H.A. was already of course an old man at the time, and one of the glories of Denmark. He complained to Gosse that there was an attack on him in some newspaper – some quite obscure newspaper.

---

[1] Novelist, playwright and critic (1883–1971).

[2] Florence St John, actress and singer (1855–1912).

121

The Beerbohms and the Craigs

"But surely, Master," said Gosse, in Danish, "such a trivial thing can't vex *you*, can it?" Hans Andersen stroked his beard: "A little, my dear," he answered.

Well, don't let Ervine hurt *you* even a little, dear Ted.

Love from us both to all  MAX

## *To William Archer*
MS. B.L.

*April 1921*                         *9 Cambridge Terrace, W.*

My dear W.A., I was glad, as I told you, that the play is such a huge success.[1] But now that I have read it I have to ask you frankly, as man to man, "How could it *not* be?" It's too exciting and brilliant *not* to be. Usually I hate reading plays. To read a play always seems to me a bastard form of study or amusement. I skim, I skip, I lay the volume aside, saying "Let me *see* this play", or rather "*Don't* let me see it". But of *The Green Goddess* I have read every page with the utmost ease and pleasure, and I say "I *must* moreover *see* this play. And why is October 1922 so far off? And couldn't there be an interim production in or about Rapallo? (With George Arliss in it if possible. And, if possible, without Herbert Waring in it. But these are details. I am ready to waive them. The play's the thing.)"[2]

I see what you meant when you said with charming Scottish detachment that the last act is "inherently weak". But the weakness only *inheres* – only sticks somewhere inside. It doesn't matter to an *audience*, I imagine; only to us old dramatic critics. You, as a fresh young dramatist, have thrown so much action and development into the last act that the inevitability of the ending doesn't extrude itself at all, I fancy, to an audience, and may even come as a surprise – the current interest being so great throughout. My only adverse criticism (a pedantic one, no doubt) is that a play compounded of comedy and melodrama ought to have A HAPPY ENDING. No doubt your Raja has certain faults of character. But he is an irresistibly sympathetic personage. And the possibility that he will be dethroned and exiled is more than I can bear. Traherne is a fine fellow. But it is impossible, somehow, to get much

---

[1] After a lifetime of drudgery in journalism Archer wrote a melodrama, *The Green Goddess*, which, with George Arliss in the chief part, was an immense success in New York in 1921 and in London in May 1923.

[2] George Arliss had played Mr Aeneas in the 1900 production of *The Happy Hypocrite*. Herbert Waring had rehearsed Lord George Hell for the New York production in 1901.

sympathy for a medical man. I want a happy sequel – the Raja's fault overlooked by H.M.'s Government; and Lucilla drawn, by an irresistible attraction, and with or without her children, back to him.

Perhaps you take a different view; but at any rate you must, in your heart, agree with me that you have written a masterly and queerly-unlike-any-other-sort-of play. *Floreat* (*hic sicut* in America) *Florebit*.

Yours ever  MAX

## *Maurice Baring[1] to Max*
### MS. Merton

*16 May 1921*           *Pickwick's Villa, Dulwich Village, S.E.21*

My dear Max, is there any chance of seeing you before you go away? I am constantly ill but I am sometimes well and always able to do anythign nice such as seeing you. As you see I I am not an expert typist but I will not rtry and correct mu mistakes that oynlu makes the matte worse. The tu th is that my bfain is quicker than my gorfinger.

Yrs etc.  maurice Baring

## *To Maurice Baring*
### MS. Jebb

*Saturday 21 May 1921*        *di Pecksniff,*

*Villino ~~Chiaro~~  Rapallo*

*S.E. 10000021*

My dear Maurice, Here I am, and have been here since last Monday, and your letter has just this moment come to me, and is a delight. I gather, from those two wondrous volumes of his letters,[2] that our dear Henry James must altogether have spent several thousands of the hours of his declining years in apologising for use of the typewriting machine. No such nonsense about *you*! You lay your gorfinger on this and that spot of your letter and say "Thou ailest here, and here", and off your letter goes with all its little ailments uncured, and is received all the more tenderly. The sun is a great healer. I have placed the little invalid on a small marble table on our small and not marble terrace. Already it begins to look rather better. It is falling into a light sleep. Hush! I raise my gorfinger to my lips and steal away on tiptoe, and sit down to write

---

[1] Poet, novelist, diplomat and man of letters (1874–1946).

[2] *The Letters of Henry James*, selected and edited by Percy Lubbock (2 vols 1920).

(in manuscript) how much I wish I had had the luck to see you while I was in London. I was there for the purpose of hanging a lot of caricatures. By the time you get this letter, you will, I daresay, have read about these in the newspapers. There were awful premonitory rumblings of a "boom" before I stepped off the Dover shingle into the little sailing-boat that nowadays takes me hither and thither.

One of the drawings that I took over from here to England was called "Experts in the Mentality of the Moujik". It represented you and Hugh Walpole and Stephen Graham – all avoiding the subject of the Moujik.[1] But I had to lay the drawing aside; for H.W. and S.G. were both away from London★, and I hadn't seen either of them for some years, and had heard that they had *altered their appearances* a good deal in the meantime; and a man who lives to displease must please be up-to-date. So my exhibition lacks a presentment of you. I hope my spelling of Moujik doesn't annoy you? You Anglo-Russians are always so particular. Mugick? Moughk? Movjhkck? Your Russian books, by the way, are the only ones I have never been able to read with delight. No fault of yours. The fault is that of the Russians – or of myself. I haven't enough imagination to be bothered about those bloody fools (as they have always appeared to me). Fabre[2] on the Insect World is very wonderful; but I do always so wish the insects were full-sized, upstanding, frank, honest, outspoken Anglo-Saxon ladies and gentlemen – or that Fabre could infect me with a little of his own wondrous insight and enthusiasm. Same feeling about you and the wretched Russians. But all your other books, all through past years and the latest year or two, prose and poetry alike, are dear to me, and treasured.

I hope that when you say you are "constantly ill" you are merely throwing out a characteristic Maurician *blague* and mystification. If you really have been, or are, at all not well, I am most sorry; and here are all wishes for quick and complete recovery and eternal wellness,

from Yrs etc  MXXX BRBEEØMH

★ H.W., as his secretary on the telephone told me, is in Cornwall; and S.G., as a forbidding charwoman on his doorstep put it, "on the continent of Europe"!

[1] Hugh Walpole, novelist (1884–1941), had spent some of the war in Russia, and two of his novels, *The Dark Forest* and *The Secret City*, were based on his experiences there. Stephen Graham (1884–1975) had travelled widely in Russia and wrote a number of books about the country and its history. Maurice Baring had spent much time in Russia and had published books about the country, its people, and its writers.

[2] Jean Henri Fabre, French entomologist (1823–1915).

# To the Editor of the Daily Herald[1]

*21 May 1921*           *Villino Chiaro*

Sir, This morning, as I sat in an attitude of the utmost refinement, surveying that restrained sea, the Mediterranean, my attention was drawn to a criticism written by J.Q.X. and published in your issue of May 18, accusing me of having been guilty of vulgarity in a prophetic drawing of a Labour Minister for Education scoffing at a penurious poet who, declaring himself a "worker", has applied to him for aid.[2]

I am not, Sir, a young man; and my work has in the course of years met with a certain amount of adverse criticism. But never till now have I been called vulgar. It has been reserved for J.Q.X. to call me that. And I must say I find the epithet immensely refreshing – all the more so because it is not undeserved. The drawing in question *is* distinctly vulgar, and so is my inscription on it.

Vulgarity has its uses. Vulgarity often cuts ice which refinement scrapes at vainly. And I like to think that some of the Labour leaders who have read J.Q.X.'s account of my shocking little drawing will visit the Leicester Galleries and be shocked themselves – shocked even into realising, as they do not yet seem to have realised, that the well-being of skilled and unskilled manual workers is not quite all that matters.

Yours obediently    MAX BEERBOHM


## To Lady Strachey[3]
### MS. B.L.

*30 May 1921*           *Villino Chiaro*

Dear Lady Strachey, A friend has told me that you went to the "Private View" of my drawings at the Leicester Galleries; and I gather moreover that the caricature of your son Lytton did not vex you. I write to say that I am deeply honoured and touched by your kindness in going – and in not being vexed!

One does what one can. I have the dubious blessing of having been

---

[1] Where it appeared on the front page of May 28, under the heading MAX ADMITS VULGARITY. The *Daily Herald* was a Labour Party and Trades Union paper.

[2] "The Patron", exhibited at the Leicester Galleries in May–June 1921 and reproduced in Max's *A Survey* in December.

[3] Jane (née Grant), widow of Sir Richard Strachey (1817–1908).

born a caricaturist; and it is always the men whom I respect most that I caricature with the greatest gusto. This is not a very satisfactory form of homage. But, such as it is, there it is.

In the course of the past two weeks, since my return to Italy, I have again read *Queen Victoria*[1] – have read it with an even deeper wonder and delight than before. There is nothing like a remote bright climate for sharpening the palate of one's appreciation of fine literature. London is all very well in its way (though I would wish to qualify this statement by saying that London always now seems to *me* extremely unwell in every way); but very assuredly, for any one who has the gift for rapture over your son's writing, some such quiet and uninterrupted place as Rapallo is the right place.

Often in the past two years I have rather regretted the instant public recognition that was given to him. This recognition was a very good sign – good, I mean, from the standpoint of a lover of the public. But I myself am a narrow and selfish sort of person. When I greatly rejoice in a thing, I want the base pleasure of feeling "superior" in connexion with it – of feeling that it needs my championship against "the giddy vulgar"; and – well, this pleasure has in this instance been withheld from me; and only through the strange outlet of caricature have I felt that there was any possible expression for me! But I console myself, in my vanity, with the belief that very, very few of all the devotees of L.S. are devoted with a sense so keen, as to the details of his work, as is possessed, dear Lady Strachey, by one who now (with apologies for so long a letter, and with gratefullest recollection of the kindness you showed him in Gordon Square, and of the vivacity which he would fain were his) signs himself          Yours sincerely   MAX BEERBOHM


## To Bohun Lynch[2]

*18 June 1921*                                                        *Villino Chiaro*

Dear Bohun Lynch, The sky is very blue here this morning, as indeed it usually is, and your letter came like a bolt from it. After I had read the first two or three lines I instinctively sat down, somewhat blasted. I then read the whole letter manfully. And now I take up my pen. But

[1] By Lytton Strachey, published on 7 April 1921.

[2] John Gilbert Bohun Lynch, author and caricaturist (1884–1928). This letter appeared as the Preface to his book *Max Beerbohm in Perspective* (1921), from which this text is taken.

I don't (it is a sign of the condition to which you've reduced me) know what to do with it. I don't quite know what to write. You are a much younger man than I am, and I think you might have waited for my demise – instead of merely hastening it. Had you said you thought of writing a little book about me, I should have said simply "Don't!" But as you give me to understand that you *intend* to write a little book about me and have already been excogitating it, what shall I say? I know, at any rate, what I shan't say. I shan't say "Do!"

I shan't offer you the slightest assistance – except of the purely negative and cautionary kind that now occurs to me. I won't supply you with any photograph of myself at *any* age, nor with any scrap of corrected manuscript, nor with any caricature of myself for a frontispiece (you yourself have done several brilliant caricatures of me, and I commend these to your notice), nor with *any* of the things you seem to think might be of interest. You must forage around for yourself. I won't even try to prevent you from using anything you may find. I eschew all responsibility whatsoever. I disclaim the horrid privilege of seeing proof-sheets. I won't read a single word till your book is published. Even if modesty didn't prevent me, worldly wisdom would. I remember several books about men who, not yet dead, had blandly aided and abetted the author; and I remember what awful asses those men seemed to me thereby to have made of themselves. Two of them were rather great men. They could afford to make awful asses of themselves. I, who am a hundred miles away from being great, cannot afford such luxuries. My gifts are small. I've used them very well and discreetly, never straining them; and the result is that I've made a charming little reputation. But that reputation is a frail plant. Don't over-attend to it, gardener Lynch! Don't drench and deluge it! The contents of a quite *small* watering-can will be quite enough. This I take to be superfluous counsel. I find much reassurance and comfort in your phrase, "a *little* book". Oh, keep it little! – in due proportion to its theme. Avoid such phrases as "It was at or about this time that the young Beerbohm" etc. My life (though to me it has been, and is, extremely interesting) is without a single point of general interest. Address yourself to my writings and drawings.

And *surtout pas de zèle*, even here! Be judicial. Make those reservations without which praise carries no weight. Don't, by dithyrambs, hasten the reaction of critics against me. Years ago, G.B.S., in a light-hearted moment, called me "the incomparable". Note that I am *not* incomparable. Compare me. Compare me as essayist (for instance) with other essayists. Point out how much less human I am than Lamb, how much less intellectual than Hazlitt, and what an ignoramus beside Belloc; and how Chesterton's high spirits and abundance shame me; how unbalanced G.S. Street must think me, and how coarse too; and how much lighter E.V. Lucas's touch is than mine; and so on, and so forth. Apply the comparative method to me also as caricaturist. Tend rather to *under*rate me – so that those who don't care for my work shall not be incensed, and those who do shall rally round me ... But I seem to be becoming guilty of just what I swore to avoid: I'm offering "positive" advice – and at such a length! Still, the advice is good; and the letter, though it will bore you in the reading, will save you trouble some day. Some day, if your future novels are as beautifully-done as your past ones (and if our civilization persists), you'll get a letter from a young man announcing that he is going to write a book about *you*; and then you will but have to post him this very screed, writing across it in blue pencil "Certainly, but please follow advice herein given" by your long-winded friend

MAX BEERBOHM

## To Lady Strachey
### MS. Merton

*19 June 1921*                 *Villino Chiaro*

Dear Lady Strachey, One line of thanks for your very delightful and kind answer to my letter. And one line of protest against a phrase that you use therein. "Greatest living master of style" – oh, believe me, Lady Strachey, that is not I, that isn't me! – *that* is your son Lytton.

I, at the age of forty-eight, have gradually, after years of flounderings and fumblings, arrived at a way of writing that is rather like the way *he* arrived at when he made his first step from the starting-point. But even now I am, and shall always be, a rather tricky writer. Whereas L. has *no* tricks – is a pure classicist who somehow makes the language play tricks *for* him – while *he* maintains a perfect dignity. It must be lovely to be L.

I expect I shall be again in London within the next year; and then I shall have with me my wife, who is at this moment in America. I shall, if I may, bring her to see you, for I think you would like her very much, and I know that she would love *you*. I am, dear Lady Strachey,

Yours very sincerely    MAX BEERBOHM

## To Bernard Shaw
MS. B.L.

*27 June 1921*                    *Villino Chiaro*

My dear G.B.S., Your book reached me this morning.[1] How good of
you to send it to me! I have spent a long day with it – the sun shining
all the while very much, but not so much as *it*. I am especially dazzled
and delighted by the "waning powers" passage at the end of the preface.[2]
Just about a quarter-of-a-century ago there was a very successful play
entitled *Gaffer Jarge*,[3] in which Cyril Maude made a great hit. (At least,
I *think* it was Cyril Maude.) I am so glad you "saw" yourself in that
part; and I have no doubt that your impersonation will have had the
effect of winning for you what you so seldom have: *une bonne presse*. But
the endearing trick wasn't needed to affect *my* remote and Italianate
judgment. I should in any case have been very solidly sure that this is
the best book that you have written. *Man and Superman* is a bad second.
I was reading that again, as it happens, a fortnight ago, after reading
some of *Plays Pleasant and Unpleasant* with a keener sense of their
untidiness and unrealness and their 1001 crudities than I had when as
a crude youth I first read them. You were always a man of genius, of
course. But you were a late developer. *M. and S.* was, I think, your first
really good piece of work (outside journalism). And that might have
been much better, if you hadn't been more of a publicist than an artist,
and hadn't felt it a civic duty to be cursory about FORM – which is
*my* way of writing the word; form would have been *your* way of writing
it. I mean that the play itself might have been ever so much better. The
intermezzo, the Hell scene (like the preface, and like the Revolutionist's
Handbook) is almost as good as it can be. In getting away from rep-
resentation of actual things, you got off your rickety little contemporary
platform and ceased your ready improvisings and sat down on the earth
and thought out a genuine work of art and achieved something beautiful
(*for once*, thought I, the other day; but *Back to Methuselah* is something
much more beautiful – or seems so to me). You gave to a dramatic work

---

1 *Back to Methuselah. A Metabiological Pentateuch* (1921).

[2] "My powers are waning; but so much the better for those who found me unbearably
brilliant when I was in my prime. It is my hope that a hundred apter and more elegant
parables by younger hands will soon leave mine as far behind as the religious pictures
of the fifteenth century left behind the first attempts of the early Christians at iconogra-
phy. In that hope I withdraw and ring up the curtain."

[3] A rustic study in one act by Alicia Ramsay, produced at the Comedy Theatre on 11
January 1896.

the FORM which you had hitherto felt compatible with your conscience only in direct ratiocinative pleading. Excellent result! There was a goblet for the wine. One didn't have to lap the liquid up off the pavement – hurting one's tongue, and not getting much of the flavour.

Good heavens! – this seems as if it were going to be a long letter. Where am I? – I who was just preaching FORM!? What I was going to begin this letter with, and what I'm full of, is this: that Act I of "In the Beginning"[1] is far and away the best thing that you have ever done. Europe and posterity will back this opinion, I'm perfectly sure. "The Gospel of the Brothers Barnabas" is as howlingly funny as anything of yours – Burge and Lubin possess my soul with laughter. And the scheme of the whole pentalogue, all through ... but no, this letter must be kept within the bounds of available note-paper, and of the time you have for reading letters and (beyond an expression of my delight that you no longer, as in "The Revolutionist's Handbook", shelter yourself behind the person of John Tanner[2] in order not to discourage old friends and comrades, but come manfully forth, saying "I, G.B.S., *know* and in my own person *assure* you that there isn't a ray of hope for the improvement of man's lot on earth" [which of course there isn't, though even poor cynical little M.B. did, when he was at Oxford or thereabouts, think there might be])* nothing shall be said by me except in thanks for just that first Adam and Eve scene. Here is high imagination – cosmic imagination; and thrilling and tender beauty. You must be glad and grateful that it has been reserved for you to do this at your age. I've no one to share my enthusiasm with, otherwise I mightn't be writing so promptly to thank you. My wife is at this moment visiting her brothers in America. She has a keener scent for fine literature than anybody I know. Bating *her* appreciation of those pages, I think I should like either Anatole France's, or that of Lytton Strachey – or, still more, that of the ghost of Heine. I suppose that, like Cunninghame Graham, you "never withdraw". I suppose that once a thing is printed you never alter a word. Otherwise I should venture to implore you to alter certain words in this masterpiece. Some of them are obviously due to carelessness; others to G.B.Sque wilfulness; and both kinds give me shudders up the spine. If it would at all interest you to know what words they are, and

* How are those two brackets, for FORM? Not very pretty, are they? And the asterisk doesn't add to their charm, does it?

[1] The opening of the Pentateuch, in which the characters are Adam, Eve, Cain and the Serpent.　　　　　　　　　　　　　　　　[2] The hero of *Man and Superman*.

where they occur, send me a post-card, and I'll tell you. I have marked them with an agonised pencil.                    Yours ever   MAX

I shall read *A and E*[1] often again. I shall return to it and linger over it much – but always, I think, with the desire to see it embodied on the stage. Its full quality would only come out *there*. I haven't been inside a theatre for years and years. Is there any possible eligible A? If so, is there an E of like kind? There may be, for aught I know.[2] But who should be the producer? Not you. I wouldn't at all trust *you* with the beauty you've created. Still less our brilliant Granville Barker. There's only one person in Europe who could produce the thing rightly; and he's just round the corner here: Gordon Craig. He is a queer and improvisible sort of fellow. I think he mightn't quite grasp the play, and he might very perfectly do so. But even if he grasped it imperfectly his production would be far more right than anybody else's. That I know.


## To A.B. Walkley[3]
MS. Virginia

*26 February 1922*                                    *Villino Chiaro*

My dear A.B.W., What nonsense, the idea that *you* should have thanked *me*! It was my business to have thanked you, long ago, for your lovely article in *The Times*[4] – the one in which you cried "*What?* Somebody has said something against my old friend Max? Intolerable! Who is this so-called Clutton? Reach me my spear! Saddle my horse! Give me my lance! *Pereat* Clutton! Strap about me flasks of balm and balsam for Max, and of oil of spikenard very precious! Brock shall have such a Benefit as he'll never forget!"[5] Well, I thank you now, and tell you how pleased and touched and honoured I was. Also, I say how glad I am

---

[1] Adam and Eve.

[2] The play's first English production was at the Birmingham Repertory Theatre in October 1923, with Colin Keith-Johnston as Adam, Gwen Ffrangçon-Davies as Eve, and Edith Evans as the Serpent.

[3] Arthur Bingham Walkley, dramatic critic and essayist (1855–1926).

[4] In *The Times* of 19 May 1921 the anonymous art-critic Arthur Clutton-Brock (1868–1924) damned Max's latest Leicester Galleries exhibition with faint praise. In *The Times* of 25 May Walkley took up the cudgels on Max's behalf.

[5] From the 1860s until the building was destroyed by fire in 1936 Brock's Fireworks Ltd gave firework displays at the Crystal Palace throughout the year. On one September day each year the display was even more spectacular than usual, and all the gate-money was paid to Brock's. Hence Brock's Benefit.

that *my* article in *The T.* didn't annoy you.[1] It was a damned dull article, but well-meant. It is the only piece of strict *journalism* that I have done in the past decade or so; and it marks the only time that I have ever thrust myself forward: I wrote to the Editor of *The T.* with mine own hand, soliciting the privilege of "doing" your book. Would that I could have "done" it more worthily! I hope you're going to have an annual – or at any rate biennial – volume of your essays? – so that one can throw away the strips that one simply can't help cutting out of *The T.* and preserving for fond re-reading ... *Re-reading* – what a word! What a shudder it will have given you! I seem to have become illiterate. The result of living in Italy, no doubt. And I shall go from bad to worse, for I have just (from the proceeds of my exhibition of last Spring) *bought* the little house where my wife and I reside; and here I shall live and die – die with Heaven knows what awful locution on my lips ... "As the sun was setting behind the purple hills that he had loved so well, Beerbohm roused himself from his coma, and his lips moved. The watchers by the bedside leaned to catch his words; and the words, the last he ever uttered, were 'I want to re-re-read A.B.W.'"

Meanwhile, I look forward with great pleasure to the arrival of Mr Theodore Byard[2] – who is quite mistaken in supposing that I have "a horror of new people". I think I twitted you, last Spring, apropos of an account you gave me of your having sat between Chesterton and Belloc at some dinner, with being over-hard to please about people whom you weren't, after all, destined to spend the whole of your life with. Heaven forbid that C. and B. should *forever* flank you! Heaven forbid that Mr Byard – but no, this is premature; for aught I know, I shall wish that Mr Byard shall *never* leave Rapallo. Anyhow, he will be most welcome for a while; and I will do all that I can to assure him of this feeling.

*Paullo majora canamus!*[3] – aren't your wife and you ever going to revisit Italy? This house is too small for us to put people up; but from morning to night we can offer very pleasant little meals. So remember and pass us not by.　　　　Your affectionate old friend　M.B.

[1] Max's review of Walkley's *Pastiche and Prejudice* appeared in *The Times* on 15 September 1921.

[2] Chairman of William Heinemann Ltd.

[3] "Let us sing of slightly more important matters" (Virgil, *Eclogues* IV i).

# To Lytton Strachey
## MS. B.L.

*June 1922*                                                              *Villino Chiaro*

My dear Lytton Strachey, I have just been reading with very deep delight your *Books and Characters*.[1] You are exquisite in controversy, and beautifully luminous and sane in criticism of the works of writers. But there are other people of whom as much as that can be said; whereas there isn't – and I protest there never was – any rival to you in the searching exposition of queer human characters, and in vivid narration of their adventures or careers, and in vivid suggestion of all their temporal background. "Voltaire and Frederick" is an abiding masterpiece. So is "Madame du Deffand". I suppose you saw last week's *Times Literary Supplement*? It (I don't mean the *T.L.S.*, but the writer of the article – whom I refuse to call "he") seemed to take a hopeful view of your case, finding that in the purely literary criticisms you had cured yourself of "a half-dramatic manner" which you "perhaps unconsciously" had allowed to mar your *E.V.* and your *Q.V.* The idiocy of the first paragraph of that article so incensed me that I sat down with the intention of writing to the *T.L.S.* But I reflected that this would be an act of impertinence to you, who are so very far from needing any champion; and I contented myself with writing a letter to Bruce Richmond,[2] in which I was as rude as I could be (and I *can* be *very* rude!) about the writer of that paragraph.

"Creevey" and "Lady Hester S[tanhope]" are lovely pieces of work. Only I wish they had both been longer. To see you at your very best, one must see you traversing a fairly long distance. I like to see you (as Boswell or somebody liked to see Burke) winding yourself into your subject like a serpent. I don't want to see the tip of your tail disappear at once, and your head emerge simultaneously on the other side, and the whole of you "harden into quick strength that has vanished".[3] By the way – concerning Lady H.S. – I wonder that you could forbear to quote that very great remark of hers, made to Dr Meryon – or was it made to Kinglake? – made, anyway, to some gentleman who mentioned

---

[1] Published on 18 May 1922.

[2] 1871–1964. Editor of the *Times Literary Supplement* 1902–37. Knighted 1935.

[3] In his essay "The End of General Gordon" in *Eminent Victorians* Strachey wrote of Gladstone: "The soft serpent coils harden into quick strength that has vanished". In Max's Rede Lecture on Strachey (1943) he quoted this passage and added: "Was ever speed so well suggested as in those eleven words?"

"principle" in the course of a political discussion with her: "Principle? What is Principle to *me*? I am a Pitt."

For the rest, I am going to read Racine. Also I shall perhaps (or perhaps not) make one little frantic second attempt at Stendhal. My first one was made, in high hopes, at Oxford, just thirty years ago. I had bought, at Blackwell's shop, a copy of *Le Rouge et le Noir* – imagining it to be a work with a strong *roulette* or *vingt-et-un* interest.

The kitten of whom I told you last year is now a confirmed cat. He is much larger than he seemed likely to become, and is vigorous and vagrant, but not, I am sorry to say, either affectionate or intelligent. It is not known that he ever caught a mouse; he dislikes rain, but has no knowledge of how to avoid it if it falls; and if one caresses him he is very likely to scratch one. He is, however, very proud of his name, and sends his respectful regards to his *Illustrissimo Eponymisto Inglese*.

Your not re-printing in your book an article which you wrote about Disraeli[1] (I never saw it – only heard of it) makes me think that perhaps you are, after all, going to write some long thing about him. I wonder. And further do I wonder whether you will ever feel yourself drawn towards the problem of Byron's character ... I don't urge; for that is the surest way to send an artist off at a tangent.

I hope your Mother is well. Please give her my best messages. I was so grateful for her kindness to me in London, last Spring, and for the great charm and vivacity of her conversation.

Yours very sincerely    MAX BEERBOHM

P.S. I don't – I daren't – suppose you would be interested to know what *I* am working at. But I may as well mention that I am engaged on an Anthology of Modern English Prose. It will be a large, thick, rather closely-printed book, consisting wholly of extracts from *Q.V.*, *E.V.*, and *B. and C.* I hope Messrs C. and W.[2] won't raise any niggling difficulties about copyright. They had better not. What is copyright to me? I am a Beerbohm.

P.P.S. I shall include also some extracts from Aldous Huxley. Don't you agree with me that he has a very exquisite sense of words and meanings?

---

[1] "Dizzy," a short review of volumes V and VI of the *Life of Disraeli*, published in the *Woman's Leader* on 16 July 1920 and reprinted in the posthumous *Characters and Commentaries* (1933).

[2] Chatto & Windus, Strachey's publishers.

## To Gordon Craig

TS. Merton

*10 September 1922*             *Grand Hôtel L'Univers, Lucca*

My dear Ted, This is the name on the façade of our present abode. But I like still better the name on the swing-doors of frosted glass: *Hôtel Royal Univers.* The universe is something, it is even much, to go on with; but when it is all royal, what more can one ask? One doesn't want to go on at all. One wants to stay forever. And one refuses to believe the news in this morning's *Tribuna* that the throne of King Constantine is in danger just because the Greeks haven't lost their inveterate habit of running away at first sight of a fez on their classic horizon.[1] Dash down yon cup of Samian wine,[2] by all means. But the crown of Constantine shall *never* be tampered with.

How are you, and how the elder and the younger Nellie, and how is the younger you? We think of you much, and talk of you much, and wish you were all here. We came hither two or three days ago from Carrara, having utterly failed to understand that place: it consists almost entirely of cafés: there is only one little hotel, and not a single restaurant but the restaurant of that hotel; there is one chemist's shop, one draper's, no grocer's, no butcher's, one shop where they sell very small ornaments of marble rimmed with red or blue velvet; and all the rest of the town consists of large cafés. The mystery is the more baffling because one never sees anybody tipsy. "Perhaps," you suggest, "the Carrarese have very strong heads." They may have, or they mayn't. One doesn't know. They never drink. The multitudinous gleaming great cafés are all quite empty, day and night. It is good to be here, in a place that one can more or less understand. The churches here are almost as many as the cafés out yonder. But there *are* worshippers in them. It is good to see San Michele again; also the Duomo; but especially San Michele, with the wonderful way that its façade and its campanile have of taking the light and looking lovelier in the afternoon than in the morning, and lovelier still in the evening, and lovelier always today than yesterday. Don't you love San Michele?

I wish there were some beautiful theatres for me to remind you of. But there aren't. The *Teatro dei Manzi*[3] is not, to my mind, beautiful. But it is, I suppose, curious, as being one of the very few remaining examples of the seicento *triangular* theatre . . .

[1] King Constantine of the Hellenes (1868–1923) succeeded his father in 1913, deposed 1917, recalled 1920, deposed 1922.      [2] Byron, *Don Juan*, Canto III.      [3] Cattle.

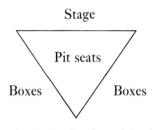

Stage

Pit seats

Boxes          Boxes

Box built for the Grand-Dukes
in the Settecento

I rather think this theatre was closed when you were here. It is practically the same as it was in the seicento – all but the added box for the Grand Dukes, and the curious sliding shutters of iron for the other, the ordinary boxes. These latter, as you know, were added by Grand Duke Carlo Pizzolomini (1742–1785) who, like Bavarian Ludwig of the following century,[1] liked to have a performance all for himself, but, unlike Ludwig, and being a man of much cheerier and more human disposition than Ludwig, liked the idea of a full house, of a drama "played to capacity", etc., and insisted therefore that every place in the boxes should be occupied, and then, when he entered his own great box at the apex of the triangle, pressed a button which caused all the sliding iron shutters to roll into position with a snap; after which the curtain rose. The inmates of the boxes were prevented from going out by sentinels posted at the door of each box. Occupants of pit seats had to stand up, facing the apex of the triangle – the men keeping their hands at the salute, the women curtseying without intermission. The performance of the play lasted usually for four hours; and the Grand Duke was sometimes pleased to encore it. I wish my little diagram of the theatre were better drawn. I am afraid Teddy the younger won't think it worth photographing.[2]

I have just asked Florence where it is that we may be going on to tomorrow – I not remembering the name of the place. But Florence has also forgotten the name ... Since I wrote the foregoing sentence, Florence has remembered. *Pistoia*. And we shall be there perhaps for a week, and then we shall see you all again. Meanwhile, with much love,

Yours ever   MAX

[1] Ludwig II of Bavaria, ruled from 1864 to 1886.
[2] The theatre was invented by Max to amuse Craig.

137

# To Mr Mearns
MS. Lilly

*26 September 1922* *Villino Chiaro*

Dear Mr Mearns, A painful picture – you wading through the "files" of me in the unquenchable hope of a reference to Charles Reade.[1] I never *have* referred to him. I wish I had, for your sake – though I hardly know what I should have said about him, never having read a line of him. I must, I shall, take a belated plunge into the troubled sea of his genius – one of these fine days. He *had* genius, hadn't he? And it *was* rather of the troubled variety, wasn't it? Or are these bad shots?

It is kind of you to be pleased by my own little products (there is certainly nothing troubled or troublous about *them*!) and I hope I shall continue to give you satisfaction. The H. about which you ask me stands – or stood – for Henry. I was christened Henry Maximilian; but the Henry and the imilian seemed to me, when I grew up, rather pointless; and so I dropped them.

With good wishes, I am yours very truly    MAX BEERBOHM

P.S. It may thrill you to know that I am not only Maximilian; but also Maxwell. At any rate I am so in the eyes of the Church of England. As you know, a child at its confirmation in the R.C. Church takes on some extra name, automatically. This isn't so in the C. of E. But soon before my confirmation I learned that, though there is no canon law in the matter, a child *can* add a name to itself, if the child be so disposed. And so, as I rather disliked the imperial imilian, I decided to be also and alternatively Maxwell. And I vaguely remember that my first published caricatures were signed H. Maxwell Beerbohm. This was a very youthful indiscretion.

---

[1] 1814–84. Author of *The Cloister and the Hearth* (1861) and many other novels and plays.

# *To Sir Michael Sadler*[1]
MS. Merton

*6 March 1923*                                                *Villino Chiaro*

Dear Sir Michael, I have just been reading your penetrating and beauti-ful essay on Matthew Arnold – both instalments of it at one and the same time. I need hardly say – though I plead as my excuse for writing to you – that I was very greatly gratified by your mention of me, your very delightful mention of me. *Too* delightful a mention. That's the trouble. That's my real motive and excuse for bothering you. I was as greatly shocked as I was gratified. I sat up. I rubbed my eyes. I asked myself, "What, in the name of Education, are these Vice-Chancellors coming to?" An "imp" I may be. An "imp" I doubtless am. But I am a conservative imp; and your suggestion that M.A. (whose intials ought to have been D.C.L.)[2] would have been the better for being the *me* "of his generation" does move me to make stern and spirited protest in his behalf.

You regret that the imp in *him* was "untimely suppressed in his childhood". Suppose it *hadn't* been! Suppose his father had said to him, "Matt, my child, in you I discern the makings of what is called an humourist. Here is a cap-and-bells. Here, moreover, is a wand-and-bladder. Make good practice with these, under God's blessing." What would have happened then? The seriousness that the child had *con-genitally* might have saved him from the horrid fate of being just a fribble and a "funny man". I myself have enough seriousness in me to prevent me from being just that – else you never would have honoured me by speaking my name. But oh, how much more amusing I should be if I were much more serious than I am! Surely it is *because* M.A. was so genuinely solemn (and even desperate) at heart that we love his outbursts of fun so much. Without the contrast of what underlies his writing, all the time, how much less delicious would be what suddenly

---

[1] Educationist (1861–1943), Vice-Chancellor of Leeds University 1911–23, Master of University College, Oxford 1923–34. Knighted 1919. His centenary essay on Matthew Arnold appeared in the February and March 1923 issues of the *Nineteenth Century*. In it he wrote:

> "If the imp had not been untimely suppressed in his childhood Matthew Arnold might have been a great and good-humoured caricaturist of the foibles and shortcomings of his time. 'Matt's sublime wagging' amused Tennyson. The author of *Friendship's Garland* should have been the Max Beerbohm of his generation. And it would have been good for that generation to have a Max Beerbohm in their midst."

[2] i.e. not Master of Arts but Doctor of Civil Law.

now and again bubbles up! "Impertinence", as you call it. Yes. But why not? Part of the joy of it, for you and me, is surely that it *was* impertinent (in the strict sense of the word, as also in the loose sense). "A flaw"? Oh, surely not! There you speak as a Vice-Chancellor, not as Michael Sadler; and the conservative imp applauds; but the thoughtful imp dissents. Think of Arnold's exquisite side-outbursts on Mr Odger, on Frederic Harrison (happily no longer with us), on Sir Daniel Gooch, on all those other flies in amber! – and maintain that these were "a flaw"![1] And maintain that their power to delight you and me, to make us really laugh aloud over the printed page, doesn't depend very much on the high seriousness of the preceding and subsequent pages!

I have come to the end of *this* page, and won't encroach on a subsequent one. I will merely apologise for an un-called-for screed from your grateful reader                                                 MAX BEERBOHM


### To Lady Desborough
MS. Hertford

*26 May 1923*                                              *40 Upper Berkeley Street, W.*

My dear Lady Desborough, It is such years and years since we met. My wife and I live all the year round in Italy, and we only come over to England on brief visits for special purposes. The special purpose this time is a little "show" of caricatures. I had a similar one two years ago, but hesitated to send a card to you, remembering that in by-gone years you used to go and see my drawings with two wonderful sons whom you have no longer; and I thought that the card might possibly distress you.[2] This time, however, I take the risk.

With all best remembrances to you,

Yours very sincerely   MAX BEERBOHM

---

[1] George Odger (1820–77), a shoemaker, who became secretary to the London Trades Council 1862. He tried to combine Trades Unionism with active political propaganda, and made five unsuccessful attempts to enter parliament. Frederic Harrison, Positivist philosopher, lawyer and prolific writer (1831–1923). Sir Daniel Gooch, engineer (1816–89). All three were treated in Arnold's *Culture and Anarchy* (1869) not as anarchists but as obstacles to sweetness and light.

[2] Lady Desborough's two elder sons, Julian and Billy Grenfell, were killed in the war.

## Postcard: To Frank Schuster[1]
### MS. N.P.G

*16 July 1923*            *8 Cambridge Terrace, W.2*

My dear Frankie Schu, I note that water-colourists at The Hut –
Sargent, Percy Anderson, Roger Fry, etc. – all tend to paint their fellow-
guests reclining on sofas, sometimes indeed pretending to read books,
but *never* doing anything useful or noble. I am sorry I have not been
able to break away from this bad tradition. Here I am. Ever so many
thanks again from Florence and me for the delightful yesterday.

Yours ever    MAX

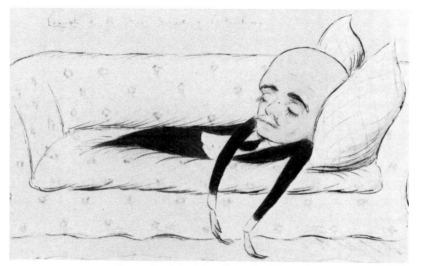

*Example* of the Max School of Portraiture.

---

[1] Wealthy music-lover and giver of parties (1840–1928). His house on the Thames near
Bray was first called The Hut and then The Long White Cloud.

# To Elinor Wylie[1]
## MS. Princeton

*November 1923*                                      *Villino Chiaro*

Dear Madam, Your publisher has been so good as to send me a copy of *Jennifer Lorn*.

I don't often read a book which I feel I should like to have written myself. But I should like very much to have written *Jennifer Lorn*. "I should rather think you *would*!" you reply. To which I rejoin that though my powers are slight enough my judgment is extremely good, and that my poor fond wish ought therefore to give you a little pleasure – even in the midst of the loud chorus of praise that (I hope) your book will have.

I am, dear Madam, Yours very ... but this letter is too short for the long journey it is going to take. My eye wanders to the copy of *Jennifer* that lies on my table. I am very much in the habit of marking, in a book that interests me, passages that I like especially; also passages that seem to me wrong. I have marked an immense number of much-liked things in *Jennifer*; and a few small lapses – or what seem to me lapses. And it is a fine afternoon, and I've nothing to do, and authors *are* rather apt to want to know what other people think; and so – though it would be much easier and more pleasant if you yourself were here – let me go through my copy of *Jennnifer* with you ... pedantically, marked page by page.

*Page 11*   The proleptic[2] touch. I believe very much in that device. I immediately became interested.

*Page 26*   Before I came to this I had become more than interested. "Here," I had said, "is a woman who can *write*" (sacred word! – and sacred function in which your sex so rarely partakes to advantage) "and is a born and made ironist, and has in virtue of her irony a keen scent for the Eighteenth Century, and has fancy, and wit, *and*," added I, after reading the passage about the gardener, "great sense of beauty and tenderness and fun."

*Page 29*   "utterly charming" – neither of these is a word of the period. Pray retract them from future editions. You do the language of the time so well; or rather, you suggest it so well. It's a thing that a modern writer had much better *suggest* than *do*. The Zounds, I-am-monstrous-glad, egad style is very quickly intolerable. Just sound good

---

[1] American poet and novelist (1885–1928). Her first novel *Jennifer Lorn* (a sedate extravaganza set in the eighteenth century) was published by Grant Richards in 1923. Max greatly admired her second novel, *The Venetian Glass Nephew* (1926).

[2] Anticipatory.

lucid formal graceful English (like yours) is the right way to suggest Eighteenth Century speech. Of course in a fantastic novel the formality can be fantasticated to any extent. And this you do delightfully, with great sensitiveness to the possible absurdities latent in language. In fact, you are utterly charming. *I* may be allowed to say that. But you should not have allowed Mr Poynyard to say it of the little Solange. They break the absurd antique spell that you have been weaving so well.

*Same page* Let the printer of future editions put an *accent grave* over *lese*.

*Page 36* A lovely first sentence. Also the proleptic touch again. Oh, there's so much to be said for that, in narrative art. But I won't bore you and me by saying it. Enough to say how poignant it makes pages 125–130.

Are you bored? No; I believe this is just the sort of letter an author likes to receive. I have never written one of the kind before. But it is *such* a fine afternoon.

*Page 37* A dead man cannot be knighted nor made a baronet. Besides, you aren't the British Sovereign. Why this attempt on the memory of Mr Horace Walpole?

*Page 82* Delightful, the reference to H.W.

*Page 84* "subsequent upon the non-arrival". Oh, good heavens! What sort of wretched muddy commercial jargon is this? *You*, with your elegance and limpidity, aren't you very much ashamed? Purify, please, for future editions. There *will* be many future editions, I am sure. Whether or not the book is an instant success, there will always in future years be discerning enthusiasts persuading a fair number of people to read it. A fantasy so well-inspired as yours, and so tightly-wrought, will not cease to be appreciated, I am very sure.

*Page 117* Another *gaffe*. "a good twenty years my deceased uncle's junior". Dreadful, isn't it? How Robert Louis Stevenson, whom by many tokens I judge that you admire, would have squirmed in reading it! But how enthusiastic he would have been about the whole work! – the delicacy and the prettiness and the endless fun of it; and (vastly important), the good solid *construction*, whereby you keep the interest up to the last page of all.

*Page 118* "an apparently wholly". Perhaps it's as well that the aforesaid Stevenson didn't live to read you and be killed by that awful collision of two adverbs. Avert such collisions. Be a good watchful pointswoman evermore.

*Pages 122–123* "In all the strange and varied trials and adventures of his later years, the memory of that night remained intact and perfect, like a pastoral scene upon a coach-panel or a classic instance modelled in tinted clay". I copy out that sentence just for the pleasure of copying it out. It is a fine example of your sure sense for cadence ... and of your amusingness, too. Not that these two things can be separated, strictly. Part of the beauty of the cadence is in its amusingness – in its expression and intensification of the fun.

*Page 123*   "The boy sat", etc. This paragraph is otiose, and not even good in itself. The one and only otiose paragraph in the book, I think. And it mars the context very much, believe me.

*Page 124*   "painted succeeded". Another awful collision – or "smash", as I believe such things are called in your country. <u>Appalling Loss of Life</u>. <u>Death of the Ghost of R.L. Stevenson</u>.

*Page 125*   "There lived no dove in any golden age
              Whose death produced a grief so exquisite
              As that which overflowed the eyes of Jennifer Lorn".
*See page 197*   "You are talking in blank verse, my lad," cried Father O'Donnell, warningly."

For "lad" read "lass", and take the Father's warning, and mine. And do forgive me these niggling criticisms. It is *because* you have such a rare notion of the architecture of sentences, and of the right ornamentation of them, that these occasional slight bungles stand out to my vision and worry me and move me to worry *you* about them. Perhaps you have more sense of proportion than I, and ask "Why is this old fool wasting his time?" I can only repeat (in a cracked senile voice) that it is a most lovely afternoon, and feebly resume:

*Page 127*   "It was simple, since the child was tired, to add a touch of rose-colour to the counterfeited cheek, instead of demanding a rouge box and a hare's foot to improve the pallor of the true one."

Those last seven words! *Brava!* Congratulations on your ear.

*Ear*: that is one of the main requisites in a writer, don't you think? What's Brain without Ear? But these are dark and difficult speculations. Return we to Jennifer.

*Page 133, second paragraph.* I don't like "frequently inconvenienced", do you? "often inconvenienced" would sound better. But, besides that, noun-verbs are beastly things, anyway. "discommoded" would be better here.

*Last line of same page.*   <u>Another Horrible Catastrophe</u>
                             <u>Ghost of R.L.S. Re-Mangled</u>
                                "consequently extremely"

144

*Pages 137–138*   The paragraph about Jennifer and Diderot. One of your most exquisitely absurd and touching things. I wonder if you like it as much as I do. Probably not. The things one likes best are, naturally, the things one couldn't have done oneself.

*Page 141, top of.*   Another great favourite of mine.

*Page 147.* "In this as in other matters the thin egg-shell of the future was transparent to his pale and voracious eye." How do you do it?

*Pages 152–153*   The Rajah's Ruby. Pauline Bonaparte. The Venetian Girl. How excellently grim in itself, this passage! And how the prolepticism of it helps the story along!

*Pages 159–160*   Sally's speech. Enchanting. "the two girls" is a very fine and pretty stroke.

*Page 164*   Jennifer reading the "Ode to Evening:" "the assurance that it occupied no more than two printed pages encouraged her to read further". How well, oh how well I know that feeling! Thank you for expressing it so tersely. For me even the best poems – and even perhaps especially the best ... but I stifle the confession. Enough that Jennifer's need of "encouragement", that glance of hers ahead, endeared her more than ever to me, and more than ever interested me in her fate therefore. I wonder if you share her weakness and are re-assured by the sight of only "two printed pages". Talking of brevity, how about this letter? Talking about two pages, here I am on my eighth! – and yet at only the 164th of your book, which has 302, and ever so many marked ones in the remainder ... Lifting my eyes, I see a slight cloud on the horizon; and I falteringly murmur, "Long live Brevity!" For her sake and yours and mine I will say no more. No more details, at any rate. Merely a general congratulation or two, on this and that. On, for example,

[*There the letter ends in the middle of a page.*]

## To E.V. Lucas[1]
MS. Clark

*28 November 1923*

My dear E.V., Your notepaper intrigues me and confounds me. What, *what* is PETTY FRANCE?[2] and how and why are you ON THE EDGE

---

[1] 1868–1938. Voluminous writer of essays, novels, books of travel, and compiler of anthologies. Edited the works of Charles Lamb. Chairman of the publishers Methuen & Co Ltd from 1924.

[2] A street in Westminster between, and parallel to, Birdcage Walk and Victoria Street.

BEERBOHM, M  ALS  N 28 23.

November 28 1923    My dear R.V.   Your note-paper intrigues me and confounds me.  What, *what* is PETTY FRANCE?  And how and why are you ON THE EDGE OF it?  Look at my simple straightforward address: VILLINO CHIARO, RAPALLO, Italy.   How plain! How frank!  How inconducive to illustration!  Do please send me an explanatory line.  I am really anxious to know.

Meanwhile I send back the "revise".  Please let the printers have it.

The division of the paragraphs by a "white line" is a great improvement, as you say.  But how absurd that it should have to be there!  Do henceforward save the firm of Methuen from the notions of "typographic experts", howsoever gifted.  Indeed, the more gifted these gentlemen are the more intent are they on dazzling one another with some chantry or eccentricity.  The reader is the last person they ever think of.  To the typographic eye, no doubt, these over-wide lines with too little space between them, and with words packed too tightly, and without any decent space

after the stops, look very nice indeed, in some arcane professional way.  But the poor dear reader! — to say nothing of the poor dear writer!  à bas l'expertise typographique!

Yours ever Max

P.S. If only he always expects, instead of trying to force over Wm. Morris, so one more volume of Tennyson, would they not learn his secret of sense and lucidity, and of the beauty of the printing? the

146

of it? Look at *my* simple straightforward address

VILLINO CHIARO, RAPALLO, Italy

How plain! How frank! How inconducive to illustration! Do please send me an explanatory line. I am really anxious to know. Meanwhile, I send back the "revise."[1] Please let the printer have it.

The division of the paragraphs by a "white line" is a great improvement, as you say. But how absurd that it should have to be there! Do henceforward save the firm of Methuen from the notions of "typographic experts", howsoever gifted. Indeed, the more gifted these gentlemen are the more intent are they on dazzling one another with some new pedantry or eccentricity. The *reader* is the last person they ever think of. To the typographic eye, no doubt, those over-wide lines with too little space between them, and with words packed too tightly, and without any decent space after the stops, *look* very nice indeed, in some arcane professional way. But the poor dear *reader!* – to say nothing of the poor dear writer! *A bas l'expertise typographique!*          Yours ever   MAX

P.S. If only the experts, instead of trying always to go one worse than William Morris, would pore over the pages of any volume of Tauchnitz,[2] how much they would learn of sense and sobriety, and of the proper aim of printing!

*To Gordon Craig*
TS. Merton

*12 February 1924*                                    V.C.

R.

L.

I.[3]

My dear Ted, I am so looking forward to the arrival of your Woodcut book;[4] so good of you to send it to me. I hope Angelo may bring it to-morrow – one never knows. I won't breathe a word about it to the Raggios.[5] How are you all? But by the way: before I ask any more questions I must answer one: the Kid's[6] address is *11 Apple Tree Yard,*

---

[1] Of "Meditations of a Refugee", Max's contribution to *The Book of the Queen's Dolls' House Library*, which was edited by E. V. Lucas and published by Methuen in 1924.

[2] The paperback editions of English books, published in Leipzig.

[3] i.e. Villino Chiaro, Rapallo, Liguria, Italy.          [4] *Woodcuts and Some Words* (1924).

[5] The Villa Raggio, very near Max's Villino, was owned by the Raggio family, but Craig had lived there since 1917. Now he had let it to Frederic Delius and his wife.

[6] Nickname of the painter William Nicholson.

*York Street, St James's, London, S.W.* I do hope the manual labourers of Genoa have not gone on making errors over your model, and that all has gone smoothly and well lately, and that Lear is well on his way to Wembley,[1] and that you all like Genoa and your special restaurant as much as ever, and as much as I *don't* like Genoa but *do* like the idea of your special restaurant.

Florence is very well, and so am I – though I have had a bad cold, and have spent several days in bed so as to get rid of it, and feel rather strange on my hind-legs, and rather *miss* recumbency and hot-water-bottles and chicken-broth and old volumes of *Punch.*

We have been seeing the Deliuses[2] (Deliuses looks wrong. How about the Delii? More classical; but not grammatical. How about Delius and Delia? *That's* more like it. It's dogged as does it. Trust the conscientious old literary hand to get there at last) from time to time, both at your house and at ours; and we find them both very sympathetic indeed. Poor fellow, it must be appalling for him to be so frail and dependent physically; but his *mind* is very good and fresh and free; and it is so essentially an *artist's* mind, of the kind that you and I like; the mind of a not unworthy tenant of the Villa Raggio. Delia is a Dane and a dear. Her only fault is an exceeding love of poultry, and a passion for ink-slinging. Your ceilings, your floors, the hangings on your walls, your books too, are splashed all over with huge jets and spurts and arabesques of ink – ink of the best quality; but still, ink. And your hens and your cock have become quite domesticated now, spending the whole day, as they do, in the drawing-room, and retiring at sunset to roost in the bedrooms. I don't think birds ought to be so domesticated as all that. Yours look very drowsy and ill. They have moulted most of their feathers; they are suffering from the pip; their eggs are all addled; they are altogether in a bad way. And besides, they are black with ink. Mrs Ted will be shocked when she sees them. So will Nellie and Master Ted.[3] So will you. They teach a great lesson: Never Let a House.

Florence and I wished more than ever yesterday that you were here. It was the day of the Fair in Rapallo, and my first outing since my cold. I hardly like to tell you of it, because you will be so envious. Who do

---

[1] A model of Craig's designs for the storm scene in *King Lear*, made by his son Teddy, was shown in the British Empire Exhibition at Wembley in 1924.

[2] Frederick Delius, the composer (1862–1934), was by now paralysed and blind.

[3] The violinist Elena (Nellie) Meo and Craig had two children, whom they confusingly named Ted and Nellie.

you think was there? Salvini, of all people.[1] The report of his death had been (as I suspected at the time) a put-up thing. The dear old man has been living in retirement on a farm near here. Yesterday was *his* first outing too. He was instantly recognised in the Piazza, and the enthusiasm was immense – *Evviva il Maestro*, etc. I am not ashamed to confess that there were tears in my eyes at sight of the dear old man bowing and waving his hat. He called for a board and a couple of trestles, and gave a magnificent performance of *Otello*. Talk of the Commedia dell'Arte! My boy, it was IT! He wasn't quite word-perfect; but Florence prompted him. And the company that he had recruited on the spur of the moment was really quite passable, in an improvising sort of way. Angelo, the postman, gave a spirited and manly interpretation of Iago; and Miss Raggio, though obviously suffering from nervousness, gave great promise in the role of Desdemona. We shall watch with interest the career of a young actress who etc. etc.

Love to all from Florence and   MAX

P.S. I send a typewritten page. Would you *really* care to have those nonsense verses in *The Mask*? They are so very unworthy, and might harm the publication, if they were incorporated in the usual way. I have therefore made a little prologue and epilogue, taking the blame off you, as it were, and on to "M.B." But even so . . . ? What do you think?[2]

## To the Rev. C. Williamson[3]
### MS. Bancroft
*July 1924*                                                    [*Villino Chiaro*]
[*on first blank page of Max's* Seven Men]

Reverend Sir, I cannot help wondering what your Bishop would say if he knew that you had sent to a man who *has not the pleasure of knowing you* a copy of a book by that man, "thanking him in anticipation" for signing it, for wrapping it up in brown paper, tying it with string,

---

[1] Tommaso Salvini, the great Italian actor, famous for his portrayal of Othello, was born in 1830 and died in 1915. This scene is Max's idea of what ought to have happened.

[2] "The Characters of Shakespeare", eight stanzas with prologue and epilogue, appeared in Craig's magazine *The Mask* in July 1924. Reprinted in *Max in Verse* (1963).

[3] I like to believe, and feel pretty sure, that this was the Rev. Charles David Robertson Williamson (1853–1943), known to his friends as Chat. Bosom-friend at Eton of the second Lord Esher, who protected him for the rest of his life. He was for a short time a Roman Catholic priest, later he dallied with gondoliers in Venice, and finally retired to his home in Perthshire. He was interested in books and may well have sent this one to Max.

addressing it, and taking it to the post-office, and posting it. What reason had you to suppose I should be so idiotically good-natured?

It appears that, with or without reason, you were right. I sign the book and send it back to you, with such Christian charity as I can muster.          Yours faithfully   MAX BEERBOHM

[on half-title]

For dear old C. Williamson – my companion in many a madcap escapade, and my accomplice in more than one rather shady transaction, in the sad bad glad mad days before he took Holy Orders.          MAX

[on verso of half-title]

P.S. I have just noticed, Reverend Sir, that the pages of this book are uncut. I do hope this fact is a sign that you have not read me at all, and *not* a sign that you are one of those appalling book-snobs who do their reading through the circulating libraries and *buy* books to keep them in such state as is most attractive to "the Trade" hereafter – "unopened edges" and the like.

I am about to cut two or three pages with my finger, so as to render your copy less exquisitely valuable.

P.P.S. I am delighted to find, on further scrutiny, that this copy is one of the "second impression" and therefore of no bibliopolic value in any case. My delight is

[on title-page]

based of course on the hypothesis that you *are* a book-snob. If you are just a simple Boeotian *author*-snob (though that is bad enough), I humbly apologise.          M.B.

[on verso of title-page]

I remember hearing, many years ago, that in the English countryside any tramp who was well-received at a house left on the gate-post of that house a cabalistic sign in chalk, whereby all subsequent tramps knew that this was a "good" house.

If you are "in with" collectors of a kind akin to your own, will you, please, warn them that any books of mine that they may send me will

[on Contents page]

be promptly chucked into the Mediterranean, where they can be dived for – or not – according to choice?          M.B.

150

# To Jessie Conrad[1]
## TS. Merton

*6 August 1924*                                               *Villino Chiaro*

Dear Mrs Conrad, I hope I am not wrong in writing to you. We did meet once – many years ago, at the Rothensteins', and I had the pleasure of sitting next to you at dinner; you may not remember this, but I take it as a reason for writing – not to offer you my sympathy in your sorrow (for of what use is sympathy, even from one's dearest friends, in anything that really matters?), but just to say how much I myself am grieving at the death of the illustrious and wondrous Joseph Conrad. I knew him so little – and yet I seemed to myself to know him so well, through his books, through thinking about him much, as every reader of his books must have thought about *him*, and through the extremely strong effect that his personal presence had upon me when I saw him.

Our meetings were only three in all. The last was a few months ago, in Theodore Byard's room at the office of the firm of Heinemann. He looked so well in health; he was so vivacious; he was so immensely courteous (he always had lovely manners: everybody was agreed about that!). I greatly valued the good luck of seeing him just by chance on a chance visit to England, and have cherished the memory of that meeting with a man of great genius whom the world had for many years neglected, whom the world (in its stupid but decent way) had at last made much of, and who (fundamentally sad though I suppose him to have been, like most men of genius) was pleased a little – ironically pleased, but genuinely pleased – by the humdrum worldly success that had overtaken him.

Dear Mrs Conrad, I think you must have been pleased by that, too, for his sake – and he for yours. You must have been glad that his greatness was at last recognised so fully.

I do not know what writings Conrad may have left behind him. Whatever posthumous work of his there may be, and however beautiful it may be, it will not make up to me for the knowledge that the noble character and example of Conrad himself are gone from the world – even though, in a sense, they remain.

I hope your sons will accept from one unknown to them the vain sympathy that I do after all venture to offer; and I am sincerely yours

MAX BEERBOHM

---

[1] Widow of the novelist Joseph Conrad, who died on 3 August 1924.

## To the Speaker of the House of Commons
MS. Texas

*14 March 1925*                                        *Villino Chiaro*

Sir, I write with great diffidence, to ask a favour which you may not be inclined to grant.

I will explain myself as briefly as possible.

I am a caricaturist; and once in every two years I have an exhibition of caricatures in London; and am having an exhibition there soon after Easter. And, with a view to that, I particularly want to visit the House of Commons and set eyes on some Members who have become illustrious since last I was there.

I wonder whether you would be willing to say something to the Serjeant-at-Arms whereby I could have a seat under the Gallery on Monday, the 23rd instant, or Tuesday the 24th? And also whether I could have a card enabling me to stand around for an hour or so in the Central Lobby?

Let me say that I am a person of respectable appearance and deportment, and that I do not want to "make sketches": I do my drawings from memory only.

If your Secretary would send me a Yea or Nay reply, I should be greatly obliged.

My address will be – *not* the above address, but

40 Upper Berkeley Street

Portman Square

London W 1

I am, Sir, Your obedient servant   MAX BEERBOHM

P.S. My reason for asking to be *under* the Gallery is that elsewhere one sees only crowns of heads, *plus* boots, and thus one is greatly misguided as to the senators' true appearances.

And my reason for troubling you, Sir, instead of some senatorial friend, is that the senatorial friend would feel compelled to ask me to a meal, and that I should feel compelled to accept, and that my visit to London will be of a "rushing and professional" kind, without proper margin for conviviality.                                        M.B.

## To Mrs John Lane[1]
### MS. Bristol

*15 March* [*1925*]                                    *Villino Chiaro*

My dear Mrs Lane, The news of the death of your husband was a great
shock and grief to me. I had had no idea that he was unwell – and had
had a charming letter from him quite recently. I offer you my deep
sympathy; though I know how poor an offering sympathy must be to
one who has suffered so grievous a loss. You have at least the memory
of all the great happiness that you brought into his life. He had always
seemed to me a very happy man; but after he met you, and thence-
forward, my impression was one of far greater happiness still.

   I shall always remember with gratitude his very many acts of kindness
to me – including his kindness in, as it were, "discovering" me when I
was an undergraduate at Oxford. It was he (and, a little later, Aubrey
Beardsley) who first urged me to become a writer. And I fancy I am but
one of many whom his acute instinct thus helped. Believe me, dear Mrs
Lane                               Yours very sincerely   MAX BEERBOHM


## To Edmund Gosse
### MS. Princeton

*30 July 1925*                                    *Villino Chiaro*

My dear Gosse, Heinemann's firm will be publishing this Autumn, if
all's well, a book of reproductions of the caricatures that were shewn at
the Leicester Galleries this year.[2] Would you be displeased at the idea
of this being dedicated to you? Glance, please, at the three pages of
type-writing that I enclose. Of these I am sending a duplicate to Bedford
Street. If you would rather *not* have the dedication, would you please
send a prompt *No* to Bedford Street? – and the typescript shall be as
though it never had been typed. Don't bother to send a *Yes* if (as of
course I am greatly hoping) my idea isn't repugnant.

   I enclose also four little pages of manuscript. In your bedroom last
spring you showed me the *Christmas Garland* as one of your bedside
books, and I was greatly pleased.

   About three years ago I too was reading that volume, and it struck
me that in the parody of Henry James there was little or nothing of the

[1] Annie E. Lane (*née* Eichberg), widow of the publisher, who died on 2 February 1925.
[2] *Observations* (1925).

great dark glow of the later manner. I hold, with you, stern views on the folly of re-writing anything that one wrote in the past. But, since H.J. himself so unaccountably indulged in the folly, surely the humble and loving parodist of him might follow in his misdirected footsteps.

At the back of the upper edge of each page you will see an unpleasant streak of brownish-yellow. This is glue. Moisten slightly with water and attach to upper edge of printed volume – page 9 of manuscript over page 9 of print, etcetera. (See Beerbohm's Hints to Bibliophiles.)[1]

To Lady Gosse,[2] to you, and to you all, affectionate greetings, in which my wife joins me.                                                         MAX

## To Edmund Gosse[3]

*18 July 1925*                                                          *Rapallo*

My dear Gosse, How many books, I wonder, have in the course of the years been dedicated to you? You must have lost count long ago. Here is a sum that could be worked out more easily: How many have *not* been dedicated to you?

The vastness of the number of authors' offerings upon your altar, though it gives the statistician pause, presents no problem at all to the seeker for reasons. Fecund though you were from the outset of your career, your own work never blunted the keen edge of your interest in the works of your coaevals; and as years passed, and men younger than yourself began to be writers, the beginnings and continuings of these younger men, and then again of men younger than these, never were without the sympathy of your eager nature; and the kindness of your pats upon young backs seemed but to be enhanced by such words of warning as you might at the same time whisper into young ears. Encouragement, with guidance thrown in – what more can the young heart need? No wonder that by throng after throng of writers have dedications been flutteringly thrust upon you, as I thrust this one.

How was I not long ago in one of those throngs? Little books of mine began to be printed in the 'nineties, and straightway you sustained and comforted me, nor did you cease to do so thereafter. I should like to give you chapter and verse, but this letter is itself the sort of thing that

[1] On 4 August 1925 Gosse wrote thanking for the extra passages and saying he had stuck them in as instructed. The volume is now at Princeton.

[2] Gosse's knighthood had been announced in January 1925.

[3] This letter was printed as the dedication of *Observations* (1925). Text from there.

154

gets into print, and I don't want to be frowned on as a braggart by the casual reader. Perhaps I always felt, by the same token, that a dedication to you would savour of braggadocio. But I think the great restraining influence has been that you must be so sick of dedications.

"Then why," you would ask if you were less courteous, "why this last straw?" And my answer would be that this is a new kind of straw. A book of caricatures has never, I believe, been added to your burden. Such a book am I handling. If you went to the Leicester Galleries last April, you will already be somewhat familiar with the contents of it. These are unworthy of you; but not of me: they are the best I can do; and to you I inscribe them.

Of course you are among them. It seems that I cannot ever do a set of drawings without introducing you into it. Time has hallowed for me this disability, and yet I do not quite understand why I have it. I grant you that the best subject for a caricaturist is someone whom he reveres. Only by reverence can he have that happy boyish sense of irreverence which is such a spur to his talent. But the spur is sharper, more conducive to caracolings, when the revered personage is of the over-serious sort – the sort that would not at all understand the workings of the caricaturist's poor dear little mind – and would probably omit the second of these three epithets. That epithet you would never omit. Those workings never have puzzled you for one instant. For there has ever been in you, as your friends can all testify, and as those who know and love you through your works alone can testify also, an admixture of levity and devilry that sometimes almost shocks them – and has always prevented you from being shocked by any caricatures of yourself, or of others, made by your affectionate                                              MAX BEERBOHM

## To E.V. Lucas
MS. Lilly

*16 October 1925*                                                           *Villino Chiaro*

My dear E.V., Life is queer! I was thinking a few days ago – not having thought of him for many years – of old Dr Stedman[1] and of his garden at Godalming. And to-day I am told by the *Times Literary Supplement* that the late Sir A. Methuen[2] was a son of his.

[1] John Buck Stedman (1820–1902). Fellow of the Royal College of Surgeons. Charterhouse is near Godalming.

[2] 1856–1924. Changed his name from Stedman to Methuen in 1899 when he started the publishing firm of Methuen & Co. Made a Baronet in 1916.

Old Stedman looked rather like this –
a fine old Victorian-Aesculapian type
But I remember even more vividly
than him the peaches on the
south wall of his great old garden.

I met Sir Algernon only once,
some twenty years ago, and with
no inkling of his relationship. Had
I had any such inkling, I should
have inferred (though doubtless
he was a genial creature to all who
knew him well) that he had been
reared on the north wall.

How are you, dear E.V.?

Yours ever    MAX BEERBOHM


*To Esther Sutro*[1]

*October 1925*                    [*Villino Chiaro*]

Dear Esther S. – I'm in distress,
It's very sad! My taste is bad.
The men that boost the work of Proust
(Those scholars and those Gentlemen,
Those erudite and splendid men,
Of whom the chief is Scott Moncrieff)
All leave me cold. Perhaps I'm old?
"The reason why, I cannot tell
I do not like thee, Doctor Fell ... "
But *why* not like the late Marcel? ...
Perhaps he wrote not very well?
This, *bien entendu*, cannot be,
He was a Prince of Paragons
(As undergraduates all agree –
Or did in nineteen-twenty-three –
With full concurrence of the Dons).

[1] Wife of Alfred Sutro. She had lent Max a copy of C. K. Scott Moncrieff's English version (1922) of Proust's *Du Côté de Chez Swann*. Text from *Celebrities and Simple Souls* by Alfred Sutro (1933).

I only know that all his Swanns
Are now, as ever, geese to me.
Pity the blindness of poor M.B.!
P.S. How sad that I'm alive!
October Nineteen-twenty-five.

## *To Henry Arthur Jones*[1]

*14 May 1926*                                                   *Villino Chiaro*

My dear Henry Arthur, I have been thinking of you much during the past horrible week or so[2] – and now I write to say how glad I am with you that England has done well. I suppose there may be difficulties yet; but they won't matter so much: the long-impending big fight has been fought and won. England has all sorts of faults – dullnesses, stupidities, heavy frivolities, constantly pointed out by you. But in politics somehow she always is – somehow slowly, dully, but splendidly – all right. I have often thought, in reading your brilliant and violent rebukes of her, that you hadn't quite as much faith in her as she deserves. You didn't overstate her dangers; but I felt that you believed not quite enough in her power to meet these and deal with these successfully in her own fumbling and muzzy way, by her own dim (damnably dim, you would say) lights. You are a die-hard, and she is a die-soft. She says mildly, "No violence, pray! I quite see your points of view, dear gentlemen all! I'm full of faults. Really I rather doubt whether I deserve to survive. Yet I hope, I even intend, to do so" ... and she *does* – the dear old thing! *Brava, bravissima*, dear silly old thing!

Dear Henry Arthur, I know how happy you are feeling – and I write to add my happiness to yours. The past week has made for my wife and me 'a goblin of the sun', and the big roses in our small garden looked horrible. In writing to me at about Christmas-time, you said I did well to be out here, because of all the trouble brewing in England. But really out here, in this alien golden clime, one feels more acutely any dangers to England. What a relief it was to us both, my wife and me, when, early in 1915, we settled down into England! And Civil War is of course much more distressing to the heart and to the imagination than war with

[1] Prolific dramatist (1851–1929). Text from *The Life and Letters of Henry Arthur Jones* by [his daughter] Doris Arthur Jones (1930).

[2] The General Strike, which lasted from 3 to 13 May 1926.

157

any number of more or less natural enemies. And oh, what paeans our hearts sing that the wretched affair is, to all intents and purposes, over – and that the right side has won.

I think King George's Message to the people very finely composed. I read it with emotion. Had you been he, the message would have been still finer, and I should have read it with still greater emotion. But it wouldn't have been so exactly right for the occasion. For the purpose of interpreting the deepest feelings of the British People, I back Hanover against Bucks every time! – though I sometimes wish Hanover had a little of Bucks's sparkle, all the same.[1]

Your affectionate MAX BEERBOHM

P.S. I never can remember the Christian or surname of anybody I haven't met constantly. Thus I forget those of the charming gifted young man who was my fellow-guest when I dined with you last May at the Athenaeum. Otherwise I would ask you to give him my kindest regards. The name of Doris does not escape me. And to her I send my love.

P.P.S. Old friendship – there's nothing very much better than that. I am reminded of this truism by my P.S. about dining with you last May at the Athenaeum. I have my faults (like England), but am sensitive to impressions and retentive of these. I do so well remember being ushered in by a waiter to that Writing-Room to the right of the hall. Up from a table rises H.A., and quickly advances, with that forward thrust of the head (that I have so often caricatured), and looking not a day older, though it was long since I had met him; and with just the same kind eager look in his eyes. And, as we shook hands, he placed his left hand over my right hand – and then I placed my left hand over *his*, in glad response.

Whatever happens to the world, things of this kind will go on. Life will always have dear good moments. M.B.

### To Henry Arthur Jones[1]

*8 August 1926* *Villino Chiaro*

My dear Henry Arthur, You had no business to write to me. I resented your letter very much. It seemed to me an impudent defiance of all the

[1] Jones was born and educated in Buckinghamshire.

[2] Text source as for previous letter.

The Shadow of Henry Irving

159

laws of convalescence. However, you have always been pugnacious, and have now reached an age when you are past all hope of reformation: doctors and daughters and nurses can but bow their heads beneath your indomitable will and place the inkpot beside the cup of chicken broth. And of course – in spite of all my disapproval – I was immensely glad to behold the Henrico-Arthurian calligraphy, and very grateful, and much touched – touched by your kindness in thanking me for that little sketch of Irving.[1] Doris (whom, please, thank from me for her delightful accompanying letter) said that you would like to use the sketch as an illustration in the course of your study of Irving. And of course it doesn't need saying that I should be very proud of seeing that sketch in such a setting. I am so glad it appealed to you. I think it *has* caught something of the subject – the Cabotin-turned-Cardinal as it were. Forgive this cheap alliteration! But you are not to tell me that you forgive it. At most, you are to dip a clean pen in the chicken-broth and write 'I forgive you' in the air. Sympathetic aerial rays will waft the message to this address. As to G.B.S., I entirely understand your feelings about his vagaries. It is very queer that a man should be so gifted as he is (in his own particular line nobody has been so gifted, I think, since Voltaire) and so liable to make a fool of himself. I never read anything of his without wishing that he had never been born *and* hoping that he will live to a very ripe old age! One of the reasons is that he, like you, is entirely free from any kind of malice. That is one of his great points. And that is why you would, I am sure, be very willing to shake hands with the demon!

Love to Doris and to all your house.

From your affectionate  MAX BEERBOHM

## To Earl E. Fisk
MS. Yale

*14 August 1926*                                               *Villino Chiaro*

My dear Mr Fisk, I am sorry to seem churlish, but – that story which you mention is a thing which I want to have in my next volume of reprinted things. And I think the author has the first call on it. And you, I am sure, will agree with him. And here he is, looking very churlish, no doubt, at first sight, but only at *first* sight, and inwardly feeling most grateful for your very pleasant letter, and being

very truly yours  MAX BEERBOHM

[1] It appeared as frontispiece to Jones's posthumously published book *The Shadow of Henry Irving* (1931). Here reproduced on page 159.

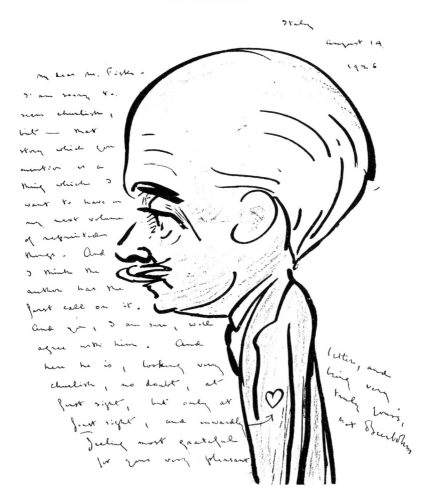

# To A.B. Walkley

MS. Virginia

*18 September 1926*                                                    *Villino Chiaro*

My dear A.B.W., This is just a line of gladness to greet you as soon as
you are reconvalescent. At the moment of its being written it is to say
how very sorry I was this morning to learn from *The Times* that you
had suffered "a relapse," and how surprised as well as sorry I was: sorry,
as an old friend with many memories of our friendship and of your
kindness through the years; and surprised as a constant reader who,
during the past few weeks, had been thinking as he read *The Times*,
"Why, he's better than ever! *Every* writer ought to fall ill! Convalescence
makes the best better!"

Reconvalesce quickly, please, dear old friend. Charles Lamb, at your
bedside, is sentimentally patient. He enjoys his sympathy with you. But
Hazlitt, whom you prefer to him, wants you to be up and doing – down
and gliding again (or, as he would prefer, *racing*) in that bath-chair
which you have made as attractive to the reader as Shakespeare made
Cleopatra's barge.

What a nuisance and curse one's manner-for-print is when one is
writing a letter! Would that I could write in the simple straightforward
"awfully-sorry" strain which would express my feelings so much more
accurately! However, no matter: you will leave wide margins around the
dreadfully literary lines. (Oh dear, oh dear! There I am, at it again!)

All best regards to Mrs Walkley, and all sympathy with her in the
anxious time she must have had.[1]                                    Yours ever   MAX

P.S. I claim a long precedence of you in the discovery of the charm of
bath-chairs. At Folkestone, when I was nine or ten years old (1881 or
1882), a relative gave me half-a-crown, and I (bless my adventurous
little boyish heart!) spent this on an hour's ride to and fro along the
Lees. And well do I remember the joy and pride of that great adventure.

---

[1] Walkley died on 7 October 1926.

## To Bohun Lynch
MS. Texas

*3 December 1926* *Villino Chiaro*

Well, my dear Jack, it is a most lovely book – inside *and* out.[1] I attribute to you the design on the side-covers: very strong and very arresting and holding, and it is with difficulty that I escape to the back-cover, where again I attribute to you the form and hue and typography of the *label* – a model to all in these days when publishers slap on any old scrap of chopped-off paper with a headline or two across it.

But of course the *inside* is what I like best. I've no doubt the book is the best book about caricature that has been written – since it is the only one that has been written by a caricaturist; and that caricaturist yourself. It is a solid, acute, sensitive, amusing, *knowing* work from first to last. And the only fault that I have to find with it is that in proportion to its length, and according to its scope, there is much too much about *me* in it. I seem to have become to you what Charles I's head was to Mr Dick![2] This is a great thing for *me*, but it makes a bulge in the otherwise impeccable form of your book; and not only one big bulge, but various little bulges: you can't praise Kapp or Quiz[3] without scolding them for not having caricatured me well, and without implying heartfelt wishes that they were both of them me! And in the great bulge itself you actually consider me "under seven heads" – every one of them a King Charles's!

The reproductions are beautifully chosen. I wish the "Petit-Coblenz" were among them. Your description of it makes my mouth water.

The moral that I draw from the book is that you and I and the rest of us caricaturists ought to be glad to have been born at about the time when we were. There seems to have been nothing in the way of caricature till towards the end of the eighteenth century: merely meaningless exaggerations of this or that deformity. The world, having got on so well without caricature during all those other centuries, is not likely to find caricature essential to its future happiness. Other mushrooms will spring up to take its place. But not in our time, O Lord!

You had given me hopes, when you were here, that you would be here again; but these weren't fulfilled – and will be fulfilled soon, I hope, dear friend.

[1] Lynch's *A History of Caricature* (1926).

[2] In *David Copperfield*.

[3] Edmond X. Kapp (1890–1978) and Powys Evans (1899–1982), caricaturists.

I hope – but I have used the word hope twice in the foregoing paragraph, so I don't hope but trust – that all your private affairs are going smoothly and well?

Your affectionate and grateful   "H.M.M.B."[1]


## To Wilfred Partington[2]
MS. Lilly

*Easter Sunday 1927*                                      *Villino Chiaro*

Dear Mr Partington, Please, like a good kind Editor, leave my name out of the forthcoming Record of Collectors. I don't collect books, nor prints, nor anything.

There seems to be a vague but widespread impression that I do collect things. And thus my life is a burden to me by reason of the torrents and torrents of catalogues that come pouring from England into this remote small house of mine. I conceive that if my name were on your Record these floods would swell yet higher. And that would be the end of me. And (for I have already said that you are good and kind) I am sure you don't desire me to cease so soon and so abruptly.

Yours truly   MAX BEERBOHM


## To Virginia Woolf
MS. Princeton

*30 December 1927*                                       *Villino Chiaro*

Dear Virginia Woolf, I can't help this familiarity: I seem to know you so well, from *The Common Reader*,[3] a book which I have read twice, and have often dipped into since, and rate above any modern book of criticism (rating it thus quite soberly, all unconfused by your habit of going out of your way to be nice about my essays!). You certainly are very like your Father.[4] With great differences, of course. What I mean is that if he had been a "Georgian" and a woman, just so would he have written.

[1] i.e. His Majesty Max Beerbohm.

[2] Author and journalist (1888–1955). Editor of the *Bookman's Journal* 1919–31.

[3] Published 1925.

[4] Leslie Stephen (1832–1904), critic, biographer, mountaineer and philosopher. Editor of the *Cornhill* and of the first twenty-six volumes of the *Dictionary of National Biography*. Knighted 1902.

*Mr Bennett and Mrs Brown*[1] is new to me – though it appears to be three years old. A friend has just sent it to me. And now I seem to know you better than ever – by reason of the first-person-singular, and of the utterance to the seeing hearers at Cambridge instead of to Great Britain and the Dominions Overseas. Was ever an audience handled with a more winning tact? or a case put more skilfully? In this lecture your powers shine out to me at their very best. I wish I had been there. Retrospectively, in the spirit, I *was* there.

I wish you were as conscious of me and the likes of me – as indulgent to the weakness of our flesh and the dulness of our spirit – in your novels as you are in your criticisms. In your novels you are so hard on us common readers. You seem to forget us and to think only of your theme and your method. Your novels beat me – black and blue. I retire howling, aching, sore; full, moreover, of an acute sense of disgrace. I return later, I re-submit myself to the discipline. No use: I am carried out half-dead. Of course I admire your creative work immensely – but only in a bemused and miserable manner. I don't really, insidious though you are, believe in your Cambridge argument that a new spirit exacts a new method. There seems to me to be only one good method of narrative – Homer's and Thackeray's method, and Tolstoi's, and Tom's, Dick's, Chaucer's, Maupassant's, and Harry's; all of them very different men spiritually, and employing the method in very different ways, but not imagining that a new method is needful, or couldn't be unhelpful, and wouldn't certainly play the deuce and all, in its own time, and might by dint of various alterations and improvements become a sure and shining instrument in the hands of the Hereafter. You may be right in thinking that we are "on the verge of one of the great ages of English Literature". I am quite unqualified to contradict. But my theory of the future is the same as the second Mrs Tanqueray's[2] (you are too Georgian to have heard of her; and she had great faults; but she had quite sound views on the future); and I believe that ten years hence and a hundred years hence fictional narrative will be thriving only on the old method about which I have been so stodgy and so longsome instead of merely thanking you from my heart, as I set out to do, for the enormous amount of pleasure that I have had from your penetrating judgments and your

[1] A paper read to the Heretics at Cambridge on 18 May 1924, published as a pamphlet 1924, reprinted in *The Captain's Death Bed* (1950).

[2] *The Second Mrs Tanqueray* by A.W. Pinero, first produced in 1893 with Mrs Patrick Campbell in the title-role. In the last act she says: "I believe the future is only the past again, entered through another gate."

sensibility and your erudition and your wit and all the other fine things in your equipment.

Thanking you from the aforesaid heart for these, I am

Yours sincerely   MAX BEERBOHM

P.S. Was Lord Macaulay *always* wrong? Will posterity agree with you that Lytton Strachey is always right?

Aren't you just a trifle over-loyal to this particular era?

I daresay posterity will agree with me that Lytton Strachey's prose is, *on the whole*, the finest English prose that has been written. Of course somebody may in the meantime write a still finer, or one as fine. But I doubt that (though I'm not in most things a great enthusiast). I think that Addison or Sir Thomas Browne or Ruskin or someone or another would already have done the trick if it were doable. As for his being less direct and forcible than Lord M., is this really due to some mysterious strategic exertions that he has had to make because of the generation he was born into? When you go to the Zoological Gardens and see there a gazelle or an antelope, do you say to Dr Chalmers Mitchell,[1] "This animal would have been, in happier circumstances, a buffalo"? Surely you have given overmuch scope to your subtlety. Lytton Strachey would have been an ironist in any period – or have been somebody else.

But here I am, argufying again. I will no more. Rest your eyes on the lovely lower half of this page[2]

## Virginia Woolf to Max
### TS. Merton

*29 January 1928*                    *52 Tavistock Square, London, W.C.1*

Dear Mr Beerbohm, Your letter reached me (at last) just as I was starting for Hardy's funeral. I had a ticket as my father's daughter. When I read your letter, I said to my husband "Now that Mr Beerbohm has praised me I have a right to half a seat on my own account."

This mood of presumption was struck down instantly. I had to go to bed for a week. Or was it the chill and the thrill of the touch of an

---

[1] Peter Chalmers Mitchell (1864–1945). Secretary to the Zoological Society of London 1903–35. Knighted 1929.

[2] Which is blank, as is the page overleaf.

immortal hand on my shoulder? Aren't you responsible for my week in bed? For you see I look upon you as one, perhaps the only one, who is withdrawn far, far above us, in a serene and cloudless air, imperishable, aloof. And then suddenly you let down a ray from your sky and it rests – behold! – upon me! If you knew how I had pored over your essays – how they fill me with marvel – how I can't conceive what it would be like to write as you do! – This is sober truth: – but I shan't attempt to say how much pleasure your letter gave me.

Can I put up any defence, though, against your most kindly criticisms? I'm afraid it's not a good one; it is simply that I can't write other than I do. I admit that when I spoke to the undergraduates I made up a plausible theory about the spirit of the age; but these theories are made after the art is done: I say to myself (as I might say about anybody's book) what made the poor woman write like that? And then I sit down and concoct something about life or literature; whereas the truth is I write these books which bruise you black and blue – you won't believe it, but so it is – simply to amuse myself. I don't defend them; I don't read them; as for expecting you to read them, the thought makes me shudder.

But I believe I could say a word in favour of freaks in general. After all, there is *Tristram Shandy*, *Gryll Grange*,[1] *Zuleika Dobson*: all my favourite works: and none of them quite in the Tom, Dick, and Chaucer, Thackeray, Harry, Homer tradition, are they? Besides, living, as you do being immortal, with the immortals, you can't measure quite the horror of rubbing shoulders daily (not physically, but mentally) with Arnold Bennett, Wells, or Galsworthy. If the tradition breeds them, with all their innumerable virtues, then to my thinking, the tradition had better be snuffed out and extinct. Let us stop writing novels altogether.

This brings me to the prayer which Lytton Strachey and I put up over the fire the other night when I read him your letter: that Mr Beerbohm should continue to write essays. We feel it to be the duty you owe us: and on that solemn note I will close.

But I can't tell, and shan't attempt to tell you, what an exhilaration it gives me to think that any word I have written has pleased you.

Yours very sincerely   VIRGINIA WOOLF

P.S. You mention my father. I am much pleased and interested that you find a likeness between us. Did you, I wonder, meet him ever, in the flesh?

[1] By Thomas Love Peacock (1861).

## To Florence Hardy[1]
MS. Yale

*14 January 1928*                                          *Villino Chiaro*

My dear Mrs Hardy, It is with great sorrow that I have just read of the death of that illustrious and beloved man. Sympathy, in your loss of him, cannot be of much avail; and on the other hand you do not need any reminder of all that you did to make happy the later years of his great life.

My wife and I have constantly talked to each other about you both – about our memories of the day when we came over from Netherton, and of the later day when you yourselves came there. My own memories of your husband go further back, back to old days at the Savile Club, at the Gosses', and so on. But dear though those memories are – memories of his youthfulness and peculiar modesty and unlikeness to anybody but himself – memories of his very beautiful manners, manners that one admired all the more because something in his eyes betrayed that his thoughts were perhaps a-roving to other and higher matters of his own – the last two memories are the dearest. It was wonderful to see, in his old age, his youthfulness merely sublimified, and his idiosyncrasies undimmed and more loveable than ever.

I am yours, dear Mrs Hardy, most sincerely    MAX BEERBOHM

## To H. A. L. Fisher[2]
MS. Bodley

*14 January 1928*                                          *Villino Chiaro*

Dear Mr Fisher, I did once have the honour of meeting you. It was only for a few moments, and many years ago; but it was under the auspices of a man whom I know that you like, Will Rothenstein, and thus I feel myself free to write and offer to you my very grateful thanks for what you have said about the political novels of Anthony Trollope. Hitherto the one and only authoritative notice of them known to me

[1] Her husband Thomas Hardy had died on 11 January 1928.

[2] Historian (1865–1940). Warden of New College, Oxford, from 1925. His essay "The Political Novel", which appeared in the January 1928 issue of the *Cornhill Magazine*, was mostly about Disraeli, but also gave generous praise to Trollope.

had been Henry James's in *Partial Portraits*.[1] And against the authority of that notice my breast rebelled hotly when, some twelve years ago, I read the lovely trilogy itself.[2] I marvelled that H.J., whose critical sense was so keen, and whose power of detaching himself from his own prejudices, whenever he set out to estimate the work of good writers, was so salient and admirable, could have allowed himself to indulge in nonsense about "the dull, impersonal rumble of the mill-wheel". H.J. knew and cared nothing about English politics. But neither did he know or care anything about the Church of England. Why should he have perceived the reality and beauty of Barchester according to St Anthony, and not those of St Stephen's equally? I gave the problem up, with much irritation against H.J. and indignation on behalf of A.T. But now all's well. *Enfin vint* H.A.L.F., after all these years, and the right canon has been promulgated and established.

A.T. is being "extensively" republished nowadays. I expect that "Planty Pal"[3] and his circle will now, by means of you, come within the rubric of what publishers think marketable. I don't possess the books – and I've no memory for names. I wish you had *named* a few more of the well-remembered personages. "The Duke of Omnium" is a name that one would fain suppress and forget. And "Gatherum Castle" – what dismal facetiousness! And yet how little such awful lapses matter *if* the novelist is a good and great one! How instantly the illusion of reality returns to the reader after he has felt that the whole show has been given away beyond redemption! Genius is that which can afford to bedevil itself without the slightest injury. (See Shakespeare and others, *passim*.) But where was I in this rambling screed? I was going to say that I wished you had paid a tribute to the *old* Duke – who, though he is only slightly done – only a bust or (say) a bas-relief – is to me as real as the Phidian-full-length Planty Pal. And I was going to say that I wished you had named P.P.'s worldly young secretary – a perfect sketch – Reggie Barrington, perhaps, the name was.[4] And the two wirepullers – who seemed to me so much more soberly "convincing"

---

[1] Published in 1888. In it James wrote that Trollope "took a suicidal satisfaction in reminding the reader that the story he was telling was only, after all, a make-believe", and declared "His political novels are distinctly dull, and I confess I have not been able to read them".

[2] Fisher refers to the political novels as a trilogy – *Phineas Finn*, *Phineas Redux* and *The Prime Minister*, whereas the series also contained *Can You Forgive Her?*, *The Eustace Diamonds*, and *The Duke's Children*.

[3] Nickname of Plantagenet Palliser in Trollope's political novels.

[4] Barrington Earle.

than Taper and Tadpole.[1] And the *arriviste* politician who was so deservedly murdered in Lansdowne Passage, on his way home from the Cosmopolitan Club.[2] Talking of topography: you know of course which of those three little tiny stuccoed and hanging-balconied houses in northern Park Lane was Madame Max Goesler's – outside which the small brown brougham of the old Duke was so often seen standing. It was the middle one.

Have you ever read *The Eustace Diamonds*? *I* think that in some ways it was the very best of all our beloved's novels. But nobody seems to know it. Possibly *you* don't. The story is much more of a *story* than one finds in the other books. It is close-knit and exciting. And Lizzie Eustace seems to me very worthy to walk arm-in-arm with Becky Sharp. Indeed, I'm not sure that she can't give Becky points in subtlety of delineation by the novelist. For she is *partly* a fool, and her adventuressshipness (if you will excuse the word) is thereby the more haunting and amusing. (And the book ends with an epilogue in which there is a sort of formal grace and irony – something rather Mozartian or Watteauesque – quite un-Trollopian. Lady Glencora and our other friends are the epiloguists.) I gave my copy of the book away years ago. Otherwise I would give myself the pleasure of sending it to you on the chance that it were unknown to you.

With many apologies for all this gabble – which is, however, a symptom of genuine gratitude –

I am sincerely yours   MAX BEERBOHM

P.S. When you speak of Disraeli's "fastidious prose" I start violently. I turn pale, I rise from my seat, and I say, with all submission, "Then may a tropical jungle be called fastidious."

P.P.S. Well, yes, of course, there *are* very many perfect sentences there, and even some perfect passages. But oh, the sentences and passages that over-climb them all around! Oh, the rot and rigmarole which are always, as one knows, those of a man of genius, *and* of a man "born in a library," and yet might more appropriately have been written by a sawny[3] born in a book!

---

[1] In Disraeli's *Coningsby*.
[2] Mr Bontsen in *Phineas Redux*.
[3] A fool.

## To Lady Gosse
MS. Brotherton

[*19 May 1928*][1]                                            *Villino Chiaro*

My dear Lady Gosse, I write to offer you my very deepest sympathy, and that of my wife also, in your great sorrow. And Tessa and Sylvia and Philip are equally in my thoughts.

Gosse had always been so wonderfully young, and so splendidly well, too. I had always thought that he was, as it were, invulnerable; and it is hard for me to believe that he is gone. I think of all the happy times I have had, during the past thirty years and more, at Delamere Terrace and at Hanover Terrace; and of all his invariable kindness to me; of his lightness and swiftness; of the clear cadences of his voice, and of the exquisite precision with which the right words always came from his lips so easily; of the glimpses that one got of his great learning; and of the delicate bouts of sheer wild fun that he indulged so much in. To be with him was always an excitement, an exhilarating privilege. I am very grateful for having been allowed to know him.

I remember that in one of Henry James's letters to him, written at a time when you were suffering some sorrow or anxiety, there occurs the phrase "I lay my hand very gently on our friend." And I say to the spirit of Henry James, "So, after all these years, do I".

Dear Lady Gosse, I wish I could say how much I feel.

Your affectionate old friend   MAX BEERBOHM

## To Sir Almeric FitzRoy[2]
TS. B.L.

*July 1928*                                                *Villino Chiaro*

Sir Almeric, This formal mode of address will warn you that you are being addressed by one who has never had the honour of meeting you. And strangers are, I admit, mostly tedious. And I expect that I myself shall be so. But I am emboldened by the fact that my name is not utterly unknown to you; and you are so good as to mention me on page 201 of your published Diary.

[1] For some unknown reason Max clearly dated this letter 19 March 1929. Edmund Gosse died on 16 May 1928, and two days later Max wrote to the editor of the *Sunday Times* regretting that he could not supply a brief obituary tribute.

[2] 1851–1935. Clerk to the Privy Council 1898–1923. His *Memoirs* were published in 1925.

I live here in Italy, rather outside the range of current books; and I am not an "omnivorous" reader; and I am always behindhand in acquaintance with what is worth-while – in devouring what is worth devouring. But when I do find the sort of prey that pleases my palate and nourishes my soul and stomach, then am I all fangs and claws and wildly-revolving eye-balls.

Such prey is your delicate and strong and altogether splendid Diary. Of course in reading it one's mind harks back to a previous Secretary to (I beg your pardon: Clerk of) the Privy Council. This is inevitable; and what is inevitable cannot be unkind. Otherwise one might rather blame oneself for unkindness to Mr Charles Greville.[1] One has always admired him, within bounds, and been grateful to him. He was infinitely industrious, there where he was, at the centre of things: nothing of the kind that he could understand did he let escape him. But how much, after all, *did* he understand? Whiggism is a fine tradition, as you say. But all things are capable of excess. Absence of morbid moisture is a Whig virtue. But morbid dryness is a Whig vice. Greville was a dreadfully dry soul. "Soul" is indeed not a word to use in connexion with him. Greville was a dreadfully dry *stick* I ought to have said. Of course his writing was technically good: very firm and lucid and succinct. His was a Roman pen; and such a pen is a rare possession. But it isn't so rare a possession as *your* pen – which I would describe as Attic. You are "undulant and diverse,"[2] you are sensitive and responsive to all manner of things, and your "style" in writing constantly varies in accordance to the theme that engages you. If one must compare you with an official predecessor, then let the comparison be made not with a Clerk of the Privy Council, but with an Inspector of Schools – Matthew Arnold, whom in many respects, whom in grace and irony and insight for example, you rather closely resemble. You are more full-blooded than he – but that is not a fatal drawback.

I hope, and suppose, that you will bequeath to the British Museum the manuscript of a diary which is of course incomplete in its now published form and is – equally of course – invaluable from the stand-point of future students of the Vict.-Ed.-Geo. era.

But it is not as a dabbler in history that I write to you: it is only as a

[1] 1794–1865. Clerk of the Council 1821–59. His *Memoirs* first appeared in 8 volumes 1874–87. Revised edition, edited by Lytton Strachey and Roger Fulford, 8 volumes, 1938.

[2] "*Certes, c'est un sujet merveilleusement vain, divers et ondoyant, que l'homme*" (Montaigne, *Essais*, book 1, chapter 1).

lover of the English language and of those men who love it and really understand it and are reverent and joyous in the use of it. I write because I wish to thank you most sincerely for the delight that I have had from your never-failing graces and felicities of expression.

I am, Sir Almeric (but I think I have now justified myself in calling you "dear" Sir Almeric),     Yours very truly  MAX BEERBOHM

## *To Gordon Craig*
TS. Merton

*Monday [c. October] 1928*              *Villino Chiaro*

My dear Ted, Mrs Ted and Nellie were here on Saturday – gave us a delightful day of their dear company. And they brought with them such a grand case of that magnificent Pilsener, the birthday present that you devised, but which oughtn't to have been given me before my seventieth-or-so birthday. I thank you from palate, throat, heart and stomach.

And they told us about your mother's will. I always look at the "Wills and Bequests" in *The Times*, but the copy of that journal which contained this will must have missed us at one of the *postes-restantes* of the various towns in which we had been sleeping and waking for a day and a night or two.[1]

Dear Ellen Terry! How cosy and jolly and soothing and warming it must have been for her to know that she – she herself – she who, like most of the open-handed and open-hearted, loveable and loved persons of this world, might have been expected to die in poverty – possessed MORE THAN £20,000! She must have often said to herself, "I've got it! – here under my pillow. How lovely! How odd! And I've gone to a lawyer about it. And it's all for Edie[2] and Ted and Nellie and others of the same sort after them. I *am* so glad." In her last days these thoughts must have been very clear to her in her clouded mind ... Everything in order ...

Such good order – such good wisdom – *brava*, E.T.! Most wills seem to me so stupid. But here was a perfectly just and right one. And Florence and I were both so immensely glad about it. And I didn't fling up my arms *very* high into the air, and didn't utter a *very* loud groan, when I gathered from the two Nellies that you were rather inclined not

[1] Ellen Terry died on 21 July 1928.
[2] Edith, Craig's elder sister. Everyone else spelt her name Edy, but perhaps Max didn't know this.

to take your share of the bequest, for I knew, I felt sure, dear Ted, that even you, with even *your* genius, and consequent lack of wisdom, and excess of impulse to do things for no possible right reason, wouldn't be so wrong-headed as to persist in the notion that had occurred to you. How could you?

But I suppose you *could* do things that aren't conceivable by a person like myself.

And this, dear friend, is why I write to you. I do so want you not to do anything foolish and wrong. I do so want you not to go and spoil the news of an absolutely right will.

It seems that you offered to Edie your share of the income. That was a good brotherly thing to do. But Edie very properly, as I think, said "No". (*Brava*, Edie!)

Your mother wished *you* to have *your* share – didn't want anybody else to have it. She wanted you, as her son, to have it; and (if I have any instinct for what passes through the minds of artists) she also wished to pay money to a man of genius to whom the rest of the world had paid precious little. Why baulk her wish?

I remember that you have once or twice told me that you thought some people had a notion that your mother was in the habit of keeping you supplied with money for current expenses. I myself had never heard anybody saying anything of the sort. But I daresay people here and there may have said it. *What matter?* Surely you aren't going to direct your course by paying attention to what some people may have said to some other people at some time or another? The fact that your mother had so much money to leave is in itself a disproof of any such silly gossip. But even plausible tittle-tattle isn't a thing that one should bother about for one instant, even at an unimportant moment in one's life. And this is an important moment in yours – *isn't it*? Not to have to fret and bother about sevenpences, as I had to until recent years! To be able to spend sevenpence without a thought, as I can now, forking it out of the left-hand waistcoat-pocket almost unconsciously! In my young days this blessing would have been bad for me. But it isn't so now in my later years. I have deserved these sevenpences, and they don't turn my head.

And oh, I do want you to have them too. I want you to share them with me – and not be a donkey, dear Ted!

I don't trust your judgment at all. Though you have often said that I am wise, I don't trust you to be guided at all by me. But I am very anxious that you should be guided by me at this moment – just at *this*

174

*one*: thereafter consider yourself free to do whatever you please – any ridiculous thing whatever.

I am so anxious that I even ask you to wire to me:

Beerbohm, Rapallo, Right

Were I a younger man, I should ask you to go to the trouble and expense of saying Right Oh. But at my age I need only the simple dignified monosyllable.[1]               Yours affectionately   MAX


## *To John Galsworthy*[2]
### TS. Merton

*5 June 1929*                                     *Villino Chiaro*

My dear John, I *am* so glad. And I hope there won't be the usual supplement to the *Gazette*, announcing that you don't want that kind of thing. For this really is something worth having; and I have for several years thought you were precisely *the* person to have it; and I am sure this has been the general opinion among cognoscenti. So don't flout us. I feel that Mrs John is on our side.

And of course don't answer this note; for you must be snowed under – or let us rather say lava'd under – with congratulations. Just tear off the appended form and have it sent to me:

---

Mr Galsworthy's seven Private Secretaries
regret
that they are suffering from writer's cramp.
They hope
to resume work shortly.

---

Ever affectionately   MAX BEERBOHM


[1] Max's concern was needless. Ellen Terry, knowing her son, left his half of her money in trust for his children Nellie and Teddie, their parents Craig and Elena to share the interest equally for their lifetimes. In an undated letter to Max Craig wrote: "I understand entirely the disadvantages of wealth. I only say I would be glad to labour under them!"

[2] Who had just been awarded the Order of Merit.

## To H.R.L. Sheppard[1]
TS. Merton

26 November 1929                                    *Villino Chiaro*

~~Dear Mr Dean~~
My dear Dick Sheppard, It is good of you to have liked me, but you
can't have liked me half as much as I liked and shall always like you and
Mrs Sheppard.

~~I am, dear Mr Dean,~~<br>always<br>Yours/ ~~very truly~~   MAX ~~BEERBOHM~~

P.S. I have only one complaint to make – but that is a grave one. You
radiantly draw one out, as the sun draws out weeds. You make one feel
that one is blossoming like the rose, so long as one is with you. It is only
after one goes away that one realises that one has been gabbling.

Next time there shall be none of that nonsense. I shall insist on
drawing *you* out.


## To Katherine Lyon Mix[2]
MS. Mix

24 June 1930                                         *Villino Chiaro*

The Yellowbook –
That's how you, dear Mrs Mix, pronounce it, isn't it? And that's how
I too pronounce it. But it's the wrong pronunciation.
The Yellow Book is the right one.
*Scene*: Cambridge Street, Pimlico.
*Time*: An afternoon in the late Autumn of 1893.
*Persons*: Aubrey Beardsley and myself.
A.B. "How are you? Sit down! Most exciting! John Lane wants to
bring out a Quarterly – Writings and Drawings – Henry Harland to be
Literary Editor – Me to be Art-Editor. Great fun. Not a thing like the

[1] 1880–1937. Vicar of St Martin-in-the-Fields 1914–27. Dean of Canterbury 1929–31,
Canon and Precentor of St Paul's from 1934. One of the founders of the Peace Pledge
Union. He and Max first met in 1929, when Sheppard and his wife visited Portofino in
search of a cure for his persistent asthma. He and Max immediately became close and
affectionate friends.
[2] American author of *A Study in Yellow: The Yellow Book and its Contributors* (1960)
and *Max and the Americans* (1974).

*Edinburgh* or the *Quarterly*. Not just a *paper* thing. A *bound* thing: a real book, bound in good thick boards. *Yellow* ones. Bright yellow. And it's going to be called *The Yellow Book*."

Aubrey's accent was, you see, on Book. The colour was important to his soul's eye, but Book (something to last longer than a quarter of a year) was the main thing. And we contributors always, in those days, spoke of The Yellow Book. I think this little side-light, or rather back-light, might be amusing material for you in your "thesis".

How well you write! How kindly and indulgently! I can't stand America at any price. But Americans (of whom my wife is one) are quite another matter; and (if Mr Mix will allow me to say so to you) I love them.                    Yours very truly,   MAX BEERBOHM

P.S. "A Peep into the Past" was a squib, never meant for publication in *The Yellow Book* or elsewhere.[1] Henry Harland was a very enlightened and fine editor. (Witness, the fact that a young lady in 1930 is interested – and thesistically interested – in the faded old venture.) And (to answer the third of your questions) I didn't first meet Aubrey Beardsley in Oxford. I fancy he never visited Oxford. Had he done so, I am sure he would have done some magical drawings on the basis of its architecture, etc.

P.P.S. I do hope your husband's Christian name isn't the same as mine. the assonance would be appalling to any sensitive ear.


## To André Raffalovich[2]
TS. Merton

*27 June 1930*                                        *Villino Chiaro*

It is most good of you, dear André Raffalovich, to be so welcoming – by letter and by telegram. I am stirrup-cupped for my pilgrimage. Thank you very much.

---

[1] On the manuscript, now in the Berg Collection of the New York Public Library, under the title Max wrote: "For the 1st No. of the *Yellow Book*", but he had clearly forgotten this.

[2] A rich Russian Jew who had been educated in France and England (1864–1934). He published verse and prose in the 1890s, and largely supported Aubrey Beardsley during the artist's last years. His great friend was the poet John Gray (1866–1934). They both became Roman Catholics, and Gray was ordained priest. They lived the last part of their lives in Edinburgh, where Gray had a parish and became a Canon. Raffalovich financed the building of St Peter's Church for him.

Bradshaw is rare, out here. But sheer intuition tells me that I reach Edinburgh at some very early hour of the morning of Wednesday, July 2 – some unearthly hour. I shall then hail a cab and drive straight to your house and ring the bell, or press the button gently, so as not to rouse you, and shall whisper to the blinking (yet respectful) servant that I am a friend of M Raffalovich, am going to be an LL.D., and should like to lie down.

Greatly looking forward to seeing you again and the Canon,

I am Yours MAX BEERBOHM

## To Lytton Strachey[1]
MS. B.L.

*17 December 1930*                                   *Great Western Royal Hotel*
                                                              *Paddington*

My dear Lytton, The deed is done: you are up for the Ath^m. (as Eminent Victorians usually wrote it, in their haste). And now all that remains to be done is that you should write to Mr Lowes Dickinson,[2] hoping he won't object to seconding a man proposed by *me*. Tell him that I am perfectly respectable. Also tell him that if he is in the country, or if he seldom goes to the Ath^m., he needs but write to the Secretary, who will enter his name for him as your seconder.

You will be a great feather in the Ath^m.'s cap; and I shall be so glad of having had a hand in placing it there.

Yours ever sincerely MAX BEERBOHM

P.S. I feared that you might shy at the notion, and was all the more pleased by your amenability.

---

[1] Max was determined to get Strachey into the Athenaeum under Rule II, which allows the committee to invite a distinguished person to become a member of the club, without need of election.

[2] Author, Fellow of King's College, Cambridge, and member of the Athenaeum (1862–1932).

## To Laurie Magnus[1]
MS. Sebag-Montefiore

My dear Mr Magnus, Before going back to Italy, I would like to thank you for all that you have done to further the good cause of Lytton Strachey. I do so hope he will get in at the next election under Rule II. All the more do I hope that he will, because if he doesn't I shall resign. This I shall do as a protest against the doltishness of a Committee that prefers essentially unimportant big-wigs to a man of genuine distinction.

I mention this firm resolve in strict confidence of course. I have mentioned it to no one except Mr Appleyard and Mr Hill.[2] But I am going to mention it by this post to Denison Ross[3] – hoping he will be able to attend the next meeting and join forces with you.

I should greatly miss the Athenaeum, which I love. But my love for the art of English prose is even deeper; and I should delight in my self-sacrifice in its cause! Also I should, I fear, take an unholy joy in sending, with my resignation, a thoroughly rude indictment of the Committee.

I need hardly say that Lytton Strachey knows nothing of my grim resolve.     Yours, with best regards, very sincerely     MAX BEERBOHM

## Lytton Strachey to Max
MS. Reichmann

*12 March 1931*                              *51 Gordon Square, W.C.1*

Dear Max, I am bringing out in May a slight and small volume of collected essays – mostly of a biographical nature – and I wonder whether you would allow me to dedicate it to you.[4] The extreme kindness you have always shown me and my great admiration for you are the combined reasons for this request. If you agree, the book will be highly honoured, while feeling itself a sadly inadequate offering. But there it is.

About two months ago I was caught by the flu, and am still not really well again. The attack itself wasn't so bad, but the recovery has been

---

[1] Journalist, publisher and author (1872–1933).     [2] Members of the club committee.
[3] Oriental scholar (1871–1940). Director of the School of Oriental Studies. Knighted 1918.
[4] *Portraits in Miniature*, published on 14 May 1931.

horribly slow and wearisome – however I am now getting slightly less ghostly every day, and before very long no doubt I shall be more or less a human being again. How are you? I hope you have both escaped this plague. I imagine you're at Rapallo, but perhaps in reality you're still lingering in the Paddington Hotel.

Among an enormous quantity of books, I've been reading W. Rothenstein's memoirs.[1] I loved your view of the Café Royal. The book seemed to me rather an ennobled version of those dizzy nineties, but with a great many interesting things in it.

Oh! Dickinson did second me for the Athenaeum – at least he said he did. But he's so unworldly that I daresay he in fact wrote my name in the Suggestion Book. No matter – we shall see what we shall see.

Yours ever    LYTTON STRACHEY

## To Lytton Strachey
MS. B.L.

*21 March 1931*                                    *Villino Chiaro*

My dear Lytton, I wasn't here when your letter arrived. It awaited me, it welcomed me, on my return this week from England. What a lovely welcome! I feel immensely proud that you should wish to dedicate a book to me. Much older though I am than you, my admiration for your prose, since first I knew it, has had the fresh wild hot quality that belongs rather to a very young man's feeling for the work of a great congenial veteran. I have always felt, and shall always feel, such a duffer and fumbler in comparison with you. But I shall be better able to disguise this feeling when my eyes shall have seen my name in your new book.

I am so very sorry you have been having influenza. My wife and I escaped the wretched thing. *The* important thing for you to do is, as you know, to remain supine and leisurely, and to eat more than you desire, long after you yourself are convinced that you are perfectly well.

Lowes Dickinson had safely written down his name. So far as anything in this world is certain, it is certain that you will be elected at the next meeting of the Committee (some time early in April). You ought to have been elected sooner. But the majority of the present Committee are stodgers – each with some stodgy old friend whom he wants to get in

---

[1] *Men and Memories*, Vol. 1, to which Max contributed a caricature of Rothenstein, Charles Conder, Oscar Wilde and Max himself at the Café Royal.

under Rule II, some Major General or Minor Canon or Chemist (and possibly Druggist). So forgive the delay. I am sure you will like the club: it has a real charm of its own.

Yours ever   MAX BEERBOHM (Receiver, *in petto*, of Dedication)

## Lytton Strachey to Max
MS. Reichmann

*27 March 1931*                                                    *51 Gordon Square*

Dear Max, I was delighted to get your far, far too kind letter. The book will I think come out early in May, and you shall be sent a copy at once.

I am beginning to feel rather excited about the Athenaeum. But at the same time I entirely sympathise with the electors and their druggist friends, so that if they firmly refuse to have anything to do with me I shall not be particularly horrified. If the rôles were reversed, should *I* elect *them*?

I am just off to the country, in the hope that the beginnings of Spring may put me to rights. Yours blushing from too many praises

LYTTON STRACHEY

## Telegram to Max

*15 April 1931*                                                              *London*

STRACHEY TOP OF THE POLL APPLEYARD ROSS MAGNUS AND HILL.

## Lytton Strachey to Max
MS. Reichmann

*18 April 1931*                     *Ham Spray House, Marlborough, Wilts.*

Dear Max, Your efforts have been crowned with success, and I've been elected to the A. under rule II! It was really most noble of you to take this trouble. I am delighted and very much obliged.

I haven't put my nose in yet. I wish you could be there to show me round. I shall feel rather like a New Boy at school.

The Gosse book[1] is full of interest. I observe that at one point he

[1] *The Life and Letters of Sir Edmund Gosse* by Evan Charteris (1931).

characteristically gives Swinburne a widow.[1] Luckily Churton Collins[2] is dead. By-the-bye, was the account of S's sex peculiarities printed or merely MS? And is it as "curious" as one imagines it ought to be?

It is perfectly disgusting here – snow at the moment – but I am sticking it out on the theory that it's good for me.

Yours ever   L Y T T O N   S T R A C H E Y

## To Lytton Strachey
### MS. B.L.

*23 April 1931*                                               *Villino Chiaro*

My dear Lytton, How charming of you to thank me! But your election under Rule II was due to your own eminence and worth, of course, and not to any "efforts" on my part. I was merely rather annoyed that it hadn't come sooner. You ought to have headed the poll at the first election. You did so, however, at this one. Of course don't happen to mention to anybody my rather rude remarks about the ruck of the committee. Atonement has now been made.

It had already occurred to me to wish I could be there to attend your début. But be assured. Very little ceremony is involved. You just walk up the steps and give your name to the hall-porter, who will excitedly conduct you to the hat-pegs. You then pass through the swing-doors of the ground-floor smoking-room, where there are usually about a dozen men. You go straight to the hearth-rug, turn your back on the fireplace, and say, "I am (Giles) Lytton Strachey, a Rule II man, and author of the following books". Having named your books and given the date of each, you ring the bell and order the waiter to bring a magnum of champagne. When this is brought, the senior man present proposes your health, and you respond briefly – *quite* briefly; ten minutes at the outside. You are then free to roam all over the premises, scowling at any one you come across, on the assumption that he is an interloper and a gate-crasher – or at all events not a Rule II man.

As I have said before, I am sure you will like the club and frequent it. Though solid and staid and tranquil, as a club should be, it is also a very genial place. I note that you call it the A. But I for my part always

[1] On p. 476 Charteris quotes a letter from Gosse to Pierre Legouis in which he refers to "the poet's widow".

[2] John Churton Collins (1848–1908), a fanatical pedant, who in the *Quarterly Review* in 1886 had pulverised Gosse's Clark Lectures *From Shakespeare to Pope*, pinpointing many gross errors.

call it the Ath (cf. Cri, Troc, Tiv, k.t.l.[1]). I daresay the room you will like best is the long room on the first floor: a very noble and restful one – though it is the one in which Trollope killed Mrs Proudie, you remember.[2]

Remember also, by the way, that though you can entertain guests for dinner in the dining-room proper, a guest for luncheon has to be headed away into that small guest-room beyond the hall. Also – what I still sometimes forget – that on entering the dining-room you don't sit comfortably down in a vacant place and order your meal from there: you go first to the steward's table and choose and write out your menu, in the bad old fashion ordained by Croker and Faraday.[3]

I haven't yet read Gosse's letters. Evan Charteris and Charles Evans[4] both promised to send me a copy; but neither of them has done anything of the sort; so I am taking the initiative. I am delighted to know from you that Gosse credits Swinburne with a widow. I do hope she is in the index? "Swinburne, Mrs A. C." I hope too that there is a reproduction of Simeon Solomon's crayon portrait of her at the time of her marriage: a lovely thing.

Yes; Gosse's account of Swinburne's abnormality was printed: just a few copies, I fancy, one of which was to be deposited in the British Museum, "for students." Gosse, I remember, sent me a proof or a typescript of it, asking my opinion. I advised that it should be suppressed. It made Swinburne (whom I revered, and liked) very ridiculous; and I should have preferred the students to be left with a

[1] Criterion, Trocadero, Tivoli. *Kai ta loipa* (Greek for etcetera).

[2] "I was sitting one morning at work upon the novel at the end of the long drawing-room of the Athenaeum Club, – as was then my wont when I had slept the previous night in London. As I was there, two clergymen, each with a magazine in his hand, seated themselves, one on one side of the fire and one on the other, close to me. They soon began to abuse what they were reading, and each was reading some part of some novel of mine. The gravamen of their complaint lay in the fact that I reintroduced the same characters so often! 'Here,' said one, 'is that archdeacon whom we have had in every novel he has ever written.' 'And here,' said the other, 'is the old duke whom he has talked about till everybody is tired of him. If I could not invent new characters, I would not write novels at all.' Then one of them fell foul of Mrs Proudie. It was impossible for me not to hear their words, and almost impossible to hear them and be quiet. I got up, and standing between them, I acknowledged myself to be the culprit. 'As to Mrs Proudie,' I said, 'I will go home and kill her before the week is over.' And so I did." (Trollope, *An Autobiography*, Vol. 2, pp. 108–9)

[3] John Wilson Croker, Irish-born politician (1780–1857), and Michael Faraday, chemist and natural philosopher (1791–1867), were two of the founders of the Athenaeum Club in 1824.

[4] Head of William Heinemann Ltd, publishers of the Gosse book and of Max.

vague notion of mere legendary wickedness. I also felt that Gosse's motive would not be understood, would be misinterpreted.[1]

Well, do forgive me for writing at such vast length. And thank you again *very* much for the dedication in the forthcoming book.

Yours ever   MAX BEERBOHM

## *To Grant Richards*[2]
MS. Clark

*16 July 1934*                                        *Villino Chiaro*

My dear Grant, I am sending back to you, registered, the "galleys" of Chapters I–XVII,[3] which are all that have arrived as yet. I've immensely enjoyed them. Vol. 2 is as good as Vol. 1,[4] I do believe. As vivid and amusing and well-observed and characteristic.

I don't think (as you do) that the bulging-out of G.B.S., in proportion to the rest, matters at all. After all, he is the most remarkable of living writers. And the fact that he is neither an artist, in any sense of the word, nor a human being in *very* many senses of the word, doesn't detract much from his immense value to the world. And one of his great good points, his genuine kindness and helpfulness, comes out strong in your account of him and in his many – his not too many – but rather too dreadfully technical and trady – letters.

My only grievance is that I have this time failed to find any mistake in a date. If you will look through the sent galleys, you will find a good deal of scribbling – but only here and there anything in the way of a suggestion.

*Author Hunting* is an excellent title. But I think there should be a hyphen between the two words. Otherwise people might think the book was an account of Anthony Trollope in his off-moments.

Yours always   MAX BEERBOHM

P.S. In the nether margin of my Shaw drawing, the *date* of the drawing should be given, as well as a repetition of the legend. The date is, I

---

[1] Gosse's account was reprinted as an appendix to Volume Six (1962) of Cecil Lang's edition of Swinburne's Letters.

[2] Publisher of fine taste but no business acumen (1872–1948). Despite several bankruptcies he was always beautifully dressed and died in Monte Carlo.

[3] Of *Author Hunting 1897–1925*, which was published by Hamish Hamilton in 1934.

[4] *Memories of a Misspent Youth 1872–1896*, 1932, introduced by Max.

think, 1912. Legend and date should be in small italic type, if possible. Or, as G.B.S. would say, "MS. caption & date on item to be plugged under in It. pica."

P.P.S. When next you see Hamish Hamilton, please remember me kindly to him. I have met him two or three times, and I liked him much.

## To Helen and Harley Granville Barker[1]
MS. Princeton

*4 January 1935*                                                    *Villino Chiaro*

Dearest Helen and Harley, Florence has already written to both of you. But I follow on, unnecessarily, to say how much we miss you – how rather empty the Casetta and Villino seem without you, and how much we hope you will come *soon* to make them seem quite full again.

   I don't know how *you* feel in the matter; but *I* feel that the four of us are somehow just right!                    Your affectionate   MAX

   Greatly glad about the unlost manuscript. *Stop*. Many thanks for telegram. *Stop*. Looking forward to publication of final clearing-up of all doubts about Hamlet's character, motives, etc. *Stop*. But am writing at bed-time and must stop. *Stop*.

## To H.R.L. Sheppard
TS. Merton

*7 February 1935*                                                  *Villino Chiaro*

My dear Dick, It's a bitter disappointment! We had so hoped, in spite of your last-but-one letter, that you would be able to come. We had so fondly looked forward to it. But down with the past tense! We do look forward to it. Surely you *will* come, ever so soon. Of course a Canon of St Paul's has heaps of duties. But oh, please, neglect them. Defy the Dean. Checkmate the Chapter. Live for pleasure. Let us know that you and Mrs Dick will be here directly. Pack your things. Whistle (it's against the law – but so much the better) for a taxi. Say "Victoria" to the driver. We will meet your train. It will do Florence and me such good. Be Christians. Florence has not yet quite recovered from influenza;

[1] Actor, playwright, stage director and writer (1877–1946). Helen Huntington was his second wife.

185

and *I* haven't been very well, either. But don't think only of us. There is the editor of that magazine: surely a deserving case. One can't *write* about writing one's reminiscences: one can only converse about it orally, by a fireside. Come for the editor's sake. There shall be a bright fire, even if the sun shines brightly.

But seriously (that dreadful phrase so often used by platform-speakers when they have just been saying something which nobody in the audience had suspected of being meant to be funny), do come as soon as ever you conveniently can. It will be all right about the guest-rooms: nobody shall have right of entry into them till you and Mrs Dick have occupied and left them.　　　　　　　　　　　　　　　Your loving　MAX

## To Ivor Novello[1]
### MS. Merton

*6 April 1936*　　　　　　　　　　　　　　　*41 Tavistock Square, W.C.1*

My dear Ivor, The Harley Granville Barkers are passing through London, on their way to America, and, as they cannot come to the first night, are very keen to be at the dress rehearsal. I feel sure you would like them to come – and I have told them so.

Sibyl Colefax rang up the other day, wanting to bring a friend with her – and has, I think, rung up the theatre. This, too, I am sure, is all right.

Florence and I are looking forward with enthusiasm to the rehearsal – believing that we too shall be welcome.

Meanwhile 10,000 best wishes and thanks, *de coeur*.

　　　　　　　　　　　　　　　　　　　Yours always　MAX

## To Winston Churchill
### MS. Texas

*11 March 1937*　　　　　　　　　　　　　　　*Villino Chiaro*

Dear Winston Churchill, Eddie Marsh[2] is rather a special case. He has done, for so many years, so much good in so enlightened and so unselfish

---

[1] Welsh actor, composer, song-writer and dramatist (1893–1951). On 8 April 1936 he presented Clemence Dane's dramatisation of *The Happy Hypocrite* at His Majesty's Theatre, with himself and Vivien Leigh in the leading parts.

[2] Edward Marsh, Civil Servant, anthologist, translator, patron of poets and painters (1872–1953). Knighted 1937.

a way that really I think he ought to be given a dinner of this kind every night of his life. When next I am in England I shall affectionately attend every one of the current meals in his honour.

Please, meanwhile, give him my fond salutations.

Yours very sincerely   MAX BEERBOHM[1]

## *To Viola Tree*[2]

Dearest Viola, Ever so many thanks for letting me see the proofs. Alan must have derived an immense amount of quiet pleasure from building up, little by little, his private Temple of Preferences. I don't suppose that he would have of his own accord opened the gates of it for the multitude to enter in and wander up and down the aisles and improve their minds among the shrines – the many shrines, great and small, grave and gay, sacred and profane. The Temple was for himself, and for you and a few others. But, though he was essentially shy, I am sure that if he could know that you and Mr Michael Burn were now opening the gates in memory of him, he would be well-pleased.

I, as one of the multitude, am very well-pleased indeed. I shall revisit the Temple often, for profit and pleasure. There are so many beautiful and delightful things in it that I hadn't known or even heard of. I rather fear that these greatly outnumber those with which I am more or less familiar. I have never read much, even in the beaten tracks of reading. Alan was an untiring, a gently passionate explorer of literature; and desultory, in the best sense; unhampered by canons; no proscriber; a welcomer, guided by nothing but his own great good taste; a scholar of the unalarming kind.

That he was a scholar, and very much so, I had known by hearsay, long before you presented me to him, in Genoa, many years ago. Middle-age is shy of youth, and ignorance nervous under the shadow of erudition; but Alan at first sight (and Alan throughout the times that were to come) made me feel entirely calm and happy. It was not long since he had

---

[1] This letter was read aloud by Will Rothenstein at a dinner of 140 in the Mayfair Hotel on 17 March to mark Eddie Marsh's retirement from the Civil Service.

[2] Her husband Alan Parsons had died in 1933, aged 44. In 1937 a selection of his commonplace books, *Alan Parsons' Book*, was published, edited by Viola Tree and Michael Burn, with Max's letter as introduction. Text from there.

come down from Oxford, and he seemed to have brought that place with him to Genoa. Somehow he did not seem to have ceased to be an undergraduate; and almost I felt that I too was one, so sympathetic was he. But I didn't then (nor at any future moment) feel that I was nearly so typical, so aromatic of Oxford as Alan was. Nor indeed can I think of any one who has seemed to me more signally Oxfordish than he. A year ago, when I was in England, I happened to revisit more than once the scenes that had shaped him, and I wondered how, if he were alive and young, he would fare among them now. Besieged, invested, invaded, infested, Nuffieldised Oxford! – with lorries incessantly shaking her to her foundations, and the pavements of St Giles's and the Corn as thronged by feverish passengers as the pavements of Oxford Street on a bargain-day at Selfridge's – Oxford, the adorable dreamer, who had "given herself so prodigally, only never to the Philistines",[1] now shrieking from her towers the latest improvements of the Mechanised Age . . . and still forming Newmans and Ruskins? Arnolds and Paters? . . . and also Alans? Let's hope, dear Viola, for the best.

Let's hope that eminent politicians of the future will be able to select from the Civil Service private secretaries who will shed on them incidentally something of Alan's engaging, discreet, unselfish lustre. I was sorry when ill-health compelled him to leave Whitehall. Had he stayed there, he would, I feel, in despite of that cramping modesty which Mr Burn so rightly stresses, have done much more justice to his powers. *A Winter in Paradise* is a delightful work. It should have been one among others. And that poem in *ottava-rima* about the tortoise-shell what exquisitely accomplished work, and how wildly funny! One desires, with a pang, many examples of that vein. As a dramatic critic, writing for a vast number of readers on the morrow, he was very important, of course. And he had real joy in the art of the theatre. But not enough of time nor enough of space was available for the right expression of his judgments. That he sent many thousands of people to good plays, and kept many thousands of people away from bad ones, is a fact that leaves me unconsoled.

Unconsoled, you will say, but garrulous. So enough! And if I need consolation, here it is, in this Alanthology – with all best wishes for which I am your always affectionate                                          MAX

---

[1] Matthew Arnold, in the Preface to his *Essays in Criticism* (1865).

## To Sydney Schiff[1]
MS. Merton

*10 December 1938*                    *62 Inverness Terrace, W.2.*

My dear Sydney, It was very kind and thoughtful of you to send me that letter of Reggie's. What a good and characteristic letter! Florence and I thank you both deeply for your sympathy in our loss of him.[2] And indeed we sympathise with *you* both in *yours* – for he loved you both and greatly valued your friendship, as you his. I had known him so long: he was the earliest of my great friends, and remained always the greatest – and will always remain so. Though I knew from his friend Orioli[3] that there was no hope that he could recover, I had not supposed that the end would come so soon. It is a blessing that he himself thought that he would recover. I have not yet heard the manner of his death, but I have no doubt at all that the doctors had kept him in an un–suffering state. I will let you know as soon as I hear from Orioli. I think his life had been on the whole a happy one, full of interest and fun. Of course he had been too sensitive an observer and feeler of things to be genuinely and uninterruptedly happy in such a world as this. But he had had a good share of happiness. And now he is beyond reach of the other thing, and is at peace, dear fellow.

It is so good of Violet and you to invite us again. Might we come to you some evening after Christmas? Any evening that would suit you.

Your affectionate   MAX

## To Sydney Schiff
MS. Merton

*22 January 1939*                    *62 Inverness Terrace*

My dear Sydney, We are intensely looking forward to Thursday. Florence is writing *minutiae* to Violet. I to you write a *minutia* of my own. I wonder whether it would at all amuse you to possess a series of seven old drawings of mine – whether they *would* amuse you a little. They

---

[1] 1868–1944. Wrote novels as Stephen Hudson. He and his wife Violet (a sister of Ada Leverson) lent the Beerbohms a cottage on their land at Abinger in Surrey. They moved there in February 1939 and lived there happily until they were bombed out in August 1944. Thereafter they stayed with friends until they returned to Rapallo in 1947.

[2] Reggie Turner died on 7 December 1938.

[3] Giuseppe (Pino) Orioli, Italian bookseller and publisher.

concern my dear old friend George Street, and I wouldn't give them to any one who would regard them as making him merely ridiculous. You would not be such a one. You would enter into the spirit of the affectionate chaff in which they were done. I gave the drawings to George at the time (1903) when they were done. When he died (1936) his old friend Alderson Horne[1] told me that George had wished that I should have them. Also another set of drawings of George done in another connexion and given by me to him. This other set I asked Alderson Horne to accept. There remains this not-other one. If you would accept it, you would have to be further burdened with an explanation of the drawings; for they don't explain themselves: they are variations on an incident which would have to be narrated. Please, dear Sydney, state a wish for or against. If "for" I will send drawings and explanation along to you. Fond love to Violet and to you.

Your affectionate   MAX

## To Sydney Schiff
MS. Merton

[*23 January 1939*]                              [*62 Inverness Terrace*]

Herewith the Prolegomena!
Lengthy but (I hope) lucid.   MAX

### Exegesis

My dear Sydney, In 1903 a pleasant and intelligent young man, Prince Pierre Wolkonski, was one of the Secretaries at the Russian Embassy here. I daresay you may have come across him, and may remember him. I was slightly acquainted with him.

One evening George Street and I were together at some play that was running at His Majesty's; and in one of the entr'actes I saw P.W. in the foyer and introduced him and G.S. to each other.

A little later:

G.S: "Seems a charming fellow, your friend."

I. "Yes, isn't he?"

G.S. "What does he do?"

I. "Oh, he's at the Embassy. And he's by way of writing poetry, I believe. And he's related to Tolstoi."

---

[1] 1863–1953. As Anmer Hall a successful actor-manager.

Later, at the Savile Club, where we supped, P.W. was again mentioned by G.S.

I. (the spirit of mischief rising in me, as it so often did in presence of G.S., who was so dignified always, and such a hater of "nonsense," and withal so good-humoured, that he was an ideal subject for mystification) – "You really did believe that he was a Russian Prince?"

G.S. "?"

I. "Splendid!"

G.S. "?"

I. "He certainly played up well. I don't wonder you were taken in!"

G.S. "?"

I. "Dear George, do forgive me! – and him. He's a young actor – Willie Culbert, a friend of mine; he has played minor parts in several productions of Herbert's. A charming fellow, as you said. And how well he nipped on to my cue! That *slightly* broken English! That grace!"

G.S. (coldly) "Really, dear Max, I don't resent your stupid little practical joke in the least. I'm merely sorry for *you*. You're thirty years old or so. You were educated at a good school, and all that. You aren't idiotic. And yet . . ."

I. "I quite see your point. But listen, George! See mine – and set your mind at rest! I have my faults, but I wouldn't have dreamt of playing any prank of *that* sort. It wouldn't have been like me. It's only *now* that I've been fooling you. Of *course* the man was the man he pretended to be – I mean, the man he *was*, and *is*. It's Willie Culbert who doesn't exist. At any rate I've never heard of him. Pierre Wolkonski is a Prince, right enough; and he *is* at the Embassy, and a relation of Tolstoi." Etc, etc.

G.S. (very coldly) "All this is entirely off the point, dear Max. The point is that you seem really to have thought that I would be rather impressed by meeting a Russian Prince. Well, really . . ." Etc, etc.

A few days later, George had returned to Kemp Town, where he was living at that time; and I received a letter in which he told me that he had lunched with A.B. Walkley at the Hotel Metropole and had recounted my joke to Walkley, who hadn't thought it even slightly amusing.

This letter moved me to do those seven drawings. George was very fond of them, and they hung always in his room. I am so glad they are deemed by you worthy of acceptance from your affectionate MAX

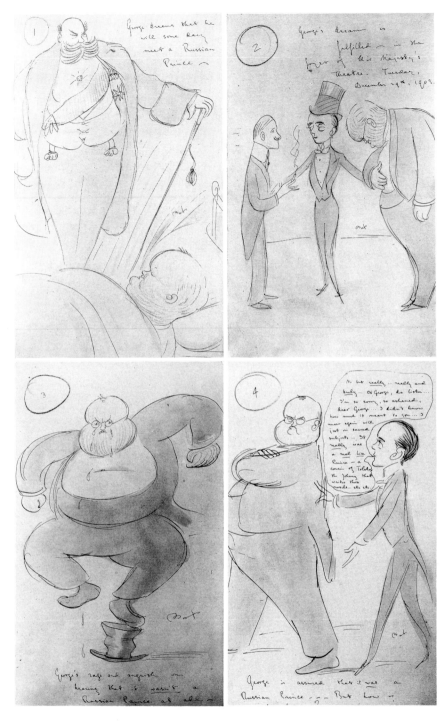

Saturn anni; and we (the Prince & I), who were young Princesses, become old & crabbed, yet never, year after year, do we leave unpaid our visit on the anniversary of George's demise to the little cemetery in Kemp Town.

193

## To Sydney Schiff
MS. Merton

*15 February 1939*        *Abinger Manor Cottage, Abinger Common,*
*Nr Dorking*

My dear Sydney, Yes, Violet's memory is quite right: you did read *Prufrock*[1] aloud to me; but I didn't recall this to you, because then you might have said you wouldn't read it to me again. Which is just what you have said now! Please reconsider this saying; for I should like to renew the delight I had in that reading. I well remember that during it I was all aglow with admiration for T.S.E. – and continued to be so, in retrospect, until I came (eagerly) in contact with another volume of his work, and – and – and realised that the glow had been due entirely to your vivacious and calorific flow of interpretation – or rather of creation. I want to renew in my breast that illusion of great merits. So do please conquer the disillusion that you seem to have been feeling, and thrill me again. I shall be as susceptible as ever.

No, I've never read *Evelina*.[2] But I shall; and if I don't really like it, I shall ask you to read me some passages, to set me going with a swing.

Florence and I have to go to Lincoln's Inn next Saturday, for a week, to welcome the Lannis[3] – the Ellis Robertses[4] having kindly offered us their rooms. We shall come and leave cards on you – neatly turned up at the corners[5] – in the course of our sojourn.

Our love meanwhile to you both.        Your affectionate   MAX


## To Sydney Schiff
MS. Merton

*15 March 1939*

My dear Sydney, It is a joy to read a letter written with such force and concision, and such insight and justice. It sums up all that I think about the vast tragic matter.[6] There is nothing left for me to say, except –

---

[1] "The Love Song of J. Alfred Prufrock" from *Prufrock and Other Observations* by T. S. Eliot (1917).        [2] By Fanny Burney (1778).        [3] Italian friends.

[4] R. Ellis Roberts, journalist and author (1879–1953), and his wife Harriet.

[5] To show that they had been brought by the person whose name they bore, and not by a footman or messenger.

[6] Presumably the German invasion of Czechoslovakia.

rather feebly – "Ditto". Without aristocracy of one kind or another there certainly can't be anything of the kind that you or I can regard as civilisation. But (here is a point that does occur to me [and there's nothing new about it!]) there can't be any sort of aristocracy without slavery. Slavery has, thank heaven! existed in England in our time, our beloved time. And now it is ceasing to exist, alas! I say "alas!" not with my *whole* heart. In a rather remote corner of that organ I am pleased that the lives of the majority of my fellow-creatures are happier than they were. You are much kinder-natured and more philanthropic than I am, and I expect you can derive from that difference greater comfort than can your affectionate                                                      MAX

P.S. Yes, it was very dear of Reggie to give me such a present, wasn't it? It came as a great surprise.[1]


## *To Douglas Cleverdon*[2]
MS. Cleverdon

*21 July 1939*                                                      *Abinger Manor Cottage*

Dear Mr Cleverdon, Many thanks for everything.
1. I think the intercalated N.E.A.C.[3] scene is all to the good. The more "action" the better. But of course I leave this point, and indeed all other points, freely in the hands of McLeverdon[4] – if I may thus portmanteauise producer and author, in order to save time!

2. So sorry I forgot to mention in my letter what had struck me in reading the Nupton extract. It had occurred to me that the phonetic spelling, though amusing in print, would be rather pointless by word of mouth and might well be given a miss. Also it might rather encourage (as a supposedly serious prophecy) the ghastly Simplified Spelling League, which was greatly encouraged the other day by a legacy of £18,000 bequeathed to it by a lunatic. But McLeverdon can decide best.

3. "So then I knew I should never be famous". Yes: necessary, I daresay.

[1] Reggie Turner had left Max £3000.

[2] Publisher and radio producer (1903–87). This letter refers to his dramatisation of "Enoch Soames", which was broadcast on 31 July 1939, with Dennis Arundell as Soames.

[3] New English Art Club.

[4] A telescoping of McLaren and Cleverdon. Moray McLaren (1901–71) was a Scottish author and radio producer.

But let it be spoken thus:– "So then I ... knew I should never be ... [very faintly] be famous".

4. The name Rothenstein must of course be pronounced in the English way: Roe-tn-stine (not with a broad German *o* or a German *sht* for *st*).

5. The substitution of *Walter Sickert* for *Beardsley* which interested you was made because W.R.[1] never liked A.B. so much as most of us did (though the two were quite passably good friends).

6. Don't, for heaven's sake, waste a photographer's time. Especially as I remember I made a serious slip in the sketch for M.McL. Soames's hair wasn't at all wild: it was meek hair.

7. I enclose, with the Soames typescript,
another typescript, which must have been
sent to me by mistake. I am inquisitive
by nature, but a gentleman by hard training,
and have repressed the impulse to read
what was not intended for my eyes.

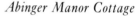

         Yours very sincerely   M.B.

## To Douglas Cleverdon
MS. Cleverdon

*1 August 1939*                       *Abinger Manor Cottage*

Dear Mr Cleverdon, I hope you were as pleased last night as were my wife and I. I thought the whole thing faultless. The "cuts" that had worried you in the making of them didn't, even to my own auctorial mind, seem to matter in the least. All the essentials were there. And the whole cast shone – especially that member of it who had the principal chance of shining, Mr Arundell.[2] I had always regarded Soames as a well-made synthetic specimen of a type that I had known well and had been annoyed by. I had never thought of him as a real human being, a pitiable fellow-creature to whom one's heart ought to go out. Mr Arundell didn't bate one jot of Soames's dismal absurdity, but he did make flesh and blood of him – insomuch that at the back of my head I rather wished the play could have a happy ending! I was, quite honestly, at the words "Neglect, failure," and in several later passages, not far from the verge of tears; *moi qui vous parle*. With many thanks for all your skill, and for all your considerateness by post.

         Yours very sincerely   MAX BEERBOHM

[1] Will Rothenstein.

[2] Dennis Arundell, actor, writer and composer (born 1898).

## To the Chairman, Aliens Tribunal
### TS. Reichmann

*October 1939*                                        *Abinger Manor Cottage*

Dear Sir, It is about twelve years since my wife and I had the pleasure of meeting, in Italy, Miss Elisabeth Jungmann, who was at that time secretary to the famous German poet and dramatist Gerhart Hauptmann. Since then we have had that pleasure year after year.

She is a woman of high intellectual attainments, and of noble and beautiful character. She is dearly beloved and deeply respected by all her friends.

I was, of course, sorry that owing to the Nazi persecution she was obliged to leave her native country; but not less glad am I that she is in England; and in England I do hope she will be free to remain always.[1]

I am, dear Sir, Yours obediently    MAX BEERBOHM

[1] She became a British subject, and worked for the Foreign Office through the war.

ELISABETH JUNGMANN

# To Douglas Cleverdon
MS. Cleverdon

*Monday [? 18 December 1939]*                    *Abinger Manor Cottage*

My dear Mr Cleverdon, Many thanks for your letters, and every good wish for the broadcast.[1] I send to you "under separate cover" the typescript of the play.[2] You will find a fair number of suggestions – mostly concerning phraseology.

The "Apollo" diversion would, I am sure, not come out well. I remember that I wrote it because I had determined that at the end of the story the mask must *melt* away. In the book it's all right. But on the air one mustn't stray so far away from one's story. I'm sure you agree. (I have slightly expanded Mr Aeneas's words about the unmeltableness, and the words should be spoken with solemn emphasis, so that the listeners shall remember them.)

*About the music.* Let there be a fair amount of it – always *subdued* of course. When Mrs Patrick Campbell produced my little version, some of the characters had a sort of *motif,* recurring from time to time. The Gambogi's motif was a French eighteenth-century drinking song, of a dashing kind. Jenny's was the "Sweet Nightingale" folk-song – less known in those days than it is now. Is it *too* well-known now? I don't think so. Do let it be used. Lord G., I think, hadn't any *motif* – a grave oversight! Let the music all be of a *simple* (and tuneful) kind.[3]

As to the cast: You needn't bother to let me know the names – for they would have no significance for me, so seldom do I enter a playhouse. Here are a few ideas, however, about what seems to me requisite:—

The Duchess must have a *full* voice, contraltoish, to distinguish her from the daughter. Tarleton's voice must be of a very different timbre from Lord G.'s, and of course the Gambogi's voice must be in vivid contrast with Jenny's.

Jenny is the most important character, I think – and the most difficult! Do any good ingénues exist? (They didn't in my time.) Jenny must have beauty of utterance, and perfect simplicity and sincerity.

The Gambogi is an easy part. But she must *not* exaggerate or clown.

[1] Of Cleverdon's radio adaptation of *The Happy Hypocrite*, which was broadcast on 13 January 1940 with Deborah Kerr (aged 15) as Jenny Mere, and Robert Farquharson (aged 62) as Lord George Hell.

[2] Max's dramatisation which had been produced at the Royalty Theatre by Mrs Patrick Campbell in 1900.

[3] The music for the broadcast was arranged by Alan Rawsthorne.

You will notice that I have deleted the sub-title – which was an invention of John Lane's, and always seemed to me rather stupid.[1]

I take it that you don't object to Mr Blackburn's[2] suggestion that "the licence to be granted to Mr Cleverdon in respect of his radio version should be for a limited period of, say, six months"? "The whole matter can," added Mr Blackburn, "be reconsidered by the end of this time if Mr Cleverdon is anxious to retain his rights".

I do so look forward to the broadcast. All best thoughts and wishes.

Yours very sincerely   MAX BEERBOHM


## To R.C. Trevelyan[3]
MS. Trinity

*Friday, 10 January 1940*                    *Abinger Manor Cottage*

My dear Bobbie, We were talking yesterday of the death of Little Nell; and after you had gone away I thought what a good and testing theme for the young would be this: "Write an account of ($\alpha$) The death of Little Nell as it would have been written by W.M. Thackeray, and ($\beta$) of the death of Colonel Newcome as it would have been rendered by Charles Dickens". And I rather think that, if when my own life is drawing to its close I have any money to leave, I shall assign to my old school (Charterhouse) a funded sum sufficient to bring in an annual interest of five shillings for a prize (The Beerbohm Prize) for the best work by a present Carthusian on the lines that I have here indicated to you. Don't you think that's rather a good idea?

If ever I am reincarnate and am again placed at Charterhouse, I fancy I might win the prize myself. Forty years or so ago I could have acquitted myself quite decently well in ($\alpha$), hard task though it is, and utterly though it would baffle me now. And, though boyhood and early youth are the time for parody, even now I find very little difficulty in ($\beta$). I will write out for you what I composed yesterday evening in my head. It would have been better if I had here a copy of *Little Nell*; *and* a copy of *Vanity Fair* to refresh my memory of Thackeray's version of the Colonel's death. I can remember only the charming Thackerayan

---

[1] *A Fairy Tale for Tired Men.*

[2] Aubrey Blackburn, theatrical agent.

[3] Poet (1872–1951), elder brother of the historian.

sentence, "*I, curre,* little white-haired gown-boy![1] God be with you, little friend", and the equally Thackerayan, the chaste and magical sentence, about Madame de Florac, "The Frenchwoman became rigid in prayer". And of course "Adsum" and "he whose heart was as that of a little child stood in the presence of his Maker".[2] These have helped me in the very disparate work that follows:

> "Old Mrs Florac knelt beside the bed, earnestly praying in her broken English that God would even now allow the Colonel, the dying man, to live for many a year – the man who in her girlish days had won her tender heart and whom she worshipped still. Into the chamber came with pattering feet the chubby grandson from the schoolroom yonder – a life beginning and a life now ceasing. Ethel was weeping hot salt tears, and Clive, her husband, sought in vain to comfort her. He too was weeping. Aye, and if Barnes himself, Barnes the black-hearted banker, had been there, not even he, with all his worldly cynicism, would not have shed some moisture from his eyes.

[1] "Go, run." Scholars, who wore gowns, were in early days called gown-boys at Charterhouse, the school of Thackeray, Max, and Colonel Newcome.

[2] The relevant passage in the final chapter of *The Newcomes* reads as follows: "*I, curre,* little white-haired gown-boy! Heaven speed you, little friend.

"After the child had gone, Thomas Newcome began to wander more and more. He talked louder; he gave the word of command, spoke Hindostanee as if to his men. Then he spoke words in French rapidly, seizing a hand that was near him, and crying, '*Toujours, toujours!*' But it was Ethel's hand which he took. Ethel and Clive and the nurse were in the room with him; the latter came to us who were sitting in the adjoining apartment; Madame de Florac was there, with my wife and Bayham.

"At the look in the woman's countenance Madame de Florac started up. 'He is very bad, he wanders a great deal,' the nurse whispered. The French lady fell instantly on her knees and remained rigid in prayer.

"Some time afterwards Ethel came in with a scared face to our pale group. 'He is calling for you again, dear lady,' she said, going up to Madame de Florac, who was still kneeling; 'and just now he said he wanted Pendennis to take care of his boy. He will not know you.' She hid her tears as she spoke.

"She went into the room, where Clive was at the bed's foot; the old man within it talked on rapidly for awhile: then again he would sigh and be still: once more I heard him say hurriedly, 'Take care of him when I'm in India;' and then with a heart-rending voice he called out 'Léonore, Léonore!' She was kneeling by his side now. The patient's voice sank into faint murmurs; only a moan now and then announced that he was not asleep.

"At the usual evening hour the chapel bell began to toll, and Thomas Newcome's hands outside the bed feebly beat a time. And just as the last bell struck, a peculiar sweet smile shone over his face, and he lifted up his head a little, and quickly said 'Adsum!' and fell back. It was the word we used at school, when names were called; and lo, he, whose heart was as that of a little child, had answered to his name, and stood in the presence of The Master."

And now, of a sudden, lo, the westering sun shone through the dormer window of the room, in crimson splendour. Simultaneously, there came the tolling of the Chapel's bell, the ancient curfew of the Pension House, that place which was for young and old alike, and where as boy the aged warrior himself had dwelt as he was dwelling now. It was the signal for the muster-roll. The Colonel heard it, and the sound found him responsive to the call of it. He sat erect and in a strong full tone uttered the old-time answer, "'Ere I am," and he whose heart was pure as driven snow stood at the golden judgment bar of Heaven and was enrolled among the host angelic, where no tears are. But they who here below knew him and loved him" ... and much more of this, no doubt.

Please give Florence's and my best messages to Mrs Trevelyan, and believe me most grateful for the joy I am deriving from your Horace and Montaigne: lovely work.     Yours ever   MAX BEERBOHM

*Erratum*! Foot of page 1. For *Little Nell* read *The Old Curiosity Shop*. A bad mistake, but better than if I had said *Quilp* – or *The Dear Old Grandpa*. M.B. [Max might have added 'For *Vanity Fair* read *The Newcomes*'.]


## To Douglas Cleverdon
MS. Cleverdon

*Thursday* [*Postmark 11 January 1940*]                    *Abinger Manor Cottage*

My dear Mr Cleverdon, I hope you'll forgive this absence of pen and ink, as I have to be in bed, there to get rid of a bad cold that has attacked me.

I am delighted to hear that Robert Farquharson[1] is going to be Lord George. Please give him my best regards and remembrances. He will be splendid in the part. But, knowing that one of his salient points is his mastery of the sinister and the macabre, I beg him to agree with me that Lord G. Hell is merely a *wicked* eighteenth-century nobleman, a straightforward blackguard, with nothing *evil* about him.

By all means, let Lord G. have that soliloquy, if rehearsal shows that it comes better than my suggested narration.

The "Announcement" is just right. Except that I would prefer, on

---

[1] Actor (1877–1966). He specialised in sinister parts. Max described him as "absolutely marvellous" as Herod in Wilde's *Salome* in 1906.

the whole, that the Announcer should interpolate the "Sir" before my name. At the time when I was knighted I wrote to the Editor of the *Radio Times*, begging that my title shouldn't be used "in direct connexion" with any work of mine; and he has loyally carried out my wish – but with rather unfortunate results: on two occasions an Announcer has referred to me as "Mr Max Beerbohm", and writers in newspapers, commenting on the broadcast, have followed suit; and several people have asked me whether I share that objection to titles which is so strongly felt by Bertrand Russell and the Sidney Webbs and other high-minded people. Whereas I am not in the least high-minded. Nothing Bloomsburyish about *me*. A simple Surrey man.

Charming of you to think I could compose a broadcast play on my own account. But I doubt whether I could – though of course I'm not so ossified yet as not to have picked up a good many hints from your scripts. There is a one-act play of mine, *A Social Success*, that George Alexander produced: quite a good little thing, which even my lack of ingenuity mightn't fail to turn on to the air tolerably well. I might try my hand at that – perhaps.

The arrangement in regard to Miss Clemence Dane is that your version shall be producible by the B.B.C. for six months; the matter to be then reconsidered. I had gathered from the B.B.C. that Mr Blackburn wished that there should be only one performance – but Mr Blackburn explained that this was a misunderstanding. (It seems that the B.B.C. is not likely to have more than one performance. But that is quite another matter. I merely objected to the idea of restriction by Mr Blackburn.)

I wonder how Miss Deborah Kerr has turned out? The name *Deborah* is promising. It suggests something not-twentieth-centuryish: something ingenuous, and something (or rather somebody) *speaking* words, instead of feebly twittering and slurring them away into inaudibility.

Give my best messages, please, to the delightful Moray McLaren. I hope he hasn't forgotten me. But this he can hardly have done, since he is in touch with the H.H.

*"Views on Eighteenth Century Pronunciation"*

Virgo – to rhyme with ergo

Sagittarius – Sadjitarious (to rhyme with various)

Nissarah – to rhyme with Kiss 'er, ah

Aeneas – accent on the second syllable, of course,
                             and English vowels

Astyanax – accent on the y – rhyme with "Hast *I* an axe?"
                             (For *Hast* read *Have*.)

St Aldred's – (Al "as in Talbot", and not "in Alfred" –
though I've no prejudice against poor Alf.)
Best wishes from                    Yours very sincerely    MAX BEERBOHM

P.S. I'm *so* glad Clinton Baddeley[1] is again me-ing!


## To J.B. Priestley
MS. Texas

*2 August 1940*                              *Abinger Manor Cottage*

Dear Priestley, Yes, please put my name down on the list: I should be
most glad to see it there, for of course I am all in sympathy with the
idea that the talents of authors in these days ought not to be looked
askance at by Whitehall.

I only wish that my own talent, such as it is, could come in useful.
But, alas, it couldn't: it's so entirely delicate and personal and ironical
and unadaptable to great cosmic issues.

I must leave *you* to speak *for* me! – as you so splendidly do, every
Sunday at 9.20. You express just what I feel as a man but couldn't for
the life of me express penfully or orally.[1]

Queer are the limitations of a style acquired in early youth! With all
good wishes, and with great admiration of you and of your works,

Yours sincerely    MAX BEERBOHM


## To G.M. Trevelyan[2]
MS. Trinity

*11 February 1941*                           *Abinger Manor Cottage*

Dear Master of Trinity, I was deeply honoured by the proposal of your
Council that I should deliver the Clark Lectures in 1942;[3] and I thank
you very much for the kind and charming wording of your letter to me.

[1] V. C. Clinton Baddeley, actor, writer, broadcaster and dramatic critic (1900–70).

[2] Priestley's immensely popular radio talks began on 5 June 1940 and continued until
October. They were published as *Postscripts* at the end of the year.

[3] Historian (1876–1962). Master of Trinity College, Cambridge, 1940–51. Text from a
copy in the hand of his brother Bob, in the library of Trinity College, Cambridge.

[4] An annual series of lectures (usually four or six) on English literature, administered
by Trinity College.

I have been hoping against hope that I might see some way of rising to the level of such an occasion. I have exhaustively searched my mind for some theme on which I might be able to discourse (not with the requisite authority, indeed, but) with the requisite copiousness. But now I am driven to confess to myself, and to you, that my search has been fruitless. I have failed to ferret out one single subject about which I know enough to enable me to say enough, or anything like enough, about it. I have views on a great number of subjects, but no great co-ordinated *body of views* on any subject. I have been rather a light-weight; and mature years have not remedied this defect. I must console myself with the fact that – well, I daresay you remember a pretty little poem of Leigh Hunt's, the last lines of which I paraphrase:

> Time, you thief, who love to get
> Sweets within your pipe, put *that* in!
> Say I'm weary, say I'm sad,
> Say I'm growing old – but add,
> G.M. Trevelyan wanted me to
>      deliver a Clark Lecture.[1]

Yours sincerely, and with deep regret,    MAX BEERBOHM

P.S. Your brother Bob often comes and delights us with his company. How entirely unlike anybody else he is! And how remarkable in all ways, and lovable!


## To Alan (Jock) Dent[2]

[1941–2]                                        *Abinger Manor Cottage*

Dear Alan Dent, I take as a great compliment your wish that I should intrude into your book; and I hasten to thank you for the shiningly good example this book would have set me if it had been published when I was as young as you still are. I should have been taught to cultivate what I, as a writer of critical articles in the old *Saturday Review*, persistently neglected: the art of modesty. You never push yourself

---

[1] Hunt's poem ends:
> "Say I'm weary, say I'm sad,
>    Say that health and wealth have missed me,
> Say I'm growing old, but add,
>    Jenny kissed me."

[2] Author, critic and journalist (1905–78). Text from his *Preludes and Studies* (1942).

forward. You merge yourself in your theme. You wish that your reader shall share your pleasure in good work that you admire, and shall incidentally learn from you just why it is admirable. My own wish was that the reader should admire *me*. And it served me right that, so far as I am aware, he didn't.

The only excuse I can find for myself is that I was never, in the true sense, a critic; never an enlightening judge of excellence. I knew what was good, but I was apt to be puzzled as to the constituents of its goodness, and was a foggy eulogist. Badness is easy game, and to badness I always turned with relief. Badness is auspicious to the shower-off. Its only drawback is that it isn't worth writing about.

I suppose that you have had to write about it from time to time. For I believe that there have been produced in recent years some bad plays (though I believe also that the general level of dramaturgy is higher, that the number of clever people who write plays is greater, than it was in my time – a time when clever people, with only four or five exceptions, never thought of writing anything in the nature of a play). But I find no depreciations included in your book, and am glad of this absence – though I have no doubt that you are as good a depreciator as I deemed myself.

As one who never was stage-struck, even in early youth, and was frightfully stage-sick long before I ceased to write dramatic criticism, but have always been keenly interested in life and all that kind of thing, I (can I *never* not thrust myself forward?) thank you most especially for your studies of men and women – Boswell and Paganini, Mrs Norton and Miss Austen, Fuseli and the rest. I knew them pretty well already. Thanks to you, I know them better now. Of the "Places" that you describe, Kew Gardens is the only one that I have seen. I was in it once, and it somehow depressed me. Now I am charmed by it. And I have a strong impulse to visit those other places of yours. That is because you write so well. Modest though you are, you can't be unconscious of your rare gift for the art of writing. But neither can I help mentioning it to you. With all good wishes, yours sincerely          MAX BEERBOHM

205

## E.M. Forster to Max
TS. Merton

[*February 1942*]                                    *West Hackhurst*

Dear Sir Max Beerbohm, I have perused with pleasure the account of Zuleika's alleged visit to Cambridge, but regret you should have lent credence to it.[1] I told you *years and years ago* what happened to her, and you have never listened to me: she was shunted into a siding at Bletchley.[2]

This letter, though an extremely important one, requires no reply.
With every good wish to Lady Beerbohm and to yourself.

Yours sincerely   E.M. FORSTER

[*Max's answer has not come to light.*]


## E.M. Forster to Max
TS. Merton

*12 March 1942*                                    *West Hackhurst*

My dear Max Beerbohm, Oh but 'wrong again' is not a scientific exclamation. To you, after a fortnight's reflection, I would rather say that, with every appearance of objectivity and with some slight inclination towards it, you have fallen into the symmetric fallacy nevertheless. You do not know what that is? You have read your Ruskin merely?[3] Very well. The symmetric fallacy is that which leads a person to be unable to conceive of Oxford without Cambridge, and to send Zuleika, at all costs, from one to the other. Ah! Life is not so balanced as that. Look into your truer self, and I feel convinced that you will agree.

Yours sincerely   E.M. FORSTER

I was aware, being a student, of Maeterlinck's relict. But she left a little baby behind her, and Melisande of Bletchley would never have stooped to that.[4]

---

[1] *Zuleika in Cambridge* by S.C. Roberts (1941), to whom Max wrote: "I had often wondered what happened when Zuleika went to Cambridge. And now I *know*, beyond any shadow of a doubt."

[2] In the old days travellers between Oxford and Cambridge had to change trains halfway at Bletchley.

[3] In his *Modern Painters* Ruskin coined the phrase "pathetic fallacy".

[4] In Maeterlinck's play *Pelléas et Mélisande* the dying heroine gives birth to a daughter.

## To E.M. Forster
MS. King's

*17 March 1942*                                    *Abinger Manor Cottage*

My dear Morgan Forster, When a man who is engaged in an uneven contest gets to talking about objectivity and Mélisande's baby and the symmetric fallacy, it is because he knows he's beaten and feels that his one chance of avoiding the knock-out blow is to throw dust in the eyes of the victor. This dust-throwing is a coward's trick. A brave man and clean fighter throws up the sponge simply and frankly.

I am investing the prize-money (or "purse", as I think they call it) in Defence Bonds and am very sincerely yours

MAX BEERBOHM

## To Violet Schiff
MS. Merton

*26 August 1942*                                    *Abinger Manor Cottage*

Dearest Violet and dearest Sydney – to the latter of whom ever so many thanks for the lovely present of lovely cigarettes (I took some of them up to London in my cigarette case on Monday afternoon, and offered a few of them impressively and unselfishly to the more fortunate of my kind hosts).

And now for the "former of whom": it is an immense pleasure to Florence and me that you are making such good progress and may be here in your home much sooner than in your letter you had expected – here away from the sounds of the "overground traffic" that seemed to you so decidedly underground. How eagerly the Manor House awaits you! – and how eagerly do we!

You said you would like to hear something of the Albemarle Street festivity.[1] Really festal it was, and very much did I enjoy it, despite the

---

[1] Jock Dent had founded an association in Max's honour and called it The Maximilians. The original members were the Seven Men (Gerald Barry, Lord Berners, James Bone, Ivor Brown, Moray McLaren, Raymond Mortimer, Alan Thomas, and Dent himself), but by the time of Max's seventieth birthday on 24 August 1942 the Maximilians numbered seventy-seven. The Grand Initial Assembly took place on that day in the tiny Players Theatre at 13 Albemarle Street, Piccadilly.

Among the answers to Dent's invitations to members were these two observations. The first from the painter Augustus John:

Recently I was moved beyond expression on hearing Max's voice on the Air. Why is this such a rare occurrence? On this occasion the Master permitted himself to indulge, though briefly, necessity of holding forth for a few minutes. I was surprised at the largeness of the number of men who had been able and willing to turn up. I suppose some 40 or 50 of the 77 were there, and they were immensely cordial. Desmond MacCarthy, as chairman, spoke beautifully about me. And before and after his and my part of the proceedings, "The Late Joys," who perform by night on the premises, gave a sort of "command performance". They are extraordinarily good: most of them quite young, but entering with infinite gusto into the spirit of the comic and of the sentimental songs of the 1860's–1880's. Truly droll and delightful. Another feature of the occasion (this an entire surprise) was the announcement of a huge presentation of wine! The carrier from Gomshall (the station via which such things are sent) will have his work cut out for him. I suppose that for members of the "Association" there must have been some entrance fee. This I had not imagined; and I feel slightly guilty – though of course I am guiltless.[1]

Thank you, dearest Sydney, for sending me Logan Pearsall Smith's[2] charming thing in the *Observer*. I had not known that he liked my work so much – though he has always been one of my encouragers. He was one of the men present, though he has for several years been in bad health, and till lately was bed-ridden.

But what a lot about myself! While it is all the time about you two that I am thinking – of you and the joy of seeing you again.

Dearest love to you both from Florence and your devoted    MAX

---

that strain of poesy which I have always suspected him of concealing and which hitherto he has kept so dark. But it was the voice of England one heard! And what a change from the jaunty standardised accents which usually reach us through the Ether and to which, I, for one, can never accustom myself. Personally I am no sound modernist. I like best old and seasoned things. Max is old and seasoned. He was born so. Hence his endurance, his indestructibility, and the inviolable innocence of his genius. With this congenital advantage he runs no danger of reaching his fatal maximum for that will always be ahead of him.

The other is self-explanatory:

In reply to your letter of the 28th April, Mr Bernard Shaw asks me to say that he suffered too much from the celebration of his own seventieth birthday sixteen years ago to make himself a party to a repetition of the same outrage at the expense of an old friend who never harmed him.

*[For Max's speech at the party, see Appendix, p. 233.]*

[1] This gift of wine became an annual event.

[2] American writer, naturalised British (1865–1949). His long and laudatory article in the *Observer* of 23 August 1942 ended: "Examining again his books of caricatures, or that masterpiece *Rossetti and his Circle*, we rub our eyes to find how time has added to their lustre. Why, a man of genius has been at work among us all the time, and we never knew it! A Genius which we feel must rank high, rank almost among the highest."

## To Sydney Schiff
MS. Merton

Dearest Sydney, What a very charming present! Ever so many thanks. I shall recur to this book constantly.[2] Those 'seventies are to me so much more congenial than these 'forties; and really I think I know much more about them. And, moreover, how immensely adroit and accomplished Tissot was in his presentment of his "world"! I rather wish James Laver had included some of the caricatures that Tissot did for Tommy Bowles.[3] The *Rochefort* and the *Napoleon III* were very powerful fantasies; and the *Leighton* was a masterpiece of admiring mockery. You may remember it? It was entitled "A Sacrifice to the Graces" – Leighton exquisitely reclining against the side of an open door at an evening party. I am glad to find the prototype of it – or a reminiscence of it? – in the painting "Too Early" (1873), which is one of the happiest compositions.

Fondest love to Violet and to you from us.   Your devoted   MAX

## To Otto Kyllmann[4]
MS. Lilly

*17 August 1944*                                         *Flint Cottage, Box Hill, Dorking*

My dear Kyllmann, How nice of you! Be assured that Florence and I are – and indeed *were* – quite all right. Neither of us received the slightest hurt or suffered from any after-effect of blast. The bomb was a direct hit on the near-by village church, and has made the Manor House and the Manor Cottage uninhabitable for the present. You must, I am sure, have visited this house in Meredith's time.[5] It now belongs

---

[1] i.e. Abinger Manor Cottage.

[2] *"Vulgar Society": the Romantic Career of James Tissot 1836–1902* by James Laver (1936).

[3] Thomas Gibson Bowles (1844–1922), M.P., journalist and author, founded *Vanity Fair* in 1868 and owned the paper. As a correspondent of the *Morning Post*, he witnessed the vain defence of Paris against the Germans in 1870 and during the siege met Tissot, a Frenchman who was fighting in the army. He survived the Commune in 1871, and in 1872 moved to England, under the auspices of Bowles. He lived in London for the next ten years, during which many of his drawings, including those mentioned by Max, appeared in *Vanity Fair*, and he exhibited regularly in the Royal Academy.

[4] 1870–1959. A partner of the publishers Constable from 1893.

[5] George Meredith lived at Flint Cottage from 1868 until his death there on 18 May 1909.

to Mr and Mrs Ralph Wood, who are kindly putting us up. We go to other neighbouring friends in a week or so.

Please give our love to Helen Waddell[1] – and also to yourself.

Yours ever   MAX BEERBOHM

P.S. None of our belongings in the cottage was injured by the action of the bomb: merely the structure itself (roof, walls, windows, etc). Bombs are strange things.

## *Evelyn Waugh to Max*[2]
MS. Reichmann

*20 May [1947]*                                    *Piers Court, Stinchcombe, Glos.*

Dear Sir Max, It was a high privilege to be allowed to visit you on Sunday. I write, first, to thank you for letting Christopher bring us; secondly, to give you our address in case you are ever near us. (For instance if you go to Bristol to broadcast this would be directly on your route and it might be convenient to stop here for refreshment of some kind.) Thirdly, to ask you to accept a copy of my last novel. I can hardly hope you will read it, still less that you will approve any of it. I bring it like a terrier putting a dead rat on the counterpane – as an act of homage.                                    Yours sincerely   EVELYN WAUGH

## *To Evelyn Waugh*
MS. Waugh

*22 May 1947*                    *Highcroft, The Edge, Stroud, Gloucestershire*

Dear Evelyn Waugh, You are wrong about the "high privilege". It was *mine*, in that the Christophers brought the Evelyns to see me. And you are wrong about "homage" too; for you are a more gifted man than ever I was. And again you are wrong in supposing that I had not read *Brideshead Revisited*: I had done so at the time when it was first published, and I remember well the great outward brilliance of it and the inward strength and depth. I shall now read it again, for I am one of "those who have the leisure to read a book for the interest of the writer's use of language". And you are a master of language when you

---

[1] Mediaevalist and writer (1889–1965). Close friend of Kyllmann.

[2] Novelist (1903–66). His *Brideshead Revisited* was published in 1945. Christopher Sykes and his wife had taken the Waughs to see Max on 18 May 1947.

write for print: it is only when you write a letter or inscribe a book that you go astray!

  With best regards to Mrs Evelyn

Yours sincerely   MAX BEERBOHM

P.S. I shall bear in mind your kind proposal that I should break my journey to Bristol, if and when I go there.


## Evelyn Waugh to Max
### MS. Reichmann

*24 May [1947]*            *Piers Court, Stinchcombe, Glos.*

Dear Sir Max, It is not for me to bandy civilities with my Master. I can only say that your letter has rendered me completely drunk.

Yours sincerely   EVELYN WAUGH


## To Douglas Cleverdon
### MS. Cleverdon

*26 February 1948*            *Villino Chiaro*

My dear Douglas Cleverdon, Your letter about *Zuleika* makes me feel rather proud of myself. But I won't go further than to admit that the book is certainly a very careful piece of work.

  Air Post is slow enough in these days, and your letter reached me only yesterday. I hope *this* letter may reach you in decent time. Not that it will contain anything of much importance.

  Your adaptation fills me with wonderment at your ingenuity and fidelity. I send eleven pages of the typescript on which I have pencilled slight and small suggestions.

  I wish the dear great Vaughan Williams could have seen his way to doing some music for Z. But, as he couldn't, here are one or two suggestions of my own about the music. I think it would be a good thing perhaps that each of the principal characters should have a *motif*, recurring now and again. *One* motif would do for the Duke; something austerely pompous and impressive. Zuleika, I think, should have two motifs – one for the gay and giddy and unscrupulous side of her, the other for the yearning and wistful side. The Duke's motif should occur first in the narrator's account of his character and career; and Zuleika's in the account of hers. The Warden might have a slight motif perhaps.

211

Not Noaks: music would not befit him. What do you think? I believe that the motifs, recurring at all crucial moments, would be of real value.[1]

In the concert scene there should certainly be some traces of Chopin's Funeral March. And perhaps in the Duke's speech at the Junta. *But not any in the scene of the undergraduates' suicide; for then it would jar on the minds of people remembering actual funeral services that they had attended.*

I think that the deleted passage on page 25 is necessary and should be restored.

I do so look forward to the Second Part. The Second Part of Goethe's *Faust* has always rather baffled people. But I'm sure the S.P. of my Z, and yours, won't do so. Yours very sincerely   MAX BEERBOHM

P.S. Let there be nothing *classical* about the first of the two Zuleika motifs. Let the Third Programme disgrace itself by something very frivolous and "catchy"!

## To Douglas Cleverdon
MS. Cleverdon

[*Postmark 9 March 1948*] *Villino Chiaro*

My dear Douglas Cleverdon, First of all, please thank "Nest"[2] (what an enchanting name!) for her letter to me, and convey to her my regrets for all those outpourings of black coffee!

Secondly, ever so many thanks for your letter about everything – the letter that you had written before you received mine.

I hope that perhaps there may meanwhile have been time for composal of little *motifs* – not for original composal of them, of course, but merely a selection of them from records in the files of the B.B.C. I do feel that some recurrent strains of music would be a great help, in keeping the narrative alive and sustaining the *fantasy* of it.

Part II seems to me as well and brilliantly done as Part I. Congratulations and thanks. I only think that perhaps Clio is given too great a space. Even in the book, for the reader, who could "skip", I felt that she rather held up the narrative. And skipping isn't a privilege allowed to the listener. I rather think she ought to be briefer. This would give time for what I feel is rather important: more attention to the *Emperor* theme (pages of typescript 66 and 94).

[1] In the end Cleverdon used the various Oxford bells as musical motifs.

[2] Mrs Douglas Cleverdon.

On page 115 I think Zuleika should say "I will go back and tell my grandfather that I have decided to take the veil – to be a nun." Without those four additional words her meaning would not carry on the air.

Otherwise, I've nothing to suggest. Except that Noaks ought to have a slightly – very slightly – Cockney accent.

Yours ever sincerely   MAX BEERBOHM

P.S. The pronunciation of the name Zuleika is a matter of vital, of tremendous importance. About that I am sending you a telegram. I am sorry it is a name of which the pronunciation is arguable and disputable – and am glad that Nest is not such a name.

## *Telegram to Douglas Cleverdon*

*[9 March 1948]*                                                   *Rapallo*

### ZULEIKA SPEAKER NOT HIKER BEERBOHM

## *To Haro Hodson*[1]
MS. Hodson

*Saturday [June 1948]*                                       *Villino Chiaro*

Dear Mr Hodson, We are so very glad you have arrived, and only sorry that you have been mystified as to our exact whereabouts.

These whereabouts are just a mile and a half away from the piazza of Rapallo. A visitor takes his courage in both hands and crosses the little bridge that runs beside the Hotel Europa, he then walks along the high road, the coast road, which has no turning (I mean, no roads leading away from it), and in due course he will see on his left-hand side a weather-cock, a small Swiss girl upstanding from a wall, and he passes her by and, a moment or two later, sees (on his left-hand side again) what looks like a garage and is the basement of this villino, and then he sees a gate which he opens, and then he comes up a flight of stone stairs, and here he is. I hope all this is lucid and unmistakeable? We shall be here all to-morrow, and we greatly hope to see you at four o'clock or so.            Yours very sincerely   MAX BEERBOHM

---

[1] Artist (born 1923).

## To Camilla Sykes[1]
MS. Georgetown

[*Early 1949*]                                                    *Villino Chiaro*

My dear Camilla, I wondered what to do in the good cause. (But first
of all let me say how greatly Florence and I rejoiced in your letter! Such
a *vocal* letter – as letters ought to be; so like your voice.) To resume, I
thought I would do a drawing of Walter Sickert: likely to be saleable
because by all the art-critics and art-students nowadays he is taken *à
plus que grand sérieux*; and is a name to conjure with even among the
non-elect, insomuch that a new block of workmen's tenements in
Camden Town is to be called "Sickert Court"! (Oh, how bewildered he
would have been, and how wildly he would have screamed with laughter,
were he still living! – he who until the last few years of his life had been
regarded by his fellow-painters and by the critics as no more than a
rather perverse experimenter and not a very gifted one.)

I will now try to be a little less inky, a little more vocal. I shan't
succeed, but I shall try. To re-resume, I did a page for you of six heads
of Walter as he was at divers times – long-haired, short-haired, clean-
shaven, enormously bearded, etc. The drawing has been mounted and
framed – and will be sent to you by registered post – but it can't be
*glazed* here; for, if it were, the parcel would then be beyond a certain
weight and all sorts of red-tape official formalities would have to be gone
through before the drawing could be legally posted out of Italy. So
please have it glazed in England – if indeed glass is procurable in
England nowadays.[2]

Love to that wondrously good writer, one of the staves of my declining
years, Christopher. And do, please, both of you, be here again with us
very soon.                                                    Yours ever   MAX

P.S. I hope you'll like the drawing. *I* think it looks rather pretty. An
*oeuvre de vieillesse,* but presentable in its funny old way.

---

[1] Daughter of Russell Pasha and wife of the writer Christopher Sykes (1907–87). She
was collecting for a charity sale at Christie's on behalf of the Young Women's Christian
Association.

[2] The drawing fetched eighteen guineas at Christie's on 24 June 1949. Its present
ownership is unknown.

## To Osbert Sitwell[1]
MS. Texas

*June 1949*                                                   *Villino Chiaro*

My dear Osbert, If I were still by way of being a caricaturist, I should do a drawing of you and Sachy on either side of Dr Edith,[2] and, from the clouds above, three sisters gazing down rather sadly and sourly.

For you three have quite definitely now surpassed the Brontës. You were very brilliant from the outset, but each of you has, throughout the passage of the years, steadily, incessantly, expanded and deepened. (And even if Anne had been as remarkable as Charlotte or Emily, she wouldn't tip the scale against the later triad.)

And I wonder what English autobiographist would tip the scale against *you*. England has produced many great histories, many great diaries, many great novels, and so on. She may have produced some great autobiographies, but they have never come my way: only some delightful ones, of no great scope and sweep, and not comparable with the work of so shiningly august a scoper and sweeper as *you*, Osbert.

I don't know what to liken these four volumes of yours to.[3] They remind me rather of Chartres Cathedral (multiplied by four). But that won't do. There's nothing *static* about *you*. You are so mobile – so grandly *processional*. A procession of Cardinals and other dignitaries in the time of the Holy Roman Empire? But no, again. They went only in one direction at a time, whereas you radiate in as many directions as the sun. And the sun can't *write*, whereas *you* ...

Yours affectionately   MAX

## To the Maximilians
MS. Texas

*June 1949*                                                   *Villino Chiaro*

My dear (I am a non-Narcissine and a modest man, fully conscious of his own unworthiness, and thus cannot give you your full name) imilians, I have received exciting news from your secretary, or ring-leader, Alan Dent. It seems that because I shall soon be seventy-seven four cases of

[1] Poet, novelist and autobiographer (1892–1969).

[2] Osbert's brother Sacheverell and their sister.

[3] *Left Hand, Right Hand!* (1945), *The Scarlet Tree* (1946), *Great Morning* (1948) and *Laughter in the Next Room* (1949). A fifth volume, *Noble Essences*, appeared in 1950.

Bordeaux and two of Cognac – seventy-two bottles in all! – have been bought in Paris and (the High Commissioner of Eire figuring somewhere mysteriously in the background) will travel southward to another capital, Rome, and thence back northward to me of all people in the world. I am puzzled but of course enchanted. I wish I were rather younger, so that I could deal with the whole gift. In the course of nature, I shall hardly be able to do that, and am therefore adding to my will a codicil directing that the residue of the gift shall go back to Rome and thence to Paris and thence to London and, Eire permitting, be divided among you in equal portions by the ring-leader.

Your grateful   M A X

## To Jim Rose[1]
MS. Rose (J)

*Tuesday 18 October 1949*                              *Villino Chiaro*

My dear Jim Rose, Thank you for your delightful letters to Florence and to me.

I think I can do something readable about *A Little Tour*,[2] and will post it to you this week, so that it would be in good time for the following week. The book of H.J.'s dramatic criticisms[3] I (or rather *me*, for even when I was in my prime I never was able to make and tie up a parcel presentably and safely – and was a constant receiver of rebukes and taunts from the Postmaster General) – I say that *me* are posting that back. To write even a very few words in addition to the countless words that I did write about the theatre would shorten the short span of my life on this earth.

The H.J. tour is very far below the level of his tours in Italy or even in England,[4] but is of course to be respected.

(By the way, since you ask me, and since in despite of American taxation the Astor family is, I like to think, still quite fairly well-off, it does seem to me that £25 isn't quite enough. But I may be wrong.)[5]

[1] Born 1909. Literary Editor of the *Observer* 1948–51.

[2] A new edition of *A Little Tour in France* by Henry James, first published in 1900. In Max's review, which appeared in the *Observer* on 13 November 1949, he described James's rewriting of his early work in old age as "a process akin to patching pale gray silk with snippets of very dark thick brown velvet. It was a strange aberration: and a wanton offence against the laws of art".   [3] *The Scenic Art*, edited by Allan Wade (1949).

[4] *English Hours* (1905). *Italian Hours* (1909).

[5] Rose was happily able to increase the fee.

I am so glad Haro Hodson's poems[1] are going to be published by the Heinemann firm, which is also *my* firm.

And now Florence and I are all the time hoping that Mrs Jim and you will soon reappear in Italy and repeat the delight that your company gave us.                    Yours very sincerely   MAX BEERBOHM

P.S. Please let the article be printed *consecutively*, when it comes. My article about the Nineties had an illustration in the middle of it, and some of the writing had to trickle narrowly down each side of the inset, rather fatally to the rhythm and the meaning of the sentences.[2]

## Telegram to Violet Schiff
### MS. Merton

[*Early January 1951*]                                    *Villino Chiaro*

DARLING  FLORENCE  RATHER  SERIOUSLY  UNWELL PLEASE TELL ELISABETH   LOVE   MAX[3]

## To Alexandra Bagshawe[4]
### MS. Clark

*25 February 1951*                                        *Villino Chiaro*

Dearest Dodie, I write in pencil because I am still weak after an attack of bronchitis which I had two days after darling Florence died. Her heart during the past few years had grown less and less strong. All that could be done by care of doctors was done. But now I am alone ... But not actually so. Florence had always wished that if she were seriously ill, dangerously ill, an old friend of hers and mine, Elisabeth Jungmann, whom we knew first when she was secretary to Gerhart Hauptmann, the poet, twenty-five years ago, and whom we have often seen here and in England during those years, should be telegraphed for. When the

---

[1] *The Visitor*, accepted in 1949, published in 1952.

[2] Max's review, in the *Observer* of 3 October 1948, of *The Eighteen-Nineties, a Period Anthology in Prose and Verse*, chosen by Martin Secker, was printed with a Beardsley drawing in the middle of its three columns.

[3] Florence died on 13 January, when Elisabeth Jungmann had already arrived to take care of Max for the rest of his life. Probably he had never been looked after so lovingly and well. Elisabeth, who adored him, was, as Eiluned Lewis wrote, "like a tree – a tall, strong tree with branches outspread to welcome and shelter".

[4] Daughter of Florence's brother Mannie.

doctors could hold out no hope that Florence could live long, I did this, without telling what the doctors had said, and she was very glad. It had always been her idea that Miss Jungmann would be able to look after me in a practical way – doing for me the many things I should be utterly incapable of doing for myself. Miss Jungmann will be able to remain here.

As I have said, I am still weak; and writing is an effort, so would you please post this letter to Nell?[1] – with my love to her, and thanks for her telegram of sorrow and sympathy.

I do so hope Robin's health will definitely improve. Love to you and to her and to George from                                          MAX


## To Ronald Boswell[2]
TS. Merton

*26 June 1952*                                                    *Villino Chiaro*

Dear Mr Boswell, Many thanks for the B.B.C.'s offer of a fee for my broadcast about Desmond MacCarthy; but on the whole I think I would rather not receive any money for having paid that little tribute to the memory of an old and dear friend.

With kind regards,            Yours sincerely   MAX BEERBOHM


## To S. N. Behrman[3]
MS. Texas

*13 July 1952*                                    *Albergo, Montallegro, Rapallo*

Dear Mr Behrman, Thank you for your charming letter.

It would be a very great pleasure for me to see you and commune with you. (*Interviewed* I can't be. I have for thirty years and more refused to be so by any one, and have offered my word of honour to every successive applicant that I wouldn't be interviewed by any other one. In the days when I was interviewed from time to time the result

---

[1] Dodie's mother.

[2] B.B.C. producer. Desmond MacCarthy died on 7 June 1952, and Max's tribute was broadcast on 22 June. It was printed in the 1957 edition of *Mainly on the Air*.

[3] American dramatist and biographer (1893–1973). This was the beginning of one of the last and happiest of Max's friendships. He was soon writing to "Dearest Sam", who later encapsulated their "communings" in his book *Conversation with Max* (1960).

was always disastrously dull. And if it was thus in the green leaf[1] ... not even so coruscating a spirit as yours would be undefeated.)

I am in weak health, and the air down in Rapallo has been stifling, and I am therefore on this higher and more salubrious level – which is reachable by motor-car or (in six minutes or so) by a funicular railway. I am looked after with very great care and kindness by Miss Elisabeth Jungmann, of whom you will have heard.

Will you please telephone to her saying when you could come to luncheon or to dinner?     Yours very sincerely   MAX BEERBOHM


## To Edward Marsh
MS. Berg

*23 August 1952*                                                    *Villino Chiaro*

My dear Eddie, I, with my pencil, have been in my time a ruthless monstrifier of men. And the bully is, proverbially, always a coward. And I have seen reproductions of Graham Sutherland's portraits of Somerset Maugham and of Lord Beaverbrook. And I feel very much honoured by the wish of the Committee of the Contemporary Arts Society that a portrait of me should be painted by him – *but* I am not one whit the less unwilling to submit and sit!

In spite of all you have done and been, I had no notion that *you* were anywhere near the age of 80. The news makes me feel that *I* must be about to be 90.                                   Yours ever   MAX

P.S. "Henry Moore", you say, "has put English sculpture on the map of Europe." This being so, the elder[2] Pitt would not now say "Roll up that map!" It has been squashed down flat for ever.


## To Laurence Irving[3]
MS. Irving

*14 September 1952*                                                  *Villino Chiaro*

Dear Laurence Irving, I had forgotten the South Down lamb at that dinner of E.V.'s,[4] but I remember (for I had never encountered them

---

[1] "For if they do these things in a green tree, what shall be done in the dry?" (St Luke, xxiii, 31).

[2] Marsh corrected this to 'younger'.

[3] Artist, author and designer for stage and film (born 1897).

[4] E. V. Lucas.

before, nor have I encountered them since) the sharks' fins. Still more clearly do I remember the very great pleasure it was for me to encounter *you*. Little did I suppose that anything that I was saying could at any future time be of the slightest use to you. And yet I gather from what you have written for the grand red Album[1] that you are under the impression that I was helpful. I hope you are right. *I*, anyway, am right in the impression – or rather the certainty – that I had in reading your biography of your grandfather,[2] that you had achieved a masterpiece. I rank it with Lockhart's life of Walter Scott, and G. O. Trevelyan's life of Macaulay. It is as perfect as they in construction, as vivid in portrayal, as sound in judgment, and as felicitous, throughout, in manner.

Yours very sincerely   MAX BEERBOHM

## To Rupert Hart-Davis[3]
MS. Hart-Davis

*20 September 1952*                                                    *Villino Chiaro*

Dear Mr Hart-Davis (though I hesitate to address you as "Mr," having often seen your perambulator in your parents' hall), Many thanks for your letter. I like very much your idea of publishing my dramatic criticisms in one large volume ("roughly 675 pages") – price 30 shillings, 15 per cent royalty, etc. I would like to see, as you suggest, a specimen page; and I am sure you will agree with me that the book should be printed in black ink on white paper (and not, as so many books are nowadays, in grey ink on sallow paper); and that there should be a proper space after full-stops, and no monkey tricks in the design of notes of interrogation and exclamation: no eccentricities of any kind; and that the printer and proof-readers shall be exhorted stringently to follow my punctuation *exactly* throughout, and that the proofs sent to me shall be in all respects absolutely faithful to the original text.
With best regards, meanwhile,

I am yours sincerely   MAX BEERBOHM

P.S. Shall you be able to run to "turn-over pages"? There must in any case be an *ample* space between every article and the next one – clearly

---

[1] This volume, filled with messages and tributes from Max's friends and admirers, was presented to him on his eightieth birthday.

[2] *Henry Irving: The Actor and his World* (1951).

[3] Max's selection of his dramatic criticisms, *Around Theatres*, had been published only in 1924 as two volumes in the expensive limited edition of his works. I had written to suggest a new edition in one volume.

indicating to the reader that a week or more has elapsed. (In the definitive edition of Bernard Shaw's dramatic criticisms the beginning of each article was jammed close up against the end of the previous one – in accordance to his own asinine principles about typography.)

P.P.S. I ought to have begun this letter with thanks to you for the copy of the Gallatin and Oliver bibliography – a most gratifying work, and awakener in me of many pleasant memories.[1]

## To Rupert Hart-Davis
MS. Hart-Davis

*22 January 1953*                                                    *Villino Chiaro*

Dear Rupert Hart-Davis, Many thanks for sending me the "Epistle Dedicatory". I find that in it I had said almost all that there was to be said by way of *Preface*. But I shall, I am sure, be able to find means to write the "little prefatory Note" of which I spoke.

Selwyn Jepson[2] has sent to me the proposed "jacket" which I like *very* much indeed. But – beautifully though the Bewick engraving comes on the page – I think that people mostly would suppose the fox to be symbolic of the character of the author whose name appears below. And this would rather worry me.[3]

Did I ever thank you for the biography of Hugh Walpole? I enjoyed and admired it deeply. He was a lovable and pitiable and enviable fellow, and his qualities could not have been shown forth more subtly and clearly than they are by you.

Very sincerely yours   MAX BEERBOHM

P.S. Many thanks also for the words inscribed on the back of the jacket. I feel honoured; and people in bookshops, will, I think, feel tempted.

[1] Although called a bibliography this book, published in 1952, was in fact simply a catalogue of A. E. Gallatin's Max collection at Harvard.

[2] Prolific novelist (born 1901). He and his wife Tania were great friends with Max in his last years and helped him greatly in literary and other business.

[3] I removed the Bewick engraving, but include overleaf a reproduction as Max first saw it. *Around Theatres* was published on 24 April 1953.

# Around

# Theatres

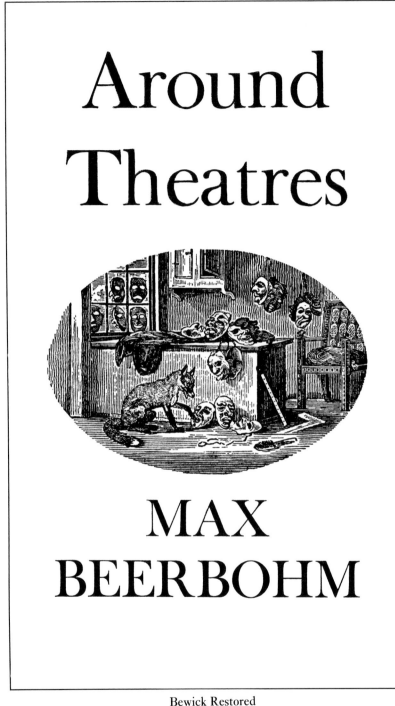

# MAX

# BEERBOHM

Bewick Restored

## To Vyvyan Holland[1]
### MS. Holland

*14 September 1953*                                      *Villino Chiaro*

My dear Vyvyan, Very many thanks for your letter, which gave me such very great pleasure. Some days before it reached me I had received a letter from Mr Eric Barton,[2] telling me about the plaque in memory of Oscar; and I enclose a copy of my answer (which will be posted to him at the same time as this letter to you).

I wish very much I could have the honour of unveiling the plaque, but I am too old to travel. I do look forward to your book.[3]

Yours ever   MAX


## To Don Patricio Gannon[4]
### TS. Draft. Reichmann

*September 1953*

Dear Patricio Gannon, Here is your book. I am so glad you have it. No one is likelier than you to appreciate the format (which so exactly suits the contents). And I am glad H. G. Wells seems to have had it too. He

---

[1] Writer and translator (1886–1967). Son of Oscar Wilde. He had asked Max to unveil the plaque outside 16 (now 34) Tite Street. Instead Max sent the following tribute, which was read out at the luncheon after the unveiling on 16 October 1954, the centenary of Oscar Wilde's birth:

"I suppose there are now few survivors among the people who had the delight of hearing Oscar Wilde talk. Of these I am one. I have had the privilege of listening also to many other masters of table-talk – Meredith and Swinburne, Edmund Gosse and Henry James, Augustine Birrell and Arthur Balfour, Gilbert Chesterton and Desmond MacCarthy and Hilaire Belloc – all of them splendid in their own way. But assuredly Oscar in *his* own way was the greatest of them all – the most spontaneous and yet the most polished, the most soothing and yet the most surprising. That his talk was mostly a monologue was not his own fault. His manners were very good; he was careful to give his guests or his fellow guests many a conversational opening; but seldom did anyone respond with more than a very few words. Nobody was willing to interrupt the music of so magnificent a virtuoso. To have heard him consoles me for not having heard Dr Johnson or Edmund Burke, Lord Brougham or Sydney Smith."

[2] Well known antiquarian bookseller.

[3] *Son of Oscar Wilde*, published in September 1954.

[4] Wealthy Argentine devotee of the writers of the Eighteen Nineties. He had just acquired and sent to Max H. G. Wells's copy of the first edition of Max's *Works*. Max returned it to him with this inscription.

223

was always very nice to me about my writings, *and* about my drawings though I used to do rather devastating caricatures of him, and though I had once made him cry. I cannot date the occasion except by saying it was very soon after the publication of *Love and Mr Lewisham*.[1] Entering the dining-room of the Savile Club at luncheon-time, I espied H. G. Wells (who had recently been elected) sitting alone at a table near the window, and went straight to him and leaned down to tell him how very beautiful I thought the book and how deeply I had been moved by it. And then, to my great embarrassment, I saw that there were tears in his eyes. He told me I was the first person who had praised the book. I suppose it was rather *because* than "though" I had made him cry that he was, ever after (intensely pugnacious and vengeful though he mostly was in his later years), so cordial to me and about me.

Elisabeth Jungmann joins me in hoping you will soon revisit Europe – and Rapallo. Most sincerely yours   MAX BEERBOHM


## To Geoffrey Bemrose[1]
### MS. Draft. Reichmann

*February* [*1954*]                                              [*Villino Chiaro*]

Dear Mr Bemrose, I am glad to know that the young Arnold's house is to be preserved in honour of him. I wish I had some tangible relic of him which I could send to you. Affection isn't a thing that can be placed in a museum. I can merely say that I was very fond of him – as indeed were all the people who knew him well. A "Card" he certainly was; but without guile; a very lovable fellow.

Yours sincerely   MAX BEERBOHM

P.S. I regard *The Old Wives' Tale* as the finest novel published in my time. Henry James, having read it, said that one asked oneself what it was all about. Well, it was, it is, all about a very important thing – the passage of youth into old age.


[1] Published in 1900.

[2] Curator of the Public Museum and Art Gallery at Hanley, Stoke-on-Trent. He had written to Max on 29 January, asking if he could contribute anything to Arnold Bennett's birthplace which was being turned into a museum by the Arnold Bennett Society.

## To Oliver Lawson Dick[1]
### MS. Draft. Reichmann

*7 June 1954*                                                    *Villino Chiaro*

Dear Mr Dick, I am sorry that I cannot be of use to you in this matter.
I did once – in 1912 or so – see a production of Russian Ballet by M.
Diaghilev, and I must confess I didn't like it. It seemed to me over-
lush.                                    Yours sincerely   MAX BEERBOHM


## To Mrs Davis
### TS. Draft. Reichmann

*15 August 1954*                                                *Villino Chiaro*

Dear Mrs Davis, I was much pleased by your charmingly kind letter,
and I wish very much that I could say in answer to it, "*Did I know* A. C.
Bradley?[2] Why, my dear Lady, I often feel that I never knew anybody
else! Such as I am, it was Bradley that made me. To him, and to him
alone, to his irradiating influence only, is due the fact that I am not (a)
a village idiot, and (b) a thoroughly bad lot." But, as a matter of fact, I
never had the pleasure of meeting him at Oxford or elsewhere, and (I
am ashamed to say) have never read any of his writings.

Please give my love to what used to be my rooms in Merton.

With all good wishes, Yours very sincerely   MAX BEERBOHM


## To Katie Lewis
### TS. Merton

*6 October 1954*                                              [*Villino Chiaro*]

Darling Katie, What an enchanting and wildly amusing letter you sent
me for my birthday! I envy you your letter-writing power. I can – or
rather used to be able to – write quite well for *print*; but I was always
one of the world's worst dullards when I wrote to a friend; and I continue
to be so.

---

[1] Who had asked Max to say something for the B.B.C. about the change that Diaghilev's
influence brought to the theatre in Europe.

[2] Andrew Cecil Bradley (1851–1935), author of *Shakespearian Tragedy* (1904) and
Professor of Poetry at Oxford 1901–6.

The book of Mrs Cameron's portraits is a lasting joy.[1] How those great men of hers do *live*! – Darwin and Sir John Herschel and Browning and Carlyle and Trollope, and the others. How finely she contrived to show the very souls of them and of their work! The whole of Barsetshire (for example) seems to be mapped out in dear old Trollope's countenance.

I am so glad you liked the William Eden book so much.[2] I wish you had been at Windlestone one night many years ago when in a neighbouring Town Hall Lady Eden and Walter Sickert played, in aid of some local charity, W. S. Gilbert's little two-act play *Engaged.* I was sitting next to him in the front row. You will remember that the scene of both acts is a very humble parlour. An immensely tall Windlestone footman bringing in a lamp, in the first scene, seemed to me to strike a false note. Still more false was the note struck by Eden, who sprang furiously to his feet, shouting "Don't put that lamp down on that table. Take it away. It would tumble over and burn the whole Hall down!" He had been very much opposed to the whole production, and indeed neither Lady Eden nor Walter Sickert showed any histrionic ability. And yet afterwards when I said something mildly complimentary about her performance he said "Well, yes. But of course a part like that didn't give her any real chance. I'd like to see her in a really good part – *La Dame aux Camélias* or something of *that* sort."

How I do hope, and so does Elisabeth, that you will be Berensonianising[3] next year and *here*-ising.

Fondest love from your devoted    MAX

## To Elisabeth Jungmann[4]
MS. Reichmann

*Friday evening* [*15 October 1954*]                              *Villino Chiaro*

Darling Elisabeth, What a beautiful letter from you this morning! And how it has moved and delighted me. I hadn't at all expected to hear so soon. I am so glad you had a whole compartment all to yourself, with

---

[1] *Victorian Photographs of Famous Men and Fair Women* by Julia Margaret Cameron, with introductions by Virginia Woolf and Roger Fry (1926).

[2] Presumably *The Tribulations of a Baronet* by Timothy Eden (1933).

[3] i.e. visiting the American art critic Bernard Berenson (1865–1959) at his home near Florence.             [4] Who was briefly visiting London.

Max in old age

no dreary persons to have to make friends with. I wonder what you have been doing to-day. *My* day has been the customary lunch in the vining-room and exercise on the terrace; and at tea-time Iris[1] came and was very good company. She goes to Rome to-morrow. I had a nice letter from "Jonah".[2] He says "Please give our love and thanks to Elisabeth, as I am now allowed to call her. Indeed I – but that would be telling." This morning a long envelope, with a bank's address on it, came for you. I have re-addressed it and it will be posted at the same time as this letter. (It is re-addressed twice – for I had made an omission at first shot.) Good night, darling, and take great care of yourself.

Your loving   MAX

## To Kenneth Rose[3]
### MS. Brudenell[4]

[*Postmark 11 December 1954*]                    *Villino Chiaro*

Dear Kenneth Rose, Further cigarettes have arrived. You are much too kind. You must cease to be so. And I must further reproach you for having sent me Mrs Cecil Woodham Smith's book about Lord Lucan and Lord Cardigan.[5] I am in the midst of reading it with intense interest. (It is as well done as the same author's *Florence Nightingale*.) Both of those Peers were (though you may hardly believe it) before my time; but I did overlap with the widow of one of them. In 1909 or so I was staying with friends within driving distance of Deene Park, and they took me to see the aged but unvenerated Lady Cardigan.[6] She wore a wig of bright gold curls and was plastered with paint, and was dressed in the fashion of a débutante in the eighteen-seventies, and held in her left hand a huge red rose. She was very arch and fluent and talked much about the Duc de Morny, and she sat down to the piano and sang to us a song entitled "Love me all in all, or not at all", by "my old friend

[1] Max's niece Iris Tree.

[2] Nickname of L. E. (Sir Lawrence) Jones, author and great admirer of Max.

[3] Biographer and journalist, born 1924.

[4] To whom Rose gave this letter, so that it might hang framed in Deene Park, the home of Lord Cardigan's family, the Brudenells.

[5] *The Reason Why* (1953).

[6] Her book *My Recollections* (1909) caused a sensation and went through many impressions. Max's caricature "Lady Cardigan's Book" (1909) bears the caption:
Early-Edwardian Era (to Early-Victorian Era):
"So! Now at last we see you in your true colours".

Julian Fane", and at the close of the song she kissed her finger-tips to us with great vivacity. It was all very strange and conducive to deep thought.     Yours very sincerely   MAX BEERBOHM


## To Gordon Craig
TS. Draft. Merton

*8 January 1955*

My dear Ted, What a delight to see your handwriting again! It always has been so immensely expressive in its variability – more like a voice than a script. You say you have been growing deaf, and I am very sorry for that — all the more so because it means that you won't hear your own voice so well as it deserves – so well as it comes out on a gramophone record that was sent to me by the kind B.B.C. – a record of what you beautifully said about me on my 80th birthday.

Ever affectionately   MAX


## To Osbert Lancaster[1]
MS. Draft. Merton

*27 January 1955*                                          *Villino Chiaro*

My dear Osbert, Your letter and the six photographs, posted on January 18th, arrived only to-day, bearing, besides the English postmark, a further one, "Valetta, Malta". I am thankful it didn't travel via Kamchatka.

The pictures are absolutely splendid. I am revelling in them, and marvelling at the beauty of them and the wit and truth of them, and vainly trying to decide which of them is my favourite. Ever so many thanks.

I haven't any reservation to make except that the moon-lit side of the quadrangle in Judas looks rather too *new*. Could you make the windows and the cornice a trifle less sharp in outline?

I long to see the rest of the photographs. Please meanwhile tell me what sort of *size* the frescoes are, what breadth and height, so that I can the better visualise them. Elisabeth Jungmann will presently be visiting

[1] Artist and writer (1908–86). Knighted 1975. He had been commissioned to paint twelve large frescoes of scenes from *Zuleika Dobson* for the ballroom of the Randolph Hotel, Oxford.

England and will certainly go to Oxford and be able to describe the general effect.

Fancy your fancying those old seventyish drawings of mine.[1] I have just been looking at the album in which they were reproduced, and I rather agree with you that they are good. I am sorry I haven't any idea of where Sir H. Vansittart and Mr Jacob Stanning may be. Perhaps in Malta?                              Yours most gratefully   MAX BEERBOHM


## To G. L. Lewin
MS. Draft. Reichmann

*14 June 1955*                                                     [*Villino Chiaro*]

Dear Mr Lewin, Julius Beerbohm was the third son of my father's first marriage, and was born in 1854. When he was quite a young man he wrote a very good book entitled *Wanderings in Patagonia*. After that he was always engaged in financial affairs, and sometimes quite rich, at others poor. He married a charming woman and had two daughters and a gifted son, who was killed in the first World War. He was known among all his friends by the nickname "Poet;" for he was constantly composing verses of either a satirical or a sentimental kind. He very seldom bothered to write a poem down, and I am not sure that any of them survives – barring that sonnet to Cecil Rhodes, which I well remember as very fine in expression and in feeling.

In a book about Herbert Beerbohm Tree (edited by me) there is a reproduction of a portrait of Julius by Zorn, the Swedish painter.

With all good wishes, Yours sincerely   MAX BEERBOHM


## To *Atticus of the* Sunday Times[2]

[*December 1955*]

Dear Atticus, I hope I don't intrude, but some of my friends have been alarmed by the recent paragraph in which you referred to the "modest circumstances" in which I face "another winter at Rapallo" and to my having "only the bare necessities of life". Let me assure you and them

---

[1] A series of sixteen portraits of imaginary luminaries of the 1870's, of which Osbert Lancaster had acquired all but two. They were all reproduced in Max's *Things New and Old* (1923).

[2] Text from the *Sunday Times* of 4 December 1955.

that I live, now as heretofore, in very great comfort and with no anxieties, and that the winter in Rapallo is always a very mild affair.

MAX BEERBOHM

## To Kenneth Rose
### MS. Rose

*17 March 1956*                                                    *Villino Chiaro*

My dear Kenneth Rose, Very many thanks for your most kind and amusing letter. I am delighted to learn from you that the ghost of my old friend Dodworth[1] walks even now here and there dispensing dignity in his own old way.

Yes, I know those memoirs of the Duke of Portland,[2] and I agree with you that such books are exhilarating in their spacious way. It would be going too far to say that lives of great grandees remind us we can make our lives sublime, but they are very jolly. (I liked very much the Duke's tale about his succession – how his batman said to the Colonel "I'm afraid Mr Bentinck wasn't quite 'correct' when he left for London this morning, sir. He went on saying something about his being the Duke of Portland.")

My favourite Duke, the most natural and monumental, is the one who had been Lord Hartington for so many years.[3] You are much too young to remember or even have heard of the Hartopp divorce case.[4] In those days such cases were reported verbatim in all the morning papers, and here is a passage which pleased me much – the opening of the Duke's evidence:

> Counsel. I think it is a fact, your Grace, that the petitioner and the respondent and the co-respondent were among a party of guests entertained

---

[1] Max's essay "T. Fenning Dodworth," a study of a pompous nonentity who wrote dull articles called "[Something] And After" and was greatly respected, was first published in the *London Mercury* in August 1921 and then in *A Variety of Things* (1928). The character may have been based on A. A. Baumann (1856–1936) who published many articles. One of his books was called *Betterment, Worsement, and Recoupment*.

[2] *Men, Women and Things* (1937) by the sixth Duke of Portland (1857–1943).

[3] The eighth Duke of Devonshire (1833–1908) was, as Lord Hartington, a Liberal cabinet minister, familiarly known as Harty-Tarty. He did not succeed to the Dukedom until he was 58.

[4] In November 1902 Sir Charles Edward Cradock-Hartopp, fifth Baronet, sued his wife Millicent, daughter of the first Lord Nunburnholme, for divorce on account of her alleged adultery with the third Earl Cowley. After a hearing which lasted fourteen days, each reported verbatim in *The Times*, the petition was dismissed, but when Sir Charles brought the same charge in April 1905 he was successful.

231

by you and the Duchess at Chatsworth House last year from January the 12th till January the 17th?

The Witness. What?

But times change, and I think you had better not suggest this as a hint to the young Duke of Kent.[1]

Elisabeth sends greetings and greatly hopes that we shall see you soon here again.                        Yours ever   MAX BEERBOHM

[1] Whom Rose had recently taken to see Max.

# APPENDIX

---

*Max's speech at his seventieth birthday party*[1]

Well, Gentlemen.

We have already listened to your delightful songs, delightfully sung. But I confess that I listened to them not without misgivings. Music always tends to make anything that comes after it fall rather flat. I hasten to say my misgivings were entirely for *myself*. I had none for my old friend Desmond MacCarthy. For Desmond's voice is in itself music. Tom Moore's Irish Melodies cannot stand comparison with Desmond's. The harp that once through Tara's Halls ... No, it won't do at all.

But as for the *matter* of his address – well, I don't say that Desmond has ever kissed the Blarney Stone – though I'm sure the Blarney Stone would love to be kissed by *him*. But I feel that in the warmth of old friendship ... and in the pathos of the sight of me reaching the Psalmist's Limit ... he has certainly over-rated me.

I don't complain. You are all here to over-rate me. And I'm immensely touched and pleased and honoured, and grateful.

But it's not for *me* to over-rate *myself*. It pains me to speak of myself at all. I wish I could say that it is not *I* whom you are here to celebrate. That is the usual, the enviable deprecation that is made by the central figure on these occasions. "In me," he says, "you are honouring not myself but the Causes to which I have devoted a long and, I hope, not useless life." (Loud cheers – rather louder perhaps than the speaker had expected, and not *quite* pleasant to his ears.) He then proceeds to name those Causes, in a slightly lowered voice; Causes political or theological or sociological, or what not.

Well, I can do nothing of *that* sort. I have never been connected with any Causes. I like Causes very much, but I have never had a burning faith in the Effects of them. I stand for nothing – except my own not very significant self. So – as I must say *something* – (at any rate Alan

[1] From a typed transcript by Jock Dent from the manuscript which Max gave him. See p. 208.

Dent told me I must) – it is with that paltry matter of self that I have dealt in the very brief little allocation that I have prepared for you.

You are all of you old enough to have heard of Tommy Bowles, the brilliant journalist and politician. Towards the end of his career, he said to a friend, said sadly and rather pompously, "I regard myself as the greatest failure of the Nineteenth Century." And the friend said, "O, come, Tommy! Say rather, the smallest success!"

Well *I* have flourished in the Nineteenth *and* the Twentieth Century, and I regard myself as the smallest success of both. What sometimes mystifies me is that I haven't been just one of the smallest failures. For whereas Tommy Bowles was extremely clever, I am not so. My brain is not at all a powerful one. To study some vast complex subject, to study it in the light of certain first principles and master it in all its details, and draw certain synthetic conclusions, and express these with such lucidity that even a child could understand them, is an achievement far beyond my powers. The act of thinking has always been up-hill work to me. And I am not sure that it is a really healthy function even for men who excel in it. These men never seem to me very happy, or even very well. I should like to have been a country gentleman, rosy and eupeptic surrounded by horses and dogs, by turnips and by mangel-worzels. Or I should like to have been a painter. I have never known a writer who liked writing. I have even known writers who didn't much like what they *had* written. But I have never known a painter who didn't love the act of painting. That is why I have always been so happy in the studios of painters despite the harshness of the large north light. They sing – or at any rate hum or whistle – at their work. They sigh when the light begins to fail, but they cheer up at the thought of being back at their easels the first thing in the morning. Who ever heard a writer even humming or whistling at his work? Alas, Nature had not equipped me to be a painter. And as I was born in London, a cadet of an entirely international family, and as I had to do something to earn a living, and as I was not of a diligent bent, and had a great love of independence and therefore a horror of being tied to any one of the learned or other professions – of having to be in some particular place at some particular time, just as though I were back at school, again – I became a writer, and at the same time went on being what I already was, what I had been since my quite early childhood: a caricaturist – a humming and whistling, even a singing, caricaturist. To the practice of caricature – and to the affection of my family, and to an immensely happy marriage, and to the kindness of a host of friends – I attribute the fact that I survived the grim labour of writing and am alive here this evening in your presence.

What I have written in my life has never been popular, but on the other hand it has always been liked by the kind of people whose good opinion is dear to me. Not long ago I read two or three of my books – or at any rate skimmed through them – with a view to finding out what virtue in them there was that had more or less atoned for my deficiency in intellect. Well, I found a good deal of sensibility to the charm of charming things and charming people. I found a rather keen observant faculty, and some intuition, and an innate distaste for any kind of hypocrisy or pretension in myself or in other people. But what especially struck me was that I had always had a great deal of common sense. It is a far less noble, but a far more useful thing than wisdom. The opinions of wise men are so very often so very foolish. *My* opinions seem to me to have been always right. I may mention that my great-grandfather on the distaff-side was a Yorkshireman. In me, beneath a southern veneer, is the sterling quality of the typical Yorkshire tyke.

As for my caricatures – well, I am not an art-critic, and I don't venture to form any estimate of them. I can't even guess how I did the earlier ones. They are so very violent, though I myself was never that. The distortions are so monstrous and so libellous. And yet that was how I *saw* my subjects, not in their presence, but afterwards, in my memory, when I sat down to draw them. And with most of them I was personally acquainted. I marvel that they did not drop my acquaintance. None of them seemed to mind. As time went on, somehow my memory of people's appearance became less tricksy. I began to remember people more or less exactly as they were, and was obliged to put in the exaggerations consciously ... There had been no recurrent snapdragon on the walls of the Oxford college in which I was an undergraduate, but even as John Henry Newman had thought he was destined to be always an Anglican, so had I believed that I should be a caricaturist to the end of my days.[1] Fate saw otherwise; and I have now meekly – but with great regret – laid aside my pencil.

[1] I left Oxford for good on Monday, February 23, 1846 ... I took leave of my first College, Trinity, which was so dear to me, and which held on its foundation so many who have been kind to me both when I was a boy, and all through my Oxford life. Trinity had never been unkind to me. There used to be much snapdragon growing on the walls opposite my freshman's rooms there, and I had for years taken it as the emblem of my own perpetual residence even unto death in my University. (Newman, *Apologia Pro Vita Sua*, Part VI.)

As for myself, apart from my work, there again I can offer no judgment. I am not a psychologist. I am not even that rather ridiculous and tedious creature, a psycho-analyst. I cannot attribute all my good and all my bad qualities to the fact that at the age of three I was rather frightened by the sight of a performing bear in the Bayswater Road. *I know quite a lot about myself*, but really I don't know whether I am on the whole a good or a bad man, or whether I have a strong character or a weak one. I can only claim for myself that I am an amiable sort of person, and that for this reason people have always been inclined rather to like me than to *dis*like me – even the people who knew me quite well. The sad thing about being seventy years old is that so many of one's best friends have died – so many of the men with whom one had laughed so much and with whom one can laugh no more. How I wish they were here to-day – such men as Reginald Turner, George Street, Charles Boyd, Bohun Lynch, Edmund Gosse, John Davidson, Evan Charteris, Walter Sickert – and many others of my coaevals or my elders. I am sorry that my dear friend Will Rothenstein is prevented by ill-health from being here. And for the same reason another dear friend is absent – Maurice Baring. But they – and others – are here in the spirit. And *you* are here actually to witness my enjoyment of this great occasion, and to receive from my lips my very sincere and heart-felt thanks.

# INDEX OF RECIPIENTS

## LETTERS TO MAX

# GENERAL INDEX